MIDDLETON AND ROWLEY

Forms of Collaboration in the Jacobean Playhouse

Can the inadvertent clashes between collaborators produce more powerful effects than their concordances? For Thomas Middleton and William Rowley, the playwriting team best known for their tragedy *The Changeling*, disagreements and friction proved quite beneficial for their work.

This first full-length study of Middleton and Rowley uses their plays to propose a new model for the study of collaborative authorship in early modern English drama. David Nicol highlights the diverse forms of collaborative relationships that factor into a play's meaning, including playwrights, actors, companies, playhouses, and patrons. This kaleidoscopic approach, which views the plays from all these perspectives, throws new light on the Middleton-Rowley oeuvre and on early modern dramatic collaboration as a whole.

DAVID NICOL is an assistant professor in the Department of Theatre at Dalhousie University.

Middleton and Rowley

Forms of Collaboration in the Jacobean Playhouse

DAVID NICOL

UNIVERSITY OF TORONTO PRESS
Toronto Buffalo London

© University of Toronto Press 2012
Toronto Buffalo London
www.utorontopress.com

Reprinted in paperback 2018

ISBN 978-1-4426-4370-3 (cloth)   ISBN 978-1-4875-2265-0 (paper)

Library and Archives Canada Cataloguing in Publication

Nicol, David, 1975–
Middleton and Rowley : forms of collaboration in the Jacobean playhouse / David Nicol.

Includes bibliographical references and index.
ISBN 978-1-4426-4370-3 (hardcover).   ISBN 978-1-4875-2265-0 (softcover)

1. Middleton, Thomas, d. 1627 – Authorship – Collaboration.   2. Rowley, William, 1585?–1642? – Authorship – Collaboration.   3. Middleton, Thomas, d. 1627 – Criticism and interpretation.   4. Rowley, William, 1585?–1642? – Criticism and interpretation.   5. Authorship – Collaboration – History – 17th century.
6. English drama – 17th century – History and criticism.   I. Title.   II. Title: Middleton & Rowley.

PR2717.N53 2012   822'.309   C2012-903673-0

This book has been published with the help of a grant from the Canadian Federation for the Humanities and Social Sciences, through the Aid to Scholarly Publications Program, using funds provided by the Social Sciences and Humanities Research Council of Canada.

University of Toronto Press acknowledges the financial assistance to its publishing program of the Canada Council for the Arts and the Ontario Arts Council, an agency of the Government of Ontario.

 Canada Council for the Arts   Conseil des Arts du Canada

 ONTARIO ARTS COUNCIL
CONSEIL DES ARTS DE L'ONTARIO
an Ontario government agency
un organisme du gouvernement de l'Ontario

Funded by the Government of Canada   Financé par le gouvernement du Canada

To Roberta, with love

Contents

Acknowledgments ix

Note on the Citation of Dramatic Texts xi

1 **Middleton *and* Rowley: Writing about Collaborative Drama** 3
   Critical Approaches to Collaboration: The Case of *The Changeling* 7
   Middleton, Rowley, and Authorship 15
   Authorial Divisions and the Process of Collaboration 21
   Analysing Collaborative Drama 32

2 **Collaborators and Individual Style: Choice and Religion in *The Changeling*** 36
   Choosing to Sin in *All's Lost by Lust* 37
   The Mind of the Sinner 42
   Calvinism and Middleton's Tragedies 47
   Collaboration and Choice in *The Changeling* 52
   Divided Authors 64

3 **The Actor as Collaborator: *Wit at Several Weapons* and the Incorporation of Personae** 66
   Rowley's Persona under Different Playwrights 72
   The Rowleyan Clown in *All's Lost by Lust* 75
   The Structure of Rowley's Clown Plots 80
   Middleton, Rowley, and the Clown: *Wit at Several Weapons* 85
   The Clown's Perspective 90

viii Contents

4 Collaborators and Playing Companies: Class and Genre in *A Fair Quarrel* 92
Middleton and the Factious Comedy 94
Rowley and Romance 98
The Double Ending of *A Fair Quarrel* 106
Duelling Genres 117

5 A Presence in the Crowd: Multiple Authorship and the Individual Voice in *The Spanish Gypsy* and *The Old Law* 120
An Actor's Presence in *The Spanish Gypsy* and *The Changeling* 125
The Patron's Presence in *The World Tossed at Tennis* and *The Old Law* 131
Epilogue: The Presence of the Absent Author 143

Appendix: A Middleton-Rowley Chronology 149

Notes 153

Bibliography 185

Index 205

Acknowledgments

Part of chapter 3 originally appeared as 'The Stage Persona of William Rowley, Jacobean Clown,' in *Cahiers Élisabéthains* 74 (2008): 23–32. Part of chapter 4 originally appeared as 'Citizens, Gentry, and the Double Ending of Rowley and Middleton's *A Fair Quarrel*,' in *SEL Studies in English Literature 1500–1900* 51, no. 2 (Spring 2011): 427–45. Both are reprinted here with permission.

I began work on this project at the University of Central England (now Birmingham City University), and I am extremely grateful to the university for its generous financial support. At UCE, I was privileged to work with Kate Aughterson, whose kindness, rigour, and encyclopedic knowledge were invaluable in helping me to shape my ideas. Judith Aldridge, Gill Day, Gordon McMullan, David Roberts, and Phil Smallwood all read and commented on my work at various points, and I am grateful for their generosity and detailed advice. Sarah Wood provided fantastic moral support.

Much of the initial research took place in Stratford-upon-Avon, using the resources of the Shakespeare Centre Library and the Shakespeare Institute Library. I am very grateful to the librarians, in particular Karin Brown at the Centre and Jim Shaw and Kate Welch at the Institute. I am also grateful to John Jowett for advice, book loans, and for sharing unpublished work; and to Martin Wiggins, whose play-reading sessions enabled me to experience some of the more obscure plays in performance.

Later work took place at Dalhousie University in Halifax, Nova Scotia. I am grateful to my colleagues past and present in the Department of Theatre for the friendly and welcoming environment. I would also like to thank the students who took my classes on Middleton and Rowley and who were remarkably enthusiastic about mouldy old plays: Rebecca Ambrosino, Simon Bloom, Brooke Fifield, Ailsa Galbreath, Andy Gouthro, Sarah Higgins, Dorian Lang, Joshua C. Law, Claire Leger, Justin Leger, Kegan Paige, Tessa Pekeles, Emily Turner, and Jennette White.

Several kind friends have gone out of their way to help me by reading parts of this book in its various incarnations or by digging up information; in particular Shannon Brownlee, Karen Kettnich, Lucy Munro, and Will Sharpe are heroes. I also owe a great debt to Ann Nicol and Diane Murray-Barker who nobly assisted with proofreading and indexing.

Part of chapter 5 was written for Richard Dutton and Kevin Curran's seminar on 'Shakespeare and the Court' at the 2008 Shakespeare Association of America Annual Meeting in Dallas, and I am grateful to the organizers and participants for their feedback. I would also like to thank Helen Ostovich, Marion O'Connor, and Anne Lancashire for helping me to organize my thoughts about the repertory of Prince Charles's Men. And although I have not met many of the following in person, I want to thank Gary Taylor, John Lavagnino, and the entire editing team of the 2007 *Thomas Middleton: The Collected Works* edition: the vast array of scholarship contained in its volumes enabled me to develop my ideas in countless new ways, and the opportunities that it has opened for the study of Middleton and his collaborators are phenomenal.

Thank you to my mother, Ann, for teaching me to enjoy reading and writing; to my father, Tim, for teaching me to enjoy the visual arts; and to my sister, Julie, for all the times I exploited her London flat.

Finally, I want to express my immense gratitude to Roberta Barker, without whose patience, love, and wisdom the whole thing would have been utterly impossible. This book is dedicated to her.

Note on the Citation of Dramatic Texts

Quotations

Unless otherwise indicated, early modern dramatic texts are quoted from the facsimiles of their earliest printed editions in the *Early English Books Online* database. Exceptions to this rule include a number of plays that exist in multiple early texts or in manuscript. *A Fair Quarrel* is quoted from the second 1617 edition (*STC* 17911a); *A Game at Chess* is quoted from the Malone Society edition, edited by T.H. Howard-Hill (1990), which is based on the Trinity Manuscript; *Hamlet* is quoted from the 1623 First Folio; *Hengist, King of Kent* is quoted from the Malone Society edition, edited by Grace Ioppolo (2003), which is based on the Portland Manuscript; and *The Second Maiden's Tragedy* (rechristened *The Lady's Tragedy* in Taylor and Lavagnino, *Thomas Middleton: The Collected Works*) is quoted from the Malone Society edition, edited by W.W. Greg (1910). Other exceptions are specified in the endnotes. For the sake of readability, features such as 'v' for 'u,' 'i' for 'j,' and the long 's' are modernized. Language, punctuation, and lineation have occasionally been corrected or modernized to aid clarity; such changes are indicated in endnotes or with square brackets. When adjustments to punctuation or lineation have been made, capitalization has been altered silently.

Act, Scene, and Line References

Act, scene, and line references to standard modern editions are provided where possible. All plays by Thomas Middleton are keyed to Gary Taylor and John Lavagnino, *Thomas Middleton: The Collected Works* (2007); non-Middletonian plays by Thomas Dekker to Fredson Bowers,

The Dramatic Works of Thomas Dekker (1953–61); non-Middletonian plays by John Webster to Anthony Hammond, David Gunby, David Carnegie, and MacDonald P. Jackson, *The Works of John Webster* (1995–2008); plays by John Fletcher to Fredson Bowers, *The Dramatic Works in the Beaumont and Fletcher Canon* (1966–96); plays by Philip Massinger to Philip Edwards and Colin Gibson, *The Plays and Poems of Philip Massinger* (1976); and plays by Shakespeare to G. Blakemore Evans, *The Riverside Shakespeare* (1974).

Plays by William Rowley not included in the texts above are keyed to the following editions:

- Charles Wharton Stork, *William Rowley: His 'All's Lost by Lust' and 'A Shoemaker a Gentleman,' with an Introduction on Rowley's Place in the Drama* (1910)
- Herman Doh, *A Critical Edition of 'Fortune by Land and Sea,' by Thomas Heywood and William Rowley* (1980)
- Trudi L. Darby, *A Critical, Old-Spelling Edition of William Rowley's 'A New Wonder, A Woman Never Vexed'* (1988)
- Michael Nolan, *'The Thracian Wonder' by William Rowley and Thomas Heywood: A Critical Edition* (1997)
- Anthony Parr, 'The Travels of the Three English Brothers,' in *Three Renaissance Travel Plays* (1995)

MIDDLETON AND ROWLEY

Chapter One

Middleton *and* Rowley: Writing about Collaborative Drama

If the criticism of any single work always consists to some extent in relating it to a total *oeuvre*, then the critics of a collaborative work must be prepared to relate it to a plurality of *oeuvres*. The essential critical point about a collaborative work is that it is the product not of one dramatic vision but of two or more; and the critic of a play like *The Changeling* who attempts seriously to account for its achievement must seek its roots not only in the Middleton canon but in the canon of William Rowley's plays as well. The crucial issue for the aesthetic appraisal of the work is how satisfactorily the multiple dramatic visions have fused into a single coherent one.[1]

Cyrus Hoy's conclusion to his 1976 article 'Critical and Aesthetic Problems of Collaboration in Renaissance Drama' encapsulates the central concerns in what has become an ongoing debate about how to read early modern collaborative plays. Hoy's simultaneous fascination with authorial plurality and aesthetic unity raises questions that remain unresolved today: Do collaborating writers retain a 'dramatic vision' related to their 'oeuvre'? And how can one describe those visions if a successful collaboration fuses them into 'a single coherent one'? These questions have polarized critics; hence, for Brian Vickers, Hoy's article is 'the most thoughtful contribution' to the question of how a critic should analyse collaborative drama, but for Jeffrey Masten, its ethos betrays 'a historically inappropriate idea of the author.'[2] The debate has centred on whether collaborative drama should be read as the interaction of recognizable and distinctive authors whose work should be applauded when their individuality is subsumed, or whether the very notion of the individual author with a distinctive style is anachronistic when applied to early modern drama.[3]

I believe that both of these approaches are problematic and indeed that they are more similar than they seem, in that both discourage investigation of the ways in which 'multiple dramatic visions' may produce impressive theatre even when they do not 'fuse.' One way to demonstrate this is to take up Hoy's challenge to read *The Changeling* – and other, lesser-known plays by the prolific playwriting team of Thomas Middleton and William Rowley – in the context of their other works. It is surprising that Middleton and Rowley feature so little in the recent debates about collaboration, since they are often considered the greatest collaborators of their age; Gary Taylor goes so far as to call them 'the best doubles team in the history of European drama.'[4] Jeffrey Masten's and Gordon McMullan's studies are primarily concerned with John Fletcher's collaborations, while Brian Vickers's and John Jowett's analyses of Middleton's collaborations are centred on his work with Shakespeare. Heather Anne Hirschfield's study of four collaborating teams includes a chapter on Middleton and Rowley but is limited to one play, *The Changeling*. A.A. Bromham and Mark Hutchings devote a chapter to Middleton and Rowley in *Middleton and His Collaborators* but discuss only three of the plays.[5] Middleton and Rowley's achievement demands greater attention.

That achievement consists of six dramatic works written over a period of about ten years, along with two others written by Middleton for performance by Rowley's playing company.[6] Middleton and Rowley began to collaborate in or around 1614, when they wrote an intrigue comedy, *Wit at Several Weapons*, for Rowley's company, Prince Charles's Men.[7] Their backgrounds were very different: the university-educated Middleton was already a prolific and successful writer of drama, poetry, and prose, most of which was of a satirical nature. Rowley, who did not have a university education, was a less prolific writer and was better known as an actor who was a leading figure in the organization of his playing company, and who specialized in clown roles. Despite these differences, the two men formed a long-lasting collaborative team that produced plays of several different genres. *Wit at Several Weapons* was followed by two tragicomedies for Prince Charles's Men: *A Fair Quarrel* (1616), and *The Old Law* (1618–19), the latter probably written in collaboration with Thomas Heywood. Next followed two masques. *The Inner Temple Masque, or, Masque of Heroes* (1619) was written entirely by Middleton, but Rowley and five other members of Prince Charles's Men performed in it; *The World Tossed at Tennis* (1619–20), a collaboration, was performed by Prince Charles's Men at a public theatre, perhaps because its court performance was cancelled. The collaborators then wrote two plays for Lady Elizabeth's Men: the first was the tragedy *The Changeling* (1622), which has become an enduring classic of the stage; the second was *The Spanish Gypsy* (1623), a tragicomedy probably co-written with Thomas Dekker and John Ford. The final project on which Middleton and Rowley are known to have worked together was the political satire *A Game at Chess* (1624), which was written entirely by Middleton but included a role for Rowley, who was by then acting with the King's Men. Middleton died the following year, and Rowley the year after.

The paucity of studies of Middleton and Rowley as collaborators does not mean that the plays themselves have been overlooked: Middleton is regarded as one of the greatest playwrights of his age, and his collaborations with Rowley have often been studied as part of his canon. But few of those studies have grappled seriously with the fact that in each of these plays, a sizeable proportion of the text, often more than half of it, was written by an obscure playwright whose solo works, such as *All's Lost by Lust* and *A Shoemaker a Gentleman*, are rarely studied. The resulting lacuna is illustrated well by the introductions to two recent editions of *The Changeling*. Both editors state, as Hoy does, that since Rowley wrote more than half of the play, his contribution must be acknowledged.[8] Yet neither suggests any way in which this knowledge should inform our reading; instead, both argue that the play is 'so closely integrated that it would be impertinent to suggest that one author was more important than the other'[9] and then proceed with readings that make no reference to its dual authorship. Crucial questions remain unanswered: if Rowley's presence must be acknowledged, it must be because a play co-written by Middleton and Rowley is different from one written by Middleton alone; but if so, *how* is it different? Is it possible to describe the effect that Rowley's presence might have had on the creation of *The Changeling*? For example, given that Thomas Middleton's plays display idiosyncratic religious and political assumptions (several studies have traced the influence of Calvinist theology and oppositional politics on his drama),[10] the recognition of Rowley's role in the creation of *The Changeling* ought to raise questions as to what *his* political and religious affiliations might have been, whether they were different from Middleton's, and if so, how this knowledge should affect interpretation of the play.

There are three reasons for the absence of studies of this kind, and Hoy's challenge hints at each of them. The first is the difficulty of determining the very oeuvres that Hoy considers important and of ascertaining how (or indeed whether) the playwrights divided the plays into authorial sections during the writing process. In fact, Middleton and Rowley have proven one of the easier collaborating teams to attribute; in the past few decades, stylistic analyses by Hoy, David J. Lake, and MacDonald P. Jackson have determined their contributions to most of the plays in question with great sophistication.[11] Despite this, Hoy's complaint that 'the criticism of collaborative drama has yet to catch up with – to make any real use of – [these] scholarly gains' largely holds true today.[12]

The second reason for the rarity of studies of Middleton and Rowley as collaborators is related to Hoy's claim that a successful collaboration is one in which 'multiple dramatic visions have fused into a single coherent one.'[13] Most studies of collaborative drama have been more interested in the coherence than in the multiplicity, and the critic who seeks to determine what unifies a collaborative play typically treats authorial distinctiveness as a problem to explain away rather than an object of study in itself. The result, I will argue, has been a tendency to elide or efface the presence of the lesser-known Rowley and to argue for the dominance of Middleton's dramatic vision.

The third reason for the lacuna is that some recent studies of collaborative drama have contested Hoy's belief that 'defining authorial shares is the necessary prerequisite to any informed critical appraisal' of collaborative drama.[14] This new approach argues that the highly collaborative nature of the early modern theatre renders the concept of the individual author a misleading critical tool, and that reading the plays as the products of individual playwrights with singular visions is anachronistic. Influenced by Michel Foucault's pronouncements on the historicity of authorship, these critics describe an alternative paradigm: in Jeffrey Masten's words, 'collaboration is ... a dispersal of author/ity, rather than a simple doubling of it; to revise the aphorism, two heads are different than one.'[15] In the following pages, I will argue that this denial of authorial distinctiveness has become so extreme that its proponents are unable to analyse the very multiplicity of voices that makes collaboration so significant to them, and their approach results in analyses that are remarkably similar to those of the searchers for unity.

I believe that the collaborating team of Middleton and Rowley has much to teach us about collaboration and authorship, but in order to learn its lessons the temptation to smooth over or elide their individual differences must be avoided. To understand these differences one must, of course, read Rowley's other plays and give them as much attention as Middleton's have received, an approach that has never been attempted with any comprehensiveness. My study is thus primarily about Middleton *and* Rowley rather than about a fused entity called 'Middleton and Rowley': I read their plays to discern the moments at which two personalities and styles rub against each other. I will argue that the collaborations of Middleton and Rowley are not always as perfectly unified as they are claimed to be. However, unlike Brian Vickers, who highlights with great skill the structural flaws of collaborative plays,[16] I do not always see disunities as failings: sometimes, the inadvertent clashes and tensions discernible within Middleton and Rowley's plays contribute toward making their drama thrilling.

My focus on one playwriting team does not mean, however, that I am only interested in collaborations between writers. In recent years, a number of scholars have proposed alternatives to grouping early modern plays by their authors, regarding entities such as playing companies, actors, and publishers as author-like owing to their influence on both the creation and reception of plays. As Lucy Munro puts it, 'In a system in which commercial plays were generally commissioned and bought outright by the companies, it seems paradoxical that the study of Elizabethan and Jacobean drama has been so often organized around dramatists, whose control over their texts was limited and local.'[17]

Treating these other entities as author-like figures can be a valuable approach, as it can draw attention to previously unnoticed voices within texts; as Munro stresses, there is no aim of 'denying the playwrights agency, but of considering the input of all those involved in the production and dissemination of plays.'[18] My study incorporates elements of this more recent approach, paying attention to other important collaborations that left their marks on the text; specifically, the playwrights' relationships with actors, playing companies, and patrons. As with my work on the playwrights, I do this not to blur the plays into perfectly unified wholes but to recognize what distinguishes these voices from each other, and hence to treat collaboration as a complex interaction between different entities.

Critical Approaches to Collaboration: The Case of *The Changeling*

Middleton and Rowley's tragedy *The Changeling* is one of the best-known plays of the early modern era and has attracted a wealth of critical commentary. Some of that commentary attempts to engage with the fact of the play's collaborative nature. *The Changeling* contains two plotlines, a tragic main plot and a comic subplot, and a consensus has emerged since the 1890s that after designing the play's plot and structure, the playwrights divided its scenes between themselves. Rowley took on the entirety of the play's subplot, a dark farce about gallants disguising themselves as madmen in order to seduce the young wife of the asylum keeper. However, the main plot, with its tale of a young aristocratic woman hiring a servant who loves her to murder her unwanted suitor, was written by both playwrights: Middleton took the middle scenes, leaving the opening and closing scenes to Rowley. This curious scenario raises many questions about the working methods of dramatists and the extent to which we can know 'who wrote what.' But before considering those questions, it is useful to observe the different ways in which critics have responded to this collaborative method.

An important, but rarely considered, problem for a critical study of the play is the extent to which the change of writer can affect the way events and characters are represented. In the case of *The Changeling*, the play was apparently divided in such a way that some of the characters – specifically, those of the main plot – were written by more than one writer: they are introduced with the words of Rowley, their characterization is developed through Middleton's words, and their climactic scene is by Rowley. A concept such as 'Middleton and Rowley's Beatrice'[19] is thus overly simplistic. Should we consider the ways in which Middleton and Rowley might have represented Beatrice's character differently?

There is a long but inconclusive history of critical debate on this matter, and the critics who have studied the problem can be divided into three camps: the disintegrators, the unifiers, and the post-structuralists. Each of these approaches attempts to study *The Changeling* with an awareness that the play is a collaboration. However, despite their differences of methodology, each has had the effect of marginalizing Rowley's presence.

The term 'disintegrators' refers to the nineteenth- and early twentieth-century critics who attempted to identify instances of revision and collaboration in early modern playtexts. The work of these critics demonstrates far more interest in the presence of diverse agents in the text than did that of their immediate successors. Indeed, the word 'disintegration' – originally used by E.K. Chambers as a pejorative term[20] – has been re-appropriated by the new textual criticism, and parallels have been drawn between Victorian disintegration and post-structuralist theory.[21] However, the original disintegrationist approach had a negative effect on Rowley's reputation because its proponents typically regarded his contributions to the plays as blots on Middleton's more sophisticated style. Edmund Gosse regarded Rowley's sentiments as 'brutal and squalid' and called Middleton 'a poet unequally yoked with one whose temper was essentially prosaic,' while A.C. Swinburne talked of Rowley's 'untimely and inharmonious' partnership with Middleton's genius.[22] As a result, some critics even advocated removing Rowley's contributions: Una Ellis-Fermor claimed that the subplot of *The Changeling* could 'be detached without much damage,' and R.H. Barker disdained to incorporate Rowley's climactic scene into his interpretation of the play, saying that it 'adds nothing to the play but a little pointless violence.'[23] T.S. Eliot wrote that Middleton could only be called a great dramatist 'after criticism has subtracted all that Rowley, all that Dekker, all that others contributed.'[24] The problem with this attitude is not that these critics distinguish Middleton from his co-author, but that they take no interest in the sections that they 'subtract.' To understand the composition of *The Changeling*, we certainly need to disintegrate it, in order to distinguish the work of the different writers; but we need also to examine the ways in which their different styles interact rather than focus exclusively on one of them.

In 1935, both William Empson and M.C. Bradbrook published work that transformed critical attitudes to *The Changeling* by emphasizing the play's formal unity. Both scholars demonstrated that the main plot and subplot are unified by a sophisticated web of parallels and contrasts. They argued that the madmen in the comic subplot embody the crazed passions of the tragic characters in the main plot, so that 'the effect of the vulgar asylum scenes is to surround the characters with a herd of lunatics ... this herd is the "people" of which the tragic characters are "heroes."'[25] Empson and Bradbrook described parallels of plotting – for example, the similarities between DeFlores in the main plot and Lollio in the subplot, both of whom try to exact rewards for service from their respective mistresses – and noted verbal parallels, such as references to the game of 'barley-break' that appear in both plotlines.[26] Empson concluded that 'however disagreeable the comic part may be it is of no use to ignore it; it is woven into the tragic part very thoroughly.'[27] A new generation of critics began to describe the play as a joint venture, a work of art that had been carefully, even intricately designed in such a way that every element contributed to a central meaning. It was a 'fully integrated artefact'[28] rather than a clumsy patchwork.[29]

This approach to *The Changeling* provides a number of valuable insights. It shows that there was a deliberate effort by the dramatists to create parallels between the two plots with the aid of repeated words, images, and staging patterns.[30] But despite this, its practitioners failed to raise Rowley's profile, instead removing him still further from consideration. Bradbrook set the tone by refusing to accept that Rowley could have written any of the main plot: 'its unity is of a kind which not even the most sympathetic collaboration could achieve.'[31] Subsequent commentators demonstrate a similar urge to treat Middleton as the sole author. Some simply ignore Rowley's presence entirely, interpreting the entire play in the context of Middleton's canon without reference to his collaborator.[32] Others avowedly subsume Rowley into Middleton: Kathleen McLuskie's chapter on collaboration in *The Revels History of Drama* does not mention the Middleton-Rowley plays, discussing them instead in a chapter on Middleton because he 'dominates them so completely';[33] Irving Ribner writes that 'Middleton's genius was the guiding spirit' and that Rowley's work was 'subsumed into the thematic unity of the whole.'[34] The most systematic attempt at effacing Rowley is that of David M. Holmes, who offers an array of unconvincing evidence that Rowley was merely 'pupil-assistant to Middleton,' so that 'Middleton's characteristic method pervades.'[35] Some disquiet at this elision is betrayed by T.B. Tomlinson, who notes that 'the ghost of William Rowley troubles readers of *The Changeling*,' but concludes that 'there is no need for this at all': Rowley's presence is irrelevant because the play is of a type that is 'virtually Middleton's own preserve.'[36] Tomlinson's comment is characteristic of a tendency to explain Rowley away rather than acknowledge his presence.

Although other critics of *The Changeling* do acknowledge Rowley's presence, they tend to describe his contribution in such a way that he is denied any independent agency. Some refer to the author as 'Middleton and Rowley' throughout, but rarely allow this formulation to complicate the interpretation of the text. As I have already noted, phrases such as 'Middleton and Rowley's Beatrice' or 'Middleton and Rowley's degraded world'[37] assume that Beatrice and the world view of the play are stable concepts, and that there is no difference in the way the two authors represent them.[38] Elsewhere, there is a tendency for critics to state that 'the collaboration was an unusually close one,'[39] a formulation that permits discussion of the text without reference to differences between the writers.

In these critical manoeuvres, one senses what Douglas A. Brooks calls, in a different context, a 'desire for univocality.'[40] The demonstration of the play's structural unity relies on the assumption that the co-authors had identical intentions or that there is no difference between the ideas and opinions of Middleton and those of Rowley. It is certainly likely that Middleton and Rowley had shared aims and intentions in writing *The Changeling*, and that they worked hard to ensure that these ideas were communicated in a coherent way. But as Gordon McMullan has stressed, collaboration is 'the condition toward which all texts tend, even if (or as) they aspire to unity and autonomy.'[41] Rather than question whether absolute unity between writers can ever be possible, critics have preferred to assume that one of the playwrights – invariably Middleton – acted as designer, organizer, and controller of the play, while the other passively obeyed his orders. The concept of the singular author is thus enforced upon the collaborative text.

This problem is especially serious in studies that attempt to analyse Middleton's distinctive political outlook. For example, in *'The Changeling' and the Years of Crisis*, A.A. Bromham and Zara Bruzzi refer to the play's author as 'Middleton and Rowley' throughout but discuss the play only in the context of Middleton's writing, without an equivalent analysis of Rowley's;[42] the unspoken assumption is that Rowley's political stance was either identical to Middleton's or is irrelevant. Similarly, Margot Heinemann's study of Middleton's Puritanism assumes 'consistency in the design and conception [of *The Changeling*] as a whole.'[43]

Even critics who seek to demonstrate the importance of Rowley's contribution to the play have often used a language and theory that blurs him with Middleton. J.L. Simmons undertakes to read *The Changeling* alongside Rowley's canon, but does so in order to demonstrate that Middleton and Rowley were both interested in the same subject matter.[44] Michael E. Mooney's important essay, which I will discuss below, theorizes that Rowley was responsible for organizing the play into a coherent whole but sees this as a process by which the dramatists effaced the differences between their individual styles and brought their work into a 'harmonic conjunction';[45] Rowley's achievement is valorized only insofar as he succeeds in merging himself with his collaborator. Similarly, Norman Rabkin argues that while Middleton and Rowley were 'doing [their] own thing' in *The Changeling*, they 'must have worked together intimately from the inception to make this strange and powerful play one.'[46] What is problematic about this approach is that it blurs intention and effect: it shows how Middleton and Rowley attempted to create ideas and images that were consistent throughout the play, but assumes that their achievement was absolutely successful.

I would argue that *absolute* harmony between writers may be impossible: collaborative texts will inevitably contain differences of style and different assumptions, regardless of the writers' efforts to remove them. This does not mean that such differences would immediately be obvious to readers or spectators; many Hollywood films are written by more than one screenwriter, and audiences are unlikely to notice the differences between their work. But close analysis may sometimes reveal differences between the writers' approaches to the subject matter. And these differences, even if unintentional, could reveal reasons for the play's effects on readers and spectators.

The problems of interpretation that I have highlighted above would be described by some post-structuralist critics as the inevitable result of applying post-Enlightenment ideas about authorship to the early modern theatre. Following Michel Foucault's influential essay 'What Is an Author?', these scholars have asked whether one can know, or should even *want* to know, 'who is speaking' at any given point.[47] Jeffrey Masten argues that much critical writing on early modern drama has 'worked to construct an authorial univocality' that is unsuited to the period; similarly, Douglas A. Brooks aspires to 'frustrate the desire for univocality that continues to generate much of the scholarship on early modern English drama.'[48] The complexities of the early modern playhouse and printing house, in which numerous agents could leave their marks on the text, can be linked to the post-structuralist argument that texts are not 'products of a singular and sovereign authorial consciousness,'[49] but rather that 'the work of art is the product of a negotiation between a creator or class of creators, equipped with a complex, communally shared repertoire of conventions, and the institutions and practices of society.'[50] In this view, the early modern playtext is a prime example of the multiple agencies that go into the creation of art; Stephen Orgel writes that 'the creation of a play was a collaborative process, with the author by no means the centre of the collaboration.'[51] The ultimate conclusion of this approach, as Gordon McMullan puts it, is to regard collaboration as 'a much more appropriate model for textual production in general than is ostensibly "solo" writing.'[52]

These arguments are important: their emphasis on the material conditions of the production of texts demonstrates that critics need to approach early modern plays armed with a good understanding of the text's origins. Furthermore, they encourage a more positive approach toward collaboration, celebrating it rather than treating it as an inferior form of writing. However, most of this work has been concerned with textual editing. When applied to literary criticism, the results are disappointing: far from revealing a multiplicity of voices, the critic tends to read the communal text for its unities. For example, Masten argues for reading collaborative plays in their entirety instead of breaking them into separate authorial fragments, and uses the phrase 'reading across the hands' to describe this process.[53] Using *Sir Thomas More* as his example, Masten criticizes those editions of Shakespeare's works that print only the 'Hand D' section of the play and which thus prevent us from seeing the continuities created by the playwriting team across the entire play. Tracing a sequence of images 'across the hands,' he advocates reading the play as a 'collective enterprise,' thereby offering a practical application of his argument that reading collaboration as the interaction of individual playwrights is ahistorical.[54] However, while *Sir Thomas More* is indeed a play whose thematic throughlines have been obscured by a critical obsession with its divided authorship, 'reading across the hands' has been the normal critical approach toward almost every other collaborative play: generations of critics have approached *The Changeling* in this way in order to deny its polyvocality, whether they are regarding it as the product of singular authorship (usually Middleton and his obedient scribe Rowley) or as a 'collective enterprise,' in which disunity is elided in the celebration of its authors' 'harmonic conjunction.' Similarly, Heather Anne Hirschfield's aim of examining 'the contexts and meanings' of Middleton and Rowley's collaboration without reference to the question of 'who wrote what' results in a study of the representation of fellowship in *The Changeling* that reads no differently from a conventional thematic reading, emphasizing as it does the 'friendly joint work' of the playwrights 'and its concomitant sharing of language, thought, and theme.'[55]

In contrast, Gary Taylor responds to Foucault's question 'What does it matter who is speaking?' by arguing that 'it matters because drama is social.' For Taylor, the cultural world is 'always pervasively dramatic, energised by the intersection of signifying agents who enter from different doors and meet in a particular space/time.'[56] The image of playwrights entering 'from different doors' is a useful metaphor for what is missing from Masten's paradigm. Masten insists that collaboration is not simply 'a more *multiple* version of authorship' but is instead 'a dispersal of author/ity,'[57] but this idealized vision of authorlessness prevents any discussion of how the different social, cultural, and educational positions of playwrights (and other agents) can create friction within a text. Because Masten denies the individuality of playwrights, he must instead blur them into an indistinguishable fog, and this blurring effaces precisely the concept that his study of collaboration raises: the idea of *diversity* within the text.

Foucault imagined a future culture in which 'fiction would be put at the disposal of everyone and would develop without passing through something like a necessary or constraining figure,' but admitted that this was 'pure romanticism.'[58] Masten acknowledges this romanticism, as does Stephen Orgel, who finds an idealized 'textual golden age,' free of authorial constraints, to be neither helpful nor realistic.[59] The celebration of the collective text fails to account for what the new textual criticism has highlighted: the presence of diverse *agents* in the construction of early modern playtexts. It can lead into a cul-de-sac in which the denial of singular authorship prevents us from being allowed to countenance the notion of collaborators interacting in a play, because to do so is to acknowledge that agents can have distinctive qualities. As McMullan puts it, this is 'the fundamental double bind of collaborative theory: that it is the existence of evidence that the text was collaboratively written which provides the critic with the opportunity to reject that evidence.'[60]

Similarly, while the post-structuralist deconstruction of authority is useful when approaching monolithic cultural constructs such as 'Shakespeare,' it can be a reactionary force when approaching texts that have not achieved canonical status. Shakespeare's amassed cultural authority and the myth of his universality have provoked valuable research into the numerous other agents that contributed to his texts, but when we turn to playwrights like Middleton, who has never had Shakespeare's god-like status, or Rowley, whose agency has barely been contemplated, this approach becomes dangerous. By ignoring Rowley's agency, we deny the possibility that the text of *The Changeling*, which has been generally treated as a stable, unified voice, might be polyvocal. In cases such as this, a failure to differentiate the agents in the text can perpetuate the marginalization of figures such as Rowley, whose importance the new textual theory could help to elaborate; as Séan Burke argues (in relation to feminist and post-colonialist theory), criticism of a previously marginalized writer should include 'a defence of the specificity of the subject, the grounding of the text in the irreducible personal and cultural experiences of its author. In each case, a rejection of the universal subject must imply a reassertion of the subject in his/her particularity.'[61]

The study of literary collaboration should focus our attention on the fact that playwrights, like all writers, are the products of their different socio-cultural situations. The presence of more than one playwright certainly denies the critic's appeal to the singular author as absolute source of meaning. But in order to break down the singular author, we must be able to describe the effects of the interaction between different agents (and therefore consider those agents as subjects), because the alternative is to turn them into a transcendent unified author, what John Jowett calls a 'collaborative essentialism, one that is achieved by blurring the specific dynamics of the text that has been described.'[62]

Any study of collaborators as distinct agents is of course faced with a number of methodological difficulties that I have thus far glossed over. These difficulties include the question of whether it is anachronistic to study early modern dramatists as authors with distinct identities; our limited knowledge of how early modern collaborating dramatists worked; and scepticism from some critics about the validity of attribution scholarship. These problems are, I believe, relatively surmountable in the case of Middleton and Rowley, making them an ideal object of study for an investigation of early modern collaborative dramatists and their work.

Middleton, Rowley, and Authorship

The theoretical and methodological problems surrounding the interpretation of collaborative drama are arguably caused not by collaboration itself, but by the application of the concept of the autonomous author to early modern drama.[63] The theatre of the period was, after all, a highly collaborative environment in which the image of the playwright as a solitary figure producing an unmediated text is inappropriate. About half of the plays of the English Renaissance may have been written by more than one playwright; plays were owned by and their transition to the stage controlled by playing companies, not by playwrights; and book-holders, printers, and booksellers had significant effects on the way those plays were represented in print.[64]

Consequently, in his provocative writing about collaboration in the period, Jeffrey Masten argues that reading collaborative plays as simply the product of two (or more) individual and distinctive authors is anachronistic, because they were 'produced before the emergence of authorship' in the English theatre.[65] Most playtexts of the period, he notes, 'began as productions in the theatre, where their writers were not known, and many of them first appeared in print without ascription of authorship (or anonymity).'[66] The concept of the playwright as author, he suggests, 'emerges from the printing house and only indirectly from the theatre,' and is 'an idea that gradually becomes attached to playtexts over the course of the seventeenth century, registered in the increasing appearance of the term in the playtexts' printed apparatus in quartos and folios.'[67] He thus argues that the notion of being able to 'discern and separate out [the work of collaborators] by examining the traces of individuality and personality' in their writing styles is a 'post-Enlightenment' one.[68]

Masten's paradigm can, however be contested; indeed, elsewhere in his book he acknowledges that the concept of dramatic authorship was not non-existent but 'open to question,' and suggests that Renaissance playwrights may demonstrate a variety of attitudes to collaboration and authorship.[69] One objection is that even if the association of plays with playwrights began in the printing house, the concept was certainly in the minds of theatregoers too. Jeffrey Knapp points out that Francis Meres's 1598 list of Shakespeare's plays 'attributes twelve plays to Shakespeare, only three of which had been published.'[70] By 1609, Thomas Dekker was advising aspiring gallants that 'by sitting on the stage, you may (without travelling for it) at the very next doore, aske whose play it is: and by that *Quest* of *Inquiry*, the law warrants you to avoid much mistaking: if you know not the author, you may raile against him: and peradventure so behave your selfe, that you may enforce the Author to know you.'[71] Apparently, even if theatrical performances were not promoted under the playwrights' names, there was an urge to identify the author among some audience members. Furthermore, even if the association of plays with playwrights was fired by the presence of printed texts with authorial information, Masten's focus on the seventeenth century obscures the fact that dramatic authorship had been appearing on title pages for decades: although anonymous publication was commoner, seventy-four playtexts were published with their playwrights' names on them between 1570 and 1599.[72]

Other criticisms of Masten's thesis have been put forward. Heather Anne Hirschfield has shown that the notion of playwrights' having distinctive styles was available in the period, and indeed was significant to the quarrels between Ben Jonson and John Marston during the Poets'

War.[73] And Knapp notes that even the concept of identifying the contributions of collaborators was not alien to the period: as early as 1565, *Gorboduc* was published with a title page explaining that 'three Actes were written by *Thomas Nortone*, and the two laste by *Thomas Sackvyle*'; and three editions of George Gascoigne's works from 1573 to 1587 provide authorial attributions for each act of the collaborative *Jocasta*.[74] This form of attribution does not appear in other dramatic texts[75] (and indeed *Gorboduc* was subsequently printed both anonymously and in a collection of Norton's works),[76] but it illustrates that the question of 'who wrote what' is not entirely the 'post-Enlightenment' concept that Masten claims it is.[77]

Indeed, some playwrights had a strong enough sense of authorial identity to want to separate themselves from their co-writers. For the publication of *Sejanus* in 1605, Ben Jonson claimed to have removed and rewritten the work of a collaborator, explaining that he had 'chosen, to put weaker (and no doubt lesse pleasing) of mine own, then to defraud so happy a Genius of his own right, by my lothed usurpation.' False modesty notwithstanding, Jonson was clearly aware of a difference between his style and that of the 'second Pen.'[78] So was Thomas Dekker when he drew the reader's attention to a speech in *The Magnificent Entertainment*: 'If there bee anye glory to be won by writting these lynes,' Dekker wrote, it was Middleton's, 'in whose braine they were begotten ... *Quae nos non fecimus ipsi, vix ea nostra voco* [That which we do not ourselves, we will never call ours]' (2184–5). John Webster more pithily differentiated his own work in the corrected state of the 1623 quarto of *The Duchess of Malfi*, which notes next to one of the songs, 'The Author disclaimes this Ditty to be his' (3.4.6.7).

In these acts of separation, Jonson, Dekker, and Webster are clearly concerned about their reputations as authors, fearing that readers will confuse their words with those of others. Furthermore, Jonson and Webster also seem to have regarded their collaborative drama as less significant than their solo plays: Jonson excluded collaborations from his 1616 Folio, and when Webster listed his 'Works' in the 1623 dedicatory epistle to *The Devil's Lawcase*, he made no mention of his collaborative plays beyond an unspecific reference to the 'others' (9–10). Noting the rarity of references to collaboration, especially positive references, Knapp argues that, *pace* Masten, 'So commanding a paradigm was *single* authorship during the Renaissance that it made the common theatrical practice of collaborative writing difficult to acknowledge, let alone extol.'[79]

Still, not all playwrights displayed this desire to differentiate their work from that of their collaborators. Middleton and Rowley expressed no views on the subject at all, but a study of their careers and their writing suggest that it is defensible to regard them as authors with a sense of individual differentiation, albeit in surprisingly different ways that may reflect their different positions in the theatre industry.

Post-Renaissance writers have often assumed that early modern dramatists collaborated because they were friends; for example, Paulina Kewes has shown how the Restoration biographer Gerard Langbaine attempted to ennoble the act of collaboration by describing a community of friends (Middleton, he wrote, was 'contemporary with those Famous Poets *Johnson, Fletcher, Massinger* and *Rowley*, in whose Friendship he had a large Share').[80] In her study of Middleton and Rowley, Hirschfield does something similar, arguing that the two men must have been close friends because they made a special effort to work together. However, Hirschfield's claim is not quite accurate, and while the playwrights' company affiliations do hint at their attitudes to collaboration, they do not necessarily indicate friendship so much as an unequal business relationship. Certainly, the collaboration was a long-lasting one (producing six plays over about ten years), and neither Middleton nor Rowley collaborated as frequently with any other playwright;[81] still, this in itself need not indicate any actual affection. More compelling is Hirschfield's claim that Middleton and Rowley deliberately 'ignored the boundaries of company affiliations to work together' in what must therefore have been 'a deliberate undertaking.'[82]

Whether Middleton had 'company affiliations' is debatable, however. Certainly, Rowley was an 'attached playwright,' in G.E. Bentley's term, one of the dramatists who 'did not easily or frequently shift their company associations, but tended to work regularly for one troupe for long periods.'[83] From 1609 to 1622, he was a sharer in Prince Charles's Men and the evidence suggests that he wrote plays almost entirely for them during this period.[84] Bentley describes Middleton, in contrast, as an 'unattached' dramatist because he does not seem to have been contracted to work for a specific company.[85] Hirschfield queries this description of Middleton, noting a pattern in his work: during the period from his first collaboration with Rowley (*Wit at Several Weapons*, ca. 1613–15) to his death, all of his solo plays for which company attributions are known were performed by the King's Men (his last solo play for another company had been *A Chaste Maid in Cheapside* for Lady Elizabeth's Men in 1613).[86] Hirschfield thus suggests that there was an association or loyalty between Middleton and the King's Men. Since Middleton's collaborations with Rowley were all written for Prince Charles's or Lady Elizabeth's companies, she theorizes that Middleton broke his association with the King's Men to write with Rowley, an act that suggests a 'deliberateness in their working relationship.'[87]

While this is a plausible interpretation, it is not the only one. Middleton's decision to submit all of his solo work to the most prestigious company in London, while writing almost all of his collaborations for Prince Charles's or Lady Elizabeth's players (the one exception was a collaboration with Webster for the King's Men in 1621),[88] could suggest that Middleton saw collaboration as *less* important than solo authorship; minor work for minor companies. Either interpretation could be true, but the possibility that Middleton was unsentimental about his collaborations with Rowley must remain conceivable.

Hirschfield claims, without explaining, that Rowley too broke a company affiliation to work with Middleton.[89] Her comment may derive from Rowley's confusing status during the mid-1620s: although he seems to have been 'attached' to Prince Charles's Men for most of his career, he co-wrote *The Changeling* for Lady Elizabeth's company in 1622. But friendship with Middleton does not explain this: after all, if they were keen to work together, why would Middleton not simply write for his friend's company? Bentley's explanation is better: he notes that *The Changeling* was written during or shortly after the period in which Prince Charles's Men left the Phoenix theatre and suggests that Rowley was fulfilling a contract with the theatre's manager.[90] Equally confusing is Rowley's behaviour after 1622, when he left Prince Charles's Men for the King's Men and began writing for both his former company and his present company, as well as for Lady Elizabeth's.[91] Rowley may have switched to freelance writing because he was not a sharer in his new company; Bentley observes that he was not sworn into the King's Men until 1625.[92] Hence, Rowley's apparent breaks with Prince Charles's Men do not necessarily indicate him placing loyalty to Middleton before all other ties.

Neither Middleton nor Rowley made any reference to their supposed friendship (in contrast, Rowley *did* call John Webster his 'friend' in a commendatory poem for *The Duchess of Malfi*; the two wrote a play together the following year). Nor did Middleton or Rowley offer any opinions about collaborative writing. Middleton wrote dedicatory epistles for two of his collaborations, *The Roaring Girl* (with Dekker, 1611) and *The World Tossed at Tennis*, but in them he neither acknowledges nor denies the presence of collaborators. In the most detailed, the *Roaring Girl* preface, he considers in the abstract what 'the excellency of a Writer' is, criticizes other unspecified playwrights, and concludes by describing what 'we rather wish' to see in plays; 'we' might refer to himself and Dekker but could simply mean the audience (22–3, 30).

In contrast to those of Middleton, Rowley's epistles suggest a hint of possessiveness toward the text and of an awareness of his own stylistic individuality. Rowley wrote epistles for *A Fair Quarrel* and *The World Tossed at Tennis* (the latter epistle appearing immediately after Middleton's).[93] In *A Fair Quarrel* he is careless of the play's authorship, telling his dedicatee 'who ever begat it, tis laid to your charge and (for ought I know) you must father and keep it too' (21–3), but in *The World Tossed at Tennis*, he writes as if he is the only 'parent' of the play, calling it 'the sonne of *Simplicitie*' after his acting role (25–6) and making no reference to his co-author, even though this conflicts with the title page and Middleton's accompanying epistle. He also goes further than Middleton when he claims in the *Fair Quarrel* epistle that his characteristic voice is recognizable in his writing: 'you see Sir, I write as I speak, & I speak as I am, & thats excuse enough for me' (15–16).

That Rowley asserts his singular authorship more forcefully than Middleton is perhaps surprising given that the majority of Rowley's plays were collaborative (only *All's Lost by Lust* and *A Shoemaker a Gentleman* have never been claimed to be collaborations). But his attitude may be explained in part by his position of responsibility in the playing company that performed the plays. Unlike Middleton, Rowley was a sharer, which meant that he had a significant role in the organization of Prince Charles's Men, with duties that included choosing new plays for the repertory, assigning parts to players, recruiting and dismissing actors, and managing the finances.[94] Although, as Masten points out, the word 'sharer' signifies collaboration rather than singular authority,[95] Rowley appears to have been the company's leader, or at least its spokesman.[96] He was probably a sharer in the company from its inception,[97] and acted as payee for court performances from 1612 to 1616.[98] When, in 1615, the Privy Council called a session to order the playing companies to stop performing during Lent, Rowley was one of the two sharers who represented Prince Charles's Men.[99] After 1616, Rowley ceased to be listed as the payee but may still have been a spokesman: in 1620, 'one of the Ordinary groomes of the Prince his chamber' travelled 'from the Courte at San James into London so far as Shoredich with a mesuage to Roulle [i.e., Rowley] one of his highnes players.'[100] Furthermore, Rowley was the principal playwright of Prince Charles's Men: all of the surviving plays from its repertory are written at least in part by him, and of those that do not survive, Rowley is known to have been involved in every one for which there is evidence of authorship until he left the company in 1623.[101]

All of this suggests that Rowley was an important, if not *the* most important figure in Prince Charles's Men, and his references to his singular authorship may thus derive from a position of influence over the process of composition. As a sharer, his role in the creation of a play would have extended beyond writing to include the casting process and the formation of the repertory that the play would be a part of; as an actor in the company's plays, he may have taken an organizational or directorial role during rehearsal.[102] This view of Rowley contrasts with the tendency of critics to dismiss him as a 'hack writer,' that is, one who writes what others order him to.[103] It is often assumed that Rowley was subservient to his collaborators: R.H. Barker writes that Rowley was '*invited* to collaborate with the more distinguished writers of the age,'[104] and Samuel Schoenbaum writes of *The Changeling* that 'Rowley was *entrusted* with the composition of the first and last scenes.'[105] In these formulations, Middleton, the more talented and therefore more powerful writer, 'invites' or 'accepts' Rowley, the less talented and therefore weaker writer, into his dramatic project. But Rowley and his company were sometimes the employers of Middleton; we should perhaps instead imagine Rowley, the powerful actor-manager, inviting or accepting Middleton into the venture. If so, it is likely that he would have had a strong sense of his own agency in the production of meaning.

I have described Rowley's position in detail because it is insufficiently acknowledged, but I do not mean to say that we should regard him as the 'singular author' *instead of* Middleton; rather, his work on *The Changeling* must be considered *in addition to* Middleton's. That work can be understood better by using stylistic analysis to study the method by which Middleton and Rowley's collaborative plays were divided and written. This evidence too shows that Rowley's role in the writing process allowed him considerable control over the meanings communicated by the plays.

Authorial Divisions and the Process of Collaboration

In order to understand how early modern collaborative writers wrote their plays, some understanding of the internal evidence for their authorship is essential. As such, my analysis of Middleton and Rowley's collaborative process is based on the results of attribution studies conducted by a number of scholars over the years. The pioneering study was Pauline G. Wiggin's 1897 *Inquiry into the Authorship of the Middleton-Rowley Plays*, based primarily on analysis of versification and parallel passages, alongside more impressionistic accounts of the authors' 'quality of wit, conception of life and human character, and dramatic technique.'[106] Other similar studies followed, the most often cited being those of C.W. Stork, Dewar M. Robb, and R.H. Barker.[107] Despite the relatively impressionistic nature of these early studies, the next wave of attribution scholars, who used more rigorous methodologies centred on stylistic analysis, produced conclusions that echoed their findings. Cyrus Hoy, David J. Lake, and MacDonald P. Jackson agree on the general overall division of authorship of *The Changeling*, *A Fair Quarrel*, and *The World Tossed at Tennis*, and their divisions typically confirm those originally identified by Wiggin, albeit with some modifications in the details. This agreement between scholars working with different methodologies, and – in the case of Lake and Jackson – working independently of each other, suggests that these perceived authorial divisions have a basis in reality and should be an important factor in discussion of those plays.

In using the findings of attribution scholars, I am contradicting the approach of some recent studies of collaboration. Jeffrey Masten has attacked stylistic analysis in the course of his argument that early modern drama should not be read as the work of individual authors; and although Masten focuses on the Beaumont and Fletcher plays, his critique is echoed by Richard L. Nochimson, who discusses Middleton and Rowley.[108] Masten objects to the central aim of attribution studies as expressed by Hoy: to be able to 'distinguish any dramatist's share in a play of dual or doubtful authorship.'[109] For Masten, this project is problematic for its assumption of the existence of singular authors with unchanging 'styles,' and for placing unwarranted faith in the univocality of the plays of 'singular authorship' that are analysed to provide the primary data.[110] Similarly, Nochimson argues that attribution scholars are more certain about their claims of authorial division than is warranted.[111] At least two recent studies have followed Masten's lead by attempting to discuss collaborative drama without making any reference to the putative divisions of authorship suggested by stylistic studies.[112]

The denial of any validity to authorship attribution is, however, an extreme response. Nochimson identifies some problems with Hoy's and Jackson's data concerning the Middleton-Rowley plays, but the rest of the considerable data continues to support the received authorial division.[113] Furthermore, these critiques misrepresent attribution scholars in claiming that they believe in clear and absolute divisions between authorial work within plays. It is true that authorship attributers can appear over-definite at times; Hoy, in particular, places apparently definitive divisions at the top of each of his play analyses, making his conclusions look simple and clear-cut. Yet Hoy makes it clear, in the lengthy explanations beneath, that there are varying degrees of certainty about each of those divisions. Hoy accepts that his stated aim of clearly dividing every play between its authors is unrealistic and makes an important comment: '[The] value to be attached to any piece of linguistic criteria is, in the end, completely relative: all depends on the *degree* of divergence between the linguistic patterns that are to be distinguished.'[114] Attribution scholars acknowledge that the degree of clarity about authorial divisions in plays can vary. The studies of Hoy, Lake, and Jackson demonstrate that *some* playwrights display extremely idiosyncratic styles while others do not; and furthermore, that *some* plays have textual histories that allow different writing styles to be seen clearly while others do not; as Jackson writes, 'The fact that in some composite plays the shares of the contributing playwrights cannot be disentangled is itself of interest, since in others the divisions are sharp and clean.'[115] Indeed, for John Jowett, one of the purposes of attribution study is 'to distinguish between the undistinguishably merged and the distinguishably separate.'[116] Hoy found, for example, that it was possible to distinguish between Fletcher and Massinger 'with virtually mathematical precision,' but that 'it is not possible ... to attribute every line or scene of *Philaster* or *The Maid's Tragedy* to either Beaumont or Fletcher.'[117] This applies to Middleton's and Rowley's plays, too: Hoy's study of *The Maid in the Mill* (by Fletcher and Rowley) demonstrates that 'linguistically, the play can be divided into two readily distinguishable parts,'[118] but his conclusions about *Wit at Several Weapons* are cautious and uncertain.[119] The fact that not every play can be divided with absolute certainty should not distract us from acknowledging that in some cases we are fortunate enough to have convincing evidence of the general pattern of division. Understanding as much as possible about how the playwrights may have worked is of fundamental importance in the study of collaboration.[120]

Another criticism is that stylistic analysis assumes that some linguistic features of a dramatist's style are unconscious rather than deliberately chosen. Norman Rabkin has written of 'the great Elizabethan disappearing act,' whereby dramatists base their writing styles on pre-existing generic models so closely that they become anonymous,[121] and Hirschfield offers the example of the three authors of *Eastward Ho*, who worked hard to tone down their individuality.[122] Indeed, Masten argues that dramatic writing is by definition Protean because it requires the replication of different patterns of speech;[123] he thus criticizes Hoy's assumption that 'a writer's use of *ye* for *you* and of contractions like *'em* for *them* is both individually distinct and remarkably constant "in whatever context,"' and suggests that such features might be deliberate decisions by the writers, perhaps reflecting class-related differences.[124] However, this ignores some of the discoveries: for example, Jackson's point that 'Middleton employs *I've* regardless of stylistic register, whereas Rowley employs it neither in his tragedy *All's Lost by Lust*, nor in his comedies *A Shoemaker, a Gentleman* and *A Woman Never Vexed*.'[125] In a recent stylistic analysis of Fletcher and Shakespeare's *Henry VIII*, Hugh Craig finds that the speeches of individual characters are written in demonstrably different styles according to which playwright is writing which scene. 'The two writers,' he concludes, 'have every interest in writing like each other, so as to produce seamless drama, and yet their character parts diverge and follow their separate patterns of function word use,' a result of unconscious preferences.[126] While playwrights may not always write consistently, there is no reason to extrapolate from this that *all* playwrights are *always* able transform their styles utterly beyond recognition.

The reason that some texts reveal clear authorial divisions and others do not is, no doubt, that methods of collaboration differ: some plays may have been quickly assembled with little discussion between the authors other than a simple planning stage, whereas others may have been carefully prepared, debated over, and revised many times, making the work of the writers indistinguishable. Jowett writes that one of the tasks of attribution studies is to 'map out, as far as possible, different and varying modes of interaction between dramatists.'[127]

These 'modes of interaction' have been much debated, as little is known about methods of writing collaborative drama in the early modern period. Nochimson castigates authorship attributers for purportedly believing that collaborators worked entirely in isolation and finds implausible the notion that plays were 'cut up into pieces, each piece to be written by a different author.'[128] Noting the parallels between the behaviour of DeFlores and Lollio in the main plot and subplot of *The Changeling*, he insists that the scenes could not have been written by Middleton and Rowley if they wrote separately, and imagines them literally writing *together* in a 'sitting-in-the-same-room-and-talking-together' situation.[129] But although modern textual criticism has rightly quashed the myth of the solitary genius, we should avoid an equally romantic vision of collaborators endlessly debating, rewriting, and swapping ideas as they write.[130] If the principal motive for collaborative writing is speed (and Henslowe's diary shows that collaborative plays could be written very quickly),[131] some degree of separate composition is necessary simply in order that the playwrights may write swiftly without interruption rather than haggling over every word.[132] This is not to claim that the dramatists worked entirely in isolation; rather, the parallels between the plots in *The Changeling* could have been produced by collaborative pre-planning rather than by writing in the same room. The planning stage of a collaboration is, of course, the most mysterious. As Lake suggests, 'The actual writing out of a play is the last stage in its composition; much of the value of the work will depend on the previous stages of plotting and arrangement of scenes; and presumably each collaborator will be involved here, in a relationship which we cannot now determine.'[133] Equally mysterious is the process by which this 'outline' was divided between the playwrights. Some scholars, notably G.E. Bentley, believed that most collaborators divided plays by act, but Nochimson is right to say that the evidence for this is very weak.[134] The evidence points to division into smaller sections than acts. Brian Vickers argues that the surviving 'plots' that break down plays into a series of short scene summaries could have aided collaborators in dividing their labours.[135] Similarly, the evidence of *Sir Thomas More* suggests that Henslowe's writers tended to divide plays by 'looking at a plot outline and selecting episodes that appealed to them.'[136] As Edward Burns notes, evidence for another method can be found in Thomas Dekker's testimony in a court case concerning a lost play, *The Late Murder in Whitechapel, or Keep the Widow Waking* (1624) written with Ford, Rowley, and Webster. Dekker testified that he 'wrote two sheetes of paper conteyning the first Act of a Play called The Late Murder in White Chapell, or Keepe the Widow waking, and a speech in the Last Scene of the Last Act of the Boy who had killed his mother.'[137] In other words, Dekker may have written a single act, but he also wrote a single speech for insertion into somebody else's scene.[138] Burns thus suggests that authorship attributers should not divide plays into scenes but into 'strands of rhetorical action' associated with things that particular dramatists were 'good at.'[139]

The situations were undoubtedly varied. McMullan notes that authorship attributers have, perhaps unwisely, assumed the basic unit of division to have been the scene, in part because quantitative analysis requires a relatively large sample of text to work with, and scenes provide a usefully sized unit.[140] But the attributers have often been successful at noticing when scenes have been broken into smaller units: examples are Lake's evidence for Middleton's authorship of the first hundred lines of scene 1.1 in *A Fair Quarrel*; Hoy's perception that lines 1–16 of *The Changeling*, scene 4.2 are by Rowley; and Gary Taylor's description of the sub-scenic units into which *The Spanish Gypsy* may have been divided.[141] It is certainly true that smaller-scale collaborative acts, such as playwrights making minute revisions to one another's work, cannot be detected by any attribution method. And, as I will show below, there is no doubt that Middleton and Rowley talked to each other and worked hard to maintain unity in their plays. But MacDonald P. Jackson insists that while their collaborations may contain 'occasional patches of mixed writing,' the stylistic differences between Middleton's and Rowley's styles are so striking that they are 'incompatible with any notion that the two men habitually worked together on actual speeches, rather than assuming separate responsibility for substantial sequences, such as scenes or acts.'[142]

Sure enough, the stylistic studies of Middleton and Rowley indicate that they sometimes utilized a distinctive collaborative method that allows for a significant degree of writing in isolation but that also allows for swift creation of coherence between these separately written sections afterwards. *The Changeling* is one of the plays written this way. The table below is based on David J. Lake's study of the play's authorship, with which the other major studies agree;[143] as always, these divisions cannot be absolute, but they can be considered accurate in a general sense.

Clearly, the playwrights did not divide *The Changeling* by acts. Instead, Rowley was responsible for the subplot (apart from the brief appearance of Alibius and Isabella in 5.2), while Middleton wrote the central section of the main plot. This pattern allowed Middleton to create the powerful tragedy of Beatrice and DeFlores, while Rowley used his comic talents to create the subplot. However, Rowley also wrote the opening and closing scenes, which means that he had a hand in both plotlines.

The Changeling (1622)
Main plot = Beatrice-Joanna's tragedy
Subplot = the madhouse

Scene	Plotline	Writer
1.1	main plot	Rowley
1.2	subplot	Rowley
2.1	main plot	Middleton
2.2	main plot	Middleton
3.1 and 3.2[144]	main plot	Middleton
3.3	subplot	Rowley
3.4	main plot	Middleton
4.1	main plot	Middleton
4.2.1–16	main plot and subplot	Rowley
4.2.17–150	main plot	Middleton
4.3	subplot	Rowley
5.1	main plot	Middleton
5.2	main plot and subplot	Middleton
5.3	main plot and subplot	Rowley

In an important study of Middleton and Rowley's collaborative method, Michael E. Mooney labels this technique 'framing.' He argues that it recognizes 'the need for a unified tone at the beginning and end' of the play, allowing one writer – Rowley – to create that unity by writing scenes from both plotlines and combining them in the final scene.[145] Noting the strange fact that Rowley appears to have written a sixteen-line section of scene 4.2, Mooney shows that these lines connect the main plot and subplots: Vermandero is describing the absence of the subplot characters Antonio and Fransiscus from his castle. For Mooney, the division of *The Changeling* thus indicates that Rowley was responsible for its 'structural organisation.'[146]

Mooney goes on to demonstrate the presence of words and stage images that recur in both plots, and to argue that the events in the two plots are designed to be compared with one another. He suggests that the division of the writing facilitated this: the links are easier to create if one writer has a hand in both plotlines. He further speculates that a 'set of words, a prepared lexicon' may have been 'added or reinforced in a final joint revision' in order to enhance the thematic unity of the plots.[147]

This 'framing' method is one way of writing a collaborative play, but it was not the only method possible. At this point, it is helpful to turn

28   Middleton and Rowley

The Maid in the Mill (1623)
Main plot = Antonio and Ismenia
Subplot = Otrante and Florimell
Clown = Bustofa's antics

Scene	Plotline	Writer
1.1	main plot	Fletcher
1.2	main plot	Fletcher
2.1	subplot and clown	Rowley
2.2	main plot, subplot, and clown	Rowley
3.1	subplot	Rowley
3.2	subplot	Fletcher
3.3	subplot	Fletcher
4.1	main plot and clown	Rowley
4.2	main plot and clown	Rowley
4.3	main plot	Rowley
5.1	main plot	Rowley
5.2.1–222	subplot	Fletcher
5.2.223–end	main plot, subplot, and clown	Rowley

away from Middleton and Rowley to compare *The Changeling* with *The Maid in the Mill* (1623), Rowley's collaboration with John Fletcher, which was written according to a very different plan. The table above is based on Hoy's study.[148] Again, there are two plotlines, and I have indicated the scenes that contain the clown.

The difference between this play and *The Changeling* is clear: the playwrights have simply divided the play into 'chunks,' each of which may contain scenes from both plotlines. The only similarity with *The Changeling* is that Rowley is responsible for all the scenes involving the clown, and that he wrote the final sequence of the play, in which the plotlines combine at the end.

This 'chunk' method appears at its clearest in *The Maid in the Mill* but is also apparent in the division of *Wit at Several Weapons*, Middleton and Rowley's first collaboration. The table below is based on Lake's study, with which the other studies broadly agree.[149] There are two plotlines, and I have noted the scenes that contain the clown. Attribution scholars are more cautious in their conclusions about this play's division; I have thus indicated with question marks those scenes for which there is a postulated author but for which either Lake or Jackson finds weak evidence or suspects mixed composition.[150]

Wit at Several Weapons (ca. 1613–15)
Main plot = Wittypate gulling his father
Subplot = Cunningham and the Niece gulling Sir Gregory
Clown = Pompey Doodle's infatuation

Scene	Plotline	Writer
1.1	main plot and subplot	Middleton
1.2	main plot	Rowley
2.1	main plot	Middleton
2.2	subplot and clown	Rowley
2.3	subplot and clown	Rowley (?)
2.4	main plot	Rowley
3.1	subplot	Middleton
4.1	main plot, subplot, and clown	Middleton
4.2	subplot	Middleton
4.3	subplot	Middleton
5.1	main plot, subplot, and clown	Rowley (?)
5.2	main plot, subplot, and clown	Rowley (?)

Here, despite the uncertain authorship of several scenes, both playwrights have clearly written a mixture of main and subplot scenes. Indeed, for half of the play they seem to have simply divided the writing by acts. Again, there is a similarity with the previous plays: if the attributions are correct, Rowley wrote most of the scenes involving the clown as well as the final scenes, which combine the main plot and subplot.

A Fair Quarrel, as Mooney notes, follows the same 'framing' pattern as *The Changeling*, although Mooney does not discuss Lake's findings, which complicate the division slightly. The play features three plotlines. Rowley was responsible for the two subplots, while Middleton wrote most of the main plot, except, as with *The Changeling*, for the opening and closing scenes. The table below is based on Lake's study; some scenes about which Jackson differs are indicated by question marks.[151]

Even taking into account the ambiguous authorship of some sections, we can see that this division is similar to that of *The Changeling*: Middleton's writing was mostly restricted to main plot scenes, while Rowley wrote the subplots and the first and last scenes. However, Lake's study suggests that two short sections of text complicate this simple division: Middleton also wrote the opening section of the first scene, and possibly the final section of the last scene.[152] This could mean that

A Fair Quarrel (1616)
Main plot = the duellists
Subplot = Jane and her father
Clown = Chough's roaring

Scene	Plotline	Writer
1.1.1–87	main plot and subplot	Middleton
1.1.88–end	main plot and subplot	Rowley
2.1	main plot	Middleton
2.2	subplot and clown	Rowley
3.1	main plot	Middleton
3.2	subplot	Rowley
3.3	main plot	Middleton
4.1	clown	Rowley
4.2	main plot	Middleton
4.3	main plot	Middleton (?)
4.4	clown	Rowley
5.1.1–392	subplot and clown	Rowley
5.1.393–end	main plot and subplot	Middleton (?)

part(s) of these scenes were rewritten by Middleton, perhaps to smooth over discrepancies. As such, *A Fair Quarrel* demonstrates that the 'framing' method used by the playwrights is not always as simple as in *The Changeling*. Nonetheless, we can see that Middleton and Rowley still divided most of the play by plotline rather than by arbitrary 'chunks.'

Mooney notes that the 'framing' pattern may also be discernible in Middleton and Rowley's *The Old Law*.[153] *The Old Law* is not an easy text to study: it survives only in a poorly printed quarto.[154] In addition, scene 5.1 may be written by a third collaborator, identified variously as Massinger or Heywood.[155] Even so, if we look at Lake's cautious conclusions (below), we can see the 'framing' pattern again (one scene about which Jackson differs is indicated by a question mark).[156] The play has two plotlines, a main plot and a clown subplot.

Once more, Rowley wrote the beginning and ending of the play and the clown plot, while Middleton was responsible for the middle scenes of the main plot. The only exception is scene 4.1, in which there are some Middleton indicators in a clown scene. Lake and Jackson both believe that Rowley wrote most of the scene, even if Middleton made some contributions to it.[157] We can therefore see that *The Old Law* is primarily based on the 'framing' method.

The Old Law (1618–19)
Main plot: the courtiers
Clown: Gnothos and Agatha

Scene	Plotline	Writer
1.1	main plot	Rowley
2.1	main plot	Middleton
2.2	main plot	Middleton
3.1	clown	Rowley
3.2	main plot	Middleton
4.1	clown	both
4.2	main plot	Middleton
5.1.1–346	main plot	third collaborator (?)
5.1.347–end	main plot and clown	Rowley

To conclude, among those Middleton-Rowley collaborations for which authorial shares can be understood with some certainty (I exclude *World Tossed at Tennis*, which is not structured as a conventional play, and *The Spanish Gypsy*, which is a four-way collaboration) there are two principal collaborative methods observable. The first, represented by *Wit at Several Weapons* (and by the Fletcher-Rowley collaboration *The Maid in the Mill*), is the simplest: after planning their play, the writers divide it into five or six 'chunks,' which they share out with no particular regard for what is contained within those chunks. They then write their shares. Having finished the writing, they join the chunks together, presumably checking through the play to remove any contradictions that may have arisen. In this system, the playwrights write an approximately equal share and take part in the creation of all of the plotlines; they are thus equally important in the play's construction, because both are performing essentially the same task.

In contrast, the 'framing' method required Rowley and his collaborator to take on quite different roles in the writing of the play. In *The Changeling*, while Middleton focuses on one long central section of the main plotline, Rowley writes an entire subplot, and also writes most of the scenes in which the plotlines are combined. Rowley's role is therefore more diverse than Middleton's: he writes a part of every plotline rather than just one. In addition, his role is an organizational one, because it involves writing the scenes that connect the disparate plotlines. This is not to describe Rowley as *the* author in any absolute sense; it does, however, show that his presence in the creation of the play was neither irrelevant nor unimportant. The fact that variants of this model appear in the earlier *A Fair Quarrel* and *The Old Law* suggest that it was a system that the two writers preferred and perhaps developed over time. Rowley's organizational role in these collaborations indicates that he should not be imagined as merely following Middleton's orders or executing plans devised entirely by Middleton.

I have defended attribution studies at length because in addition to determining which texts are associated with Middleton and which with Rowley, they can also offer insights into the process by which collaborative plays were written by demonstrating the presence of recurring patterns in the divisions of authorship within the texts.[158] But what can we do with this information? Hoy writes that critics have found it difficult to translate the results of authorship studies into meaningful interpretations of the plays; to discuss how, in Jowett's words, 'a hypothesis about divided authorship can constructively feed into a critical, interpretive practice.'[159] As Jowett does, I think this can be done if the critic takes the uncomfortable step of looking at where collaborators *fail*, rather than succeed, in generating unity.

Analysing Collaborative Drama

If the problem with the disintegrationist approach is that it advocates detaching and discarding pieces of texts, and if the failure of the unifiers and the post-structuralists is that they blur collaborators into a single author, I propose two solutions: reading collaborative texts for their disunities, and grouping the texts through multiple author-like figures beyond the playwrights.

The first solution – studying the ways in which distinctive authorial traits cause disharmony and inconsistency within playtexts – is the only way to appreciate how distinctive playwrights worked together without falling back into romantic ideas of authorial and/or textual unity. There have been moves toward such an approach. By far the most detailed is Brian Vickers's exhaustive study of the discordant plotting, characterization, and linguistic structures in Shakespeare's collaborations.[160] This approach can, of course, seem unappealing: Vickers's conclusions are usually negative, as he meticulously shows how each of Shakespeare's collaborative plays is defective. This is in part unavoidable: as John Jowett puts it, 'collaboration is only visible at the points where it fails to produce a harmonious meshing of the playwrights' contributions,' so that 'the marks of collaboration are easily translated as the marks of failure.'[161] Gordon McMullan notes that 'the quest *either* to merge together *or* to differentiate between collaborators is inevitably a destructive one,' as the critic must choose between destroying the distinctive qualities of the playwrights by merging them together or breaking up the text into competing authorial sections and destroying its illusion of coherence, a conclusion that McMullan finds painful.[162]

But Jowett sees the positive side of this approach. Contesting the common argument that inconsistencies in collaborative plays are likely to be ignored in performance, he argues that 'effects that might not register consciously can still contribute strongly to the play's impact.'[163] In his edition of *Timon of Athens*, Jowett notes differences in the ways in which Middleton and Shakespeare represent the title character. These differences cause a 'central and vital ambiguity of the role' that has 'a strong bearing on critical and theatrical responses' to it.[164] Jowett's important insight is that disunities can sometimes be theatrically effective, even when inadvertent.

A rare example of such an approach to *The Changeling* is Raymond Pentzell's study, which argues that the first and last scenes are 'unmistakably different in style ... from Middleton's scenes.' Pentzell suggests that Rowley's scenes of the main plot are more 'formal' and less 'realistic' than Middleton's, and claims that Rowley wrote in 'neat, old-fashioned verse at times reminiscent of Spenser and Lyly.'[165] Although I do not agree with this assessment of Rowley's verse, Pentzell is unusual in suggesting that *differences* between Middleton and Rowley might contribute to the effects of the main plot. Pentzell argues that formalist criticism obscures the wild disjunctions in the play, a play that he sees as 'a tonal thrill-show, a roller-coaster ride on hills of many heights and many angles of steepness.'[166] However, Pentzell's approach differs from mine in his assumption that the play's disjunctions are deliberate choices by the playwrights; that Middleton and Rowley were aware of their different styles and structured their plays accordingly. For my purposes, the inadvertent contradictions are just as valuable as any deliberate ones that might exist.

My first approach, therefore, is to read collaborative texts doubly: to acknowledge where the playwrights are attempting to efface their differences, but also to observe where their differences appear to cause unintentional effects. Following from this approach, I will analyse the plays with these principles in mind:

1. Playwrights may strive to minimize the fact of their collaboration, but may not perfectly achieve this.
2. The failure to achieve unity or coherence between authorial voices does not inherently entail theatrical failure.

By bearing these principles in mind, it is possible to analyse collaborative plays in such a way that the presence of more than one author both destabilizes our view of the text's unity and provides us with an understanding of each author's distinctive qualities. These distinctions, in turn, can reveal and explain aspects of the text that may otherwise be overlooked. In chapters 2 and 4 of this book, I attempt to do just that with Middleton and Rowley's best-known plays, *The Changeling* and *A Fair Quarrel*.

This methodology is not appropriate for every collaborative playtext; it can only be used on those for which convincing authorial divisions can be produced. And it is not, of course, the only way to read these texts. Since not all texts can be divided convincingly – *The Old Law* and *The Spanish Gypsy* present exceptional difficulties – one must use other methods to learn about Middleton and Rowley indirectly. For this reason, my second approach is to broaden the scope of authorship by considering other ways of grouping texts.

As we have seen, scepticism about the significance of authorial agency has encouraged the grouping of the plays in alternative ways. In her study of the Children of the Queen's Revels, Lucy Munro argues not for 'denying the playwright's agency' but for 'considering the input of all those involved in the production and dissemination of plays: dramatists, actors, shareholders, playhouse functionaries, patrons, audiences and publishers.' The value is in 'acknowledging the compromises which writers make when they engage with institutions such as the early modern theatre industry.'[167]

The best-explored alternative to grouping texts by authorship is repertory study. In recent years, studies by Rosalyn L. Knutson, Scott McMillin and Sally-Beth MacLean, Mary Bly, and Andrew Gurr have demonstrated that reading the repertories of individual playing companies 'with the kinds of critical and textual attention that are normally reserved for the canons of the playwrights'[168] can yield fresh insights into the companies and their plays.[169] The study of individual actors is another fruitful area: David Wiles's *Shakespeare's Clown* illustrates the importance of understanding the qualities of the clown actors whose distinctive presence playwrights were obliged to incorporate into their plays.[170] And since audiences seem to have considered particular playhouses to have distinct identities, Alexander Leggatt, in *Jacobean Public Theatre*, experiments with identifying plays by their playhouse rather than by author.[171] Of course, each of these approaches creates what Foucault called a 'constraining figure' similar to that of the author;[172] indeed Bly, in her study of the Whitefriars repertory, acknowledges that in drawing connections between the company's plays, she is turning the Whitefriars syndicate into an 'author figure.' The value of these approaches, Bly argues, is their broadening of our understanding of the network of agencies involved in the creation of plays, and hence their complication of the idea of the singular author.[173] The synthesis of many of these approaches, viewing the texts through different lenses, is one way to accrue a more sophisticated understanding of early modern plays. For example, studying the clown roles written by Rowley is less illuminating than comparing the roles he wrote to perform himself with those that were written for him by others, including Middleton. Studying the class politics of Middleton and Rowley's plays as a whole is less illuminating than studying the differences between those written for Rowley's company and those for other companies. For this reason, my study of *Wit at Several Weapons* in chapter 3 discusses the significance of Rowley's stage persona for the structure of that play, and in chapter 5 I demonstrate the importance of a popular boy actor's persona to *The Spanish Gypsy*; my examination of *A Fair Quarrel* in chapter 4 emphasizes the importance of the playing companies for which the playwrights were working; and my analysis of *The World Tossed at Tennis* and *The Old Law* in chapter 5 focuses on the significance of the company's patron, Prince Charles. As such, while taking up Hoy's challenge to study Middleton *and* Rowley, I hope to broaden the scope of study in order to avoid a simplistic focus on individual authors, while still allowing them a degree of individual distinction.

Chapter Two

Collaborators and Individual Style: Choice and Religion in *The Changeling*

In one of the few readings of *The Changeling* to consider the implications of its dual authorship, Arthur Symons attempted in 1910 to describe the process of the collaboration and its effect on the characterization of the play's tragic protagonists. Symons notes that Rowley 'begins the play, and thus introduces the characters of Beatrice and De Flores.' He describes Middleton as having 'both hands upon' the story for the middle acts and then says that in the conclusion, 'Rowley seems to snatch the whole web out of his hands and to twist it into an abrupt end.'[1] During this process, Symons claims, 'De Flores seems to grow greater as he passes from one to the other of the two playwrights, as they collaborate visibly at his creation.'[2] Symons's analysis, generalized though it is, hints at fascinating questions: How does the change of playwright affect DeFlores's 'greatness' (however that is defined)? Is not the character's perceived 'growth' due to the plot rather than the collaborative process? When do the playwrights 'collaborate visibly'? Unfortunately, Symons does not examine these ideas further. Instead, he offers a theory that in *The Changeling*, Middleton's and Rowley's talents became fused into a new, hybrid form. Rowley, he argues, aspired to write drama with 'great passions and a loftiness in good and evil' but lacked the poetic skills to match his grand ambitions. Middleton, meanwhile, was a better poet but needed the inspiration of Rowley to raise his writing to a more emotional pitch.[3] Of the great scene 3.4 in *The Changeling*, in which DeFlores comes to Beatrice-Joanna to claim his reward for murder, Symons writes that Middleton 'has distilled into it the essence of his own genius and of the genius of Rowley': it is 'at once tragical, probable and poetical.'[4] Here, Symons is demonstrating the common tendency that I described in the previous chapter, in which the critic imagines collaborators fusing into a transcendent singular author. In this chapter, however, I will elaborate on Symons's first idea and explore how Middleton's and Rowley's different sensibilities could affect the ways in which we interpret the characters as they pass from playwright to playwright. I suggested in the previous chapter that it can be valuable to study the inconsistencies caused by collaboration in order to understand the distinctive qualities of each writer, while still remembering that such inconsistencies need not render the play theatrically unsatisfying. Here I will argue that some of the most powerful effects of the main plot of *The Changeling* are created by disunities resulting from the shifts from one playwright's work to that of the other.

I will focus on a fundamental disunity in *The Changeling* that arises from the different ways in which Middleton and Rowley represent characters in the act of making moral choices. Reading the non-collaborative tragedies of both playwrights reveals that they were remarkably different in their depiction of characters who decide to perform actions that are sinful. This difference is symptomatic of a profound dissimilarity in the writers' representation of the process by which sin is conceived and enacted, and can be identified with opposing attitudes current in the theological debates of the time.

In order to demonstrate this, I will begin with an analysis of Rowley's only non-collaborative tragedy, *All's Lost by Lust*, a play that illustrates powerfully the decision-making moments that are central to this chapter. I will then explain the ways in which the representation of these 'decision points' reflects early modern theological debates and show that such scenes are handled differently in Middleton's non-collaborative tragedies, which are influenced by Calvinist theology more than are Rowley's. Finally, I will turn to *The Changeling* and explain how these differences of approach generate some of that play's effects.

Choosing to Sin in *All's Lost by Lust*

William Rowley wrote *All's Lost by Lust* (1618–20) a few years before *The Changeling*.[5] As its title suggests, the play includes a number of scenes in which characters are shown making a catastrophic decision to act upon their illicit desires. An example is the scene in which the nobleman Antonio decides to betray his low-born wife, Margaretta, by committing bigamy with Dionyzia. Guilt-ridden, Antonio suffers an inner struggle that he describes as a 'wound,' as 'paine,' and as 'a bed of snakes [that] struggle within me' (2.6.13, 39, 36). In his turmoil, Antonio shifts between two contrary impulses: at first, he refuses to enact his desires; then he gives in and flirts with Dionyzia; then he once more feels 'lost,' crying, 'oh Margaretta' (172, 174).

The sequence has two significant characteristics. First, Antonio's decision takes place gradually, over an entire scene. This has the effect of focusing the audience's attention on his indecision, which manifests as a mental conflict between opposing desires. Second, when Antonio finally resolves to betray his wife, he is depicted as walking knowingly into a situation that will cause his damnation:

> 'Tis now concluded in me, I will on,
> I must, although I meet destruction:
> Downe hill we run, climbe upward a slow pace:
> Easie discents to hell, steepe steps to grace. (182–5)

This image of the sinner knowingly running to hell recurs throughout the play and recalls Ovid's paradox, often cited by Renaissance thinkers, *video meliora proboque, deteriora sequor* (*Metamorphoses*, 7.20–1), which describes Medea proceeding to act upon her desire for Jason despite her knowledge that restraint would be better.[6] The paradox reappears when Margaretta shifts between opposing impulses as she prepares to strangle the sleeping man that she (wrongly) believes to be Antonio. At first determined to be a 'cruell executioner' (4.2.7), Margaretta is unsettled when her maid vows to be the 'Prologue to *Antonios* Tragedy' (10). Margaretta has second thoughts:

> *Antonios* Tragedy! that very Name
> Should strike even sparkes of pitty from the flint:
> *Antonio*! husband *Antonio*. (4.2.11–13)

But the maid persuades her to continue, and Margaretta resolves herself in language similar to that of Antonio:

> ... thus I begin. [*Pulls at the halter*]
> And follow thus and thus, now I am in,
> Nothing shall pull me back. (20–2)

Like Antonio, Margaretta decides to proceed with her actions even though they will send her to hell. Vowing to 'smile / Upon my dreadfull Executioner,' she says, 'Tis needy mischiefe, and hee's basely bent / That dares doe ill, yet feare the punishment' (51–5). Both characters suffer mental anguish, and both are aware of the consequences of their actions when they resolve to endure the punishment that awaits them in hell.

When, in the play's other plotline, King Roderick rapes Jacinta, Rowley emphasizes his 'decision point' in a different way. Roderick does not suffer conflicting impulses, but he still makes his decision in the full knowledge that it will send him to hell, because Jacinta delivers a speech in which she warns him,

> It is not love you seeke;
> But an Antipathy as dissonant
> As heaven and hell, the musique of the spheares
> Comparde with gnashings, and the howles below.
> Can lust be cal'd love[?] then let men seeke hell,
> For there that fiery diety doth dwell. (2.1.107–12)

Roderick is careless of the consequences, telling Jacinta that his misery must be ended in spite of morality: 'Cal't as you please, / We have a burning feaver, and the disease / You must lay balsum to' (120–2).

In each of these scenes, a character chooses to enact a desire despite certain knowledge that he or she will be damned by it. As several critics have noted, such moments challenge easy divisions of humanity into good and evil.[7] Alan Sinfield writes of Macbeth (who vacillates as Rowley's characters do), 'If immediate revulsion at the thought of evil is a test of moral sensitivity then Macbeth is the most moral person in the play.'[8] It was the opinion of Aristotle that people do not perform evil actions knowingly; they do so either because they mistakenly believe such actions to be good or because they are self-deceiving.[9] But the characters in *All's Lost* commit evil without making any such mistakes; their actions suggest that moral instruction is powerless to prevent evil.

Structuring the 'decision points' in this way is a simple method for creating dramatic tension, because if the character clearly understands the difference between good and evil, the possibility is raised that he or she may choose good; the character possesses what Margaretta calls 'sparkes of pitty' (4.2.12) that might pull them back from the brink. This possibility is important to Rowley's play, because two of its sequences dramatize a moral about the potential of reason and willpower to defeat sinful desires.

The first sequence involves Jacinta's father, one of Roderick's generals, who is leading an army against the invading Moors. The raped Jacinta travels in disguise to her father's military camp. There, she informs him that she is a woman who has been raped and asks him what he would do had such a thing happened to his daughter. Julianus responds with what sounds like disinterested common sense:

> O tis too hard a question to resolve,
> Without a solemne Councell held within
> Of mans best understanding faculties:
> There must be love, and fatherhood, and griefe,
> And rage, and many passions, and they must all
> Beget a thing call'd vengeance; but they must sit upon't. (4.1.76–81)

Julianus postulates a conflict, like those suffered by Antonio and Margaretta, between 'many passions' and the 'understanding faculties.' But he also permits emotions such as 'love, and fatherhood, and griefe, / And rage,' as long as they are informed by a 'solemne Councell held within.' The result of this, in Julianus's opinion, is that an ideal course of action will be found, without the distractions of emotion. It is a speech that advocates the supremacy of reason over passion.

However, Julianus's detachment lasts only as long as he believes the woman in front of him to be a stranger. When Jacinta reveals that she really *is* his daughter and that King Roderick was the rapist, his self-control evaporates. 'See you my daughter?' he roars to the assembled lords. 'She sounds the Trumpet, which draws forth my sword / To be revengde[!]' (107–9). The lords try to calm him down, reminding him of the need for rational thought before he acts:

> Digest your choller into temperance:
> Give your considerate thoughts the upper hand,
> In your hot passions, twill asswage the swelling
> Of your big heart. (110–13)

But Julianus suffers more 'fighting passions' and even faints with sorrow (120–1) before whipping the lords into a fervour for revenge against their king. In this passionate state, he develops a foolhardy plan: he sets free his captured enemy, the King of the Moors, and invites him to unite in an attack on Roderick. The Moor agrees, but he is only exploiting the crazed general, and once Roderick has been deposed, the Moor betrays Julianus.

Rowley's second sequence about the control of the passions by the 'understanding faculties' is the culmination of an extended symbol of the rewards of patience that he develops throughout the play. At the heart of Roderick's castle is a sealed room that has been left unopened by twenty of his predecessors, who 'added each a locke to guard it more' (1.1.53). The room's contents are a mystery, and 'fearefull prophesies predict / Fatall events to *Spaine*' if the room is opened before 'fate hath runne / Her owne wasting period' (58–9, 60–1). If, on the other hand, fate is permitted to run its course,

> Auspitiously they promise, that wreathes are kept
> In the fore-dooming Court of destiny,
> To binde us ever in a happy conquest.   (62–4)

Roderick's patience snaps when the Moors march on his palace, and he breaks the locks. When thunder rolls, Roderick recognizes the warning, but chooses damnation regardless: 'Hell wakens, yet Ile on … If this doore thither lead, Ile enter hell' (5.1.33–5). Again Rowley presents us with the image of a character going 'on' despite knowledge of the consequences. Within the 'fatall chamber,' Roderick sees a vision of himself being forced to kneel to the Moor, who wears the Spanish crown (5.2.16–19); his punishment for breaking into the room is thus not only the loss of Spain but also to see his own fate performed before him. The breaking down of the doors can be read as a symbolic re-enactment of the rape of Jacinta: the locked room represents her body.[10] But Roderick's actions also function as a parallel to the other characters in the play who walk knowingly into damnation. The magic room is a symbol of the rewards of rational self-control.

All's Lost by Lust thus depicts several scenes in which characters struggle to control their passions, and proposes the tempering of emotion by reason as an alternative. Most of the 'decision points' are structured according to an assumption that the character's mind is divided into reasoning and passionate faculties, so that it is possible for the character to knowingly make the wrong choice. As such, these moments are premised on the notion that the mind of the sinner is capable of understanding the laws of God, even it fails to obey them. Such assumptions were not, however, taken for granted in post-Reformation England, and in order to appreciate the psychology represented in *All's Lost*, it is necessary to understand contemporary debates about the location of God's grace within his creation, as Middleton's tragedies seem written under a very different system of beliefs than that suggested by *All's Lost by Lust*.

The Mind of the Sinner

The theological shifts of the English Reformation, and in particular the dominance of Calvinism in the English church during the late sixteenth and early seventeenth centuries, generated new ideas about the ways in which the mind functions during the decision to commit a sin. Especially important to these new ideas was the doctrine of double predestination, according to which humanity is divided into the elect (who are given God's grace and are predestined to heaven) and the reprobates (who have not been given God's grace and are therefore predestined to hell). In this schema, a person's ability to repent, choose good, and achieve salvation is determined by God's providence prior to her or his birth and not by thoughts and actions during life. Equally, those predestined to be refused grace are evil without the possibility of altering their moral state; there is no sense in which they can, by an act of will, achieve grace through their choices. As the preacher Arthur Dent succinctly explained, 'We beleeve, because wee are elected: and not therefore elected, because we beleeve.'[11]

This doctrine did not go unquestioned in the 1610s and 1620s, and the opposing argument – that grace is attainable by human self-will – was available from numerous sources. Recusant Catholicism was one obvious source, but even within the English church there was continual debate between those ministers who adhered strictly to the doctrine of double predestination and those who allowed some scope for the importance of 'human efforts and good works.'[12] Indeed, the difficulty of explaining and justifying predestination to parishioners meant that even hard-line Calvinists tended in their sermons to imply an element of choice in the gaining of grace.[13] Furthermore, the anti-Calvinist movement of Arminianism – associated by its opponents with a belief in 'God's universal grace and the free will of all men to obtain salvation'[14] – had become a subject for debate in England by the time *All's Lost* and *The Changeling* were written.[15] There were other, less sophisticated sources of anti-Calvinist thought. The simple Pelagian assumption that those who did good works would be saved was common among uneducated people even during the years of Calvinist dominance in the church.[16] Popular religious ballads tended to emphasize the availability of grace to all, particularly to those who repent at the last minute.[17] And even devout Protestants could get confused: Rowley's acquaintance John Taylor the Water-Poet continually expounded his identity as a 'plain Protestant' and yet 'appears to have thought ... that people were free to accept or reject the saving grace offered by God.'[18]

These two theological perspectives – the traditional belief in the efficacy of good works, and the Calvinist insistence on predestination as the cause of election – parallel two common early modern ideas about the structure of the mind and the location of sinful thoughts within it. William Bouwsma describes these contrasting psychological theories. The first was a 'traditional conception of human being as a hierarchy of discrete faculties in which the will, the passions, and the body are properly subordinated to the mind.' The second, associated by Bouwsma with both humanism and Calvinism, concerned 'what is *central* rather than what is *highest* in the self' and 'represented the self as a mysterious unity rather than a hierarchy of discrete faculties.'[19] Bouwsma suggests that these two theories 'existed uneasily side by side in the minds of most Renaissance thinkers.'[20]

In the traditional theory, which originated in the scholastic tradition, the human subject is defined by competition between the soul and the body; moral decisions therefore involve a battle between the reasoning faculties (located in the soul), and the passions, or humours (located in the body). In this schema, the reasoning faculties are entirely separate from the rest of the mind and body; as the English Jesuit Thomas Wright put it, 'Passions are drowned in corporall organs and instruments, as well as sense; reason dependeth of no corporal subject, but as a Princesse in her throne, considereth the state of her kingdome.'[21] Moral decisions derive from an inner dialogue known as *synderesis*, which results in 'conscience,' the inner voice that tells a person how to behave in a particular situation.[22] A fundamental assumption in this theory is the existence of 'natural law,' that is, the notion that the laws of God are known by the souls of all humans. While some people are more dominated by their passions than others, all have the *potential* for good, because all contain the voice of reason somewhere within them.[23]

Bouwsma connects the competing theory – that of the mind and body as unity rather than hierarchy – with Calvinism because it echoed Calvin's belief that far from being the site of a tussle between opposing forces, the human subject is fundamentally evil unless it has been awarded God's grace. Although Calvin could be inconsistent about the presence or otherwise of natural law in the soul, his overall approach was to distrust human capacity for reason. For Calvin, mankind's natural state is that of ignorance, and reason is so 'choked with greate thickness of ignorance, that y^t canne not effectuallye gette abroade,' so that human will 'can covet no good thynge.'[24] The faculties of reason and passion are thus not separate, and the human soul is governed from a central point; as Bouwsma puts it, 'there is no *privileged* area of the personality left untouched by original sin, notably including operations of the mind.'[25] This thinking is apparent in the writings of English Calvinist clergymen: William Perkins wrote that 'a wicked man, when he sinneth in his heart he giveth ful consent to the sinne'; and Daniel Dyke elaborated, 'The will and affections of an ungodly man doe not holde backe, or make any resistance, when hee is tempted to sinne: for they are wholly carnall, and have not either the least hatred of the sinne forbidden, or love of the Law forbidding it.'[26] Lacking God's grace, the reprobate has nothing to make him or her hesitate before committing a sinful action. Dyke thus equates the sinner's identity entirely with his or her sinfulness: reprobates cannot claim as an excuse that it is *'not wee, but the flesh,'* for this is merely to say it is *'not wee, but we.'* Dyke scorns those who follow Augustine in saying 'we of our selves have good wils to doe otherwise, we like, and approve of the best things, but the *flesh* overmasters us,' accusing them of being 'nothing but *flesh*'; he thus explicitly rejects the hierarchical conception of the human mind in favour of its uniformity.[27]

Bouwsma's note that the two psychological schemas he describes 'existed uneasily side by side' is evident when we observe that Calvinist writers sometimes wrote about the mind as if it did have multiple, conflicting faculties. However, these inner conflicts are typically depicted as a quality that distinguishes the elect from the reprobate. William Perkins explained the special structure of the minds of the elect: 'the godly though they fall into the same sinnes with the wicked, yet they never give full consent: for they are in their mindes, wils, and affections partly regenerate, and partly unregenerate, and therefore their wils doe partly will, and partly abhorre that which is evill.'[28] This understanding of the mind is also evident when Calvinist preachers exhort their flocks to self-examination and self-criticism. As Martha Tuck Rozett notes, when a seventeenth-century diarist writes that he must 'look more diligently to my selfe then I have done,' the word 'self' refers to everything in the mind except the critical faculty ('I') that is examining it.[29] Again, this division of the mind is considered to be a quality of the elect, made possible by God's grace. Arthur Dent wrote that the elect are defined by 'deniall of our selves' (that is, maintaining a critical attitude toward the behaviour of their 'self'), whereas a symptom of reprobate identity is 'trusting to our selves' (that is, not analysing one's 'self').[30] In other words, the difference between the elect and the damned is precisely the potential for mental conflict in the elect that in the traditional psychological system is available to everyone.

Similar ideas are apparent in Calvinist descriptions of the operation of 'conscience,' which use the word differently than the traditional conception of conscience as the result of *synderesis*. Calvin did not see conscience as a process by which humans make moral decisions but rather as 'a feling of Gods jugement as a witnesse adjoined w^t them, which doth not suffer them to hide their siñes, but y^t they be brought accused to ye judgeme[n]t seate of God.'[31] As R.S. White puts it, Calvin sees conscience as more of 'a punitive and corrective faculty than an active instrument choosing between good and evil in actual situations.'[32] Dyke explained that the elect suffer inner conflicts when contemplating sin because 'every part of their soule is partly carnall, partly spirituall,' whereas the reprobates are only affected by 'conscience,' which makes them 'see the terror of the punishment' but provides no active love for good to restrain them.[33] Despite the existence of this tormenting conscience, the reprobate soul is distinguished by its inability to engage in the mental conflicts that characterize the elect.

To which of these philosophies does *All's Lost by Lust* seem most indebted? I will argue that it seems indebted to the traditional psychological schema, not to Calvinism. However, since some scholars would claim otherwise, it is necessary first to consider the alternative viewpoint. A Calvinist influence has been claimed for plays like *Macbeth* (and, by extension, *All's Lost*) that focus on a sinner's struggle with his or her conscience. Richard Waswo and John Stachniewski interpret Macbeth as a Calvinist reprobate, explaining his inward conflicts by referring to Calvin's admission that there may be a 'naturall desire of good in manne' but that men are unable to choose good because they lack reason (see Calvin, *Institution of Christian Religion*, 2.2.26).[34] This interpretation does not, however, fit with Calvin's subsequent insistence that the awareness of good is only present in the elect; that the 'spirit is not of nature, but of regeneration' (*Institution of Christian Religion*, 2.2.27). When Martha Tuck Rozett uses William Perkins's description (quoted above) of the elect sinners who 'partly will, and partly abhorre' sin to argue that Macbeth's inner conflicts could have been inspired by Calvinist doctrine, she notes that 'in this respect [Macbeth] resembles the elect.'[35] To interpret *Macbeth* as Calvinist, one must assume that the protagonist is in possession of God's grace and thus destined for heaven, but Rozett does not elaborate on why Shakespeare might have imagined a regicide as one of God's chosen few.[36] Such an idea, problematic enough in Shakespeare's play, is even harder to apply to *All's Lost*, in which many of the characters – including a bigamist, a usurper, and a murderess – are represented as suffering the inward conflicts that mark the elect. It would also conflict with the final image of that play, in which the Moor – who symbolizes the devil[37] – sits on a throne in triumph over the dead protagonists, a conclusion that would be inappropriate if the characters were all considered to be elect.

If we assume the protagonists of *All's Lost* to be reprobates, their inner conflicts would be incompatible with Calvinist doctrine, as their sinful desires do not determine all aspects of their identity. Antonio says, 'my hearts / A rebell to me,' in which 'me' refers to the 'I' of utterance, distinguished from the 'heart' that lusts after Dionyzia. The same idea appears when Antonio says, 'My conscience / And my affection warre about this quarell, / My conscience saith the first, but my affection, / The second' (3.3.175–8); and when Julianus loses his self-control, his 'best understanding faculties' are opposed to the 'swelling' of his 'big heart' (4.1.78, 112–13). Antonio and Julianus are represented as having an identity separate from their 'hearts,' an idea reminiscent of Wright's description of reason observing the body from a detached perspective. Both characters are therefore represented as possessing a 'good' side to their personality that understands the laws of God and is strong enough to offer resistance to sin, but is not always powerful enough to prevent strong passions from usurping its authority.

R.S. White argues that although in many plays 'individuals choose to turn away from the righteous path,' this 'does not mean that they do so without struggle involving reason and conscience,' and that such struggles demonstrate a human potential for good: 'a fragile but real state within corrigible but vulnerable protagonists.' White cites *Hamlet*, *Macbeth*, *The Duchess of Malfi*, and *'Tis Pity She's a Whore* as examples of such plays.[38] To this list I would add *All's Lost by Lust*, which similarly implies the *possibility* that the protagonists might earn God's grace. Even though they never do attain it, the characterization has the effect of suggesting that they might have been able to choose the path of goodness had they fought harder.

However, in arguing for this underlying optimism in Renaissance tragedy, White does not consider the tragedies written by Thomas Middleton, which seem to offer precisely the doctrinaire Calvinist vision that he claims not to exist. Middleton structures his characterizations as if most humans were predestined to sin and possess no inner sparks of reason. When White denies that Jacobean tragedies 'abandon men and women to ignorant and blind courses of evil action in a fallen world,'³⁹ he is inadvertently describing the effect of Thomas Middleton's dramaturgy.

Calvinism and Middleton's Tragedies

Unlike those of most early modern playwrights, Middleton's religious sympathies are well documented: his pamphlet *The Two Gates of Salvation* (1609), reissued in 1620 as *The Marriage of the Old and New Testament*, indicates that he took an active interest in theology and was a Calvinist who subscribed to the doctrines of election and of double predestination.⁴⁰ In addition, both John Stachniewski and Herbert Jack Heller have argued for a Calvinist influence on Middleton's drama.⁴¹ Margot Heinemann's claim that Middleton can be labelled a Puritan (that is, an anti-establishment extremist Protestant) has been discredited,⁴² but as Heller points out, one could be a Calvinist without having Puritan political convictions.⁴³

The style of characterization in Middleton's tragedies accords with Calvinist ideas about the structure of the mind. Edward Engleberg calls Middleton's tragedies 'a terrible vision of life. And its terror lies in the nightmarish defencelessness of the blinded characters who are so quickly, so mercilessly, ambushed by their afflictions.'⁴⁴ Stachniewski compares this 'vision of life' with Calvin's assertion that after the Fall, human will is incapable of choosing good.⁴⁵ I suggest that Middleton's distinctive 'vision' in his tragedies is generated in part by his representation of the characters' 'decision points.' Unlike Rowley in *All's Lost*, Middleton tends not to draw out his protagonists' decision-making or represent them suffering mental conflict. Instead, he tends to restrict the characters' anguish to the period *after* the sinful act has been performed.

The Revenger's Tragedy (1606) has long been recognized as a parody of the revenge tragedy genre: its emblematic characters are ostentatiously wicked to the point of absurdity.⁴⁶ As such, it serves as an extreme introduction to Middleton's approach. Lussurioso offers a moral *sententia* at one point:

> It is our bloud to erre, tho hell gapte lowde[;]
> Ladies know *Lucifer* fell, yet still are proude! (1.3.74–5)

This is the Ovidian paradox dramatized so often in *All's Lost*, in which characters go on with an action despite knowing that it will damn them. But in *All's Lost*, knowledge of damnation causes intense mental torments, whereas in *Revenger's Tragedy*, Lussurioso's speech is an expression of delight at the ease of corrupting virgins, and he shows no desire for things to be different. Indeed, for the characters in *Revenger's Tragedy*, the notion that they are damned is almost invigorating. Their minds have what Calvinists called 'security,' a word used to mean 'imperviousness to spiritual peril':[47] they suffer no anguish when contemplating sin, no hesitation, and no remorse. Each sinner operates with no more indecision than Ambitioso when he decides to kill his brother: 'Excellent, / Then am I heire – Duke in a minute[!]' (3.1.12–13). There is only one 'decision point' comparable to those in *All's Lost*: Spurio momentarily recoils from the Duchess's sexual advances, protesting, 'you are my fathers wife,' before resolving to do the deed as a revenge on his father and 'call foule Incest but a Veniall sinne' (1.2.130, 169). Even here, there is no sense of the attractions of virtue and only a momentary flicker of inner conflict. And the only virtuous character, Castiza, is simply the opposite of the other characters; as George C. Herndl puts it, virtue in the play 'stands always isolated, absolute, wholly unrelated and out of tune with all about it.'[48] The play thus echoes the Calvinist doctrine that 'it is not possible that either the elect should always be without care to do well or that the reprobate should have any will thereunto. For to have either good will or good work is a testimony of the spirit of God, which is given to the elect only.'[49]

There is only one scene of extended mental conflict in the play, and it occurs during repentance *after* sin rather than during the initial decision to commit it. Vindice is shocked when his mother, Gratiana, is swiftly overcome by temptation to prostitute Castiza (2.1.103). But when Vindice later shames Gratiana for it, Middleton shows her gradually revealing an understanding of goodness, praying to heaven to 'Take this infectious spot out of my soule' and finally claiming to be 'recoverd of that foule disease' of sin (4.4.52, 122). If Gratiana has been revealed as one of the elect, Middleton follows Calvinist doctrine in depicting grace as caused by God, not by human actions: Gratiana laments, 'To weepe, is to our sexe naturally given: / But to weepe truely thats a gift from heaven' (55–6).[50] As we will see, this sequence is characteristic of Middleton's approach in his later plays in depicting mental anguish as something that happens after the crime, not before.

The characters in *Women Beware Women* (ca. 1621) are more complex than those in *Revenger's Tragedy* in that they change as the play progresses. In particular, Leantio and Bianca move from a state of relative idealism to one of commitment to sin; the audience is invited to understand that the characters are propelled toward sin as a result of their disillusionment at the corruption and violence they discover in the court. Yet despite this increased complexity, Middleton's handling of the 'decision points' remains similar to that in *Revenger's Tragedy*: the characters' moral states result from their essential nature, not from inward decision-making; as David L. Frost puts it, 'Beyond the degrees of social and economic determinism suggested by the action of the play is a deeper determinism.'[51]

The play contains incidents that at first glance seem reminiscent of *All's Lost*: in particular, there are several scenes in which a character is warned by another that his or her actions are damnable. For example, just as Jacinta warns Roderick of the fires of hell, Bianca warns the rapist Duke that his actions are against religion (2.2.347–57).[52] However, in Rowley's play Roderick understands Jacinta's warning but announces that it makes no difference to him, whereas in Middleton's play, the Duke assumes that his victim is only affecting unwillingness in order to tease him: 'Sure I think / Thou know'st the way to please me. I affect / A passionate pleading, 'bove an easie yeilding' (357–9). The Duke thus remains entirely blind to the consequences.

Similar scenes recur throughout the play. The Lord Cardinal tries to persuade the Duke to repent of his fornication by warning of its consequences:

> How dare you venture on eternal pain,
> That cannot bear a minuts reprehension? (4.1.232–3)

The Duke appears to understand this warning and promises to live virtuously:

> If I ere keep woman more unlawfully,
> May I want penitence, at my greatest need.
> And wisemen know there is no barren place,
> Threatens more famine, [than] a dearth in grace. (256–9)

But he does not respond by suppressing his desires for Bianca, as the Cardinal wishes; instead, he murders her husband so that he can marry her and therefore make their relationship 'moral.' Middleton highlights the absurdity of the Duke's belief that semantic juggling can excuse him from hellfire:

> Her husband dies to night, or at the most,
> Lives not to see the morning spent to morrow;
> Then will I make her lawfully mine own,
> Without this sin and horror. (272–5)

The Duke is shown to exercise a form of self-deceit, in which he uses sophistry to convince himself that his actions are not immoral. He shifts himself into a state of ignorance and maintains it until the very end of the play.[53]

Self-deceit like that practised by the Duke is a common theme in Calvinist writing. In *The Mystery of Selfe-Deceiving*, Daniel Dyke describes those who are 'grossely tainted with many horrible sinnes, which yet in no case they wil be brought to see, or acknowledge[;] nay so far are they blinded through *selfe-love*, and *selfe deceit*, that they will be at daggers drawing with any that shall offer to lay such matters to their charge.'[54] Arthur Dent describes the devil's ability to 'delude and bewitch our inward senses & the naturall faculties of our soules,' so that we 'thinke we are that which we are not, see that which we see not, & feele that which we feele not,' adding that 'onely the elect do feele it, & therefore onely the elect do beleeve it.'[55] Whereas Rowley's Roderick knowingly chooses hellfire, Middleton's characters do not believe they are evil. They do not follow the advice of Dyke and other preachers to engage in self-examination and to study the scriptures in order to understand their own minds. Damnation is rarely an issue to them; they remember it in flashes and then dismiss it with a joke: 'Though sin be death,' says Leantio, 'I had di'd, if I had not sin'd' (1.1.40). And although the conflict between reason and passion is mentioned at times (for instance, when Leantio forces himself to go to work rather than stay in bed with Bianca; 1.3.41–2), the characters never go through this dialogue at the crucial 'decision points' in their tragedies; *synderesis* never appears to operate at the appropriate moments.

There is an exception, however: Hippolito holds back from declaring his incestuous love for Isabella because 'Heaven has forbid it, / And 'tis most meet, that I should rather perish / [Than] the Decree Divine receive least blemish' (1.2.155–7). When he decides that he cannot restrain himself, he offers only the fatalistic reasoning that 'ev'ry man has something / To bring him to his end' (190–1). This sequence is reminiscent of the way Rowley structures the 'decision points' in *All's Lost* as following from a character's demonstration that he or she is deliberately choosing a path that is sinful. However, Hippolito is the only character in *Women Beware* to demonstrate such awareness. His moment of foresight highlights further the blindness of the others, a point that Middleton emphasizes by giving Hippolito a moralizing speech at the end: 'Lust, and forgetfulness has been amongst us, / And we are brought to nothing' (5.1.184–5). 'Forgetfulness' of heaven has certainly been the undoing of the other characters, as they demonstrate no awareness of moral structures until it is too late; perhaps Middleton is suggesting that Hippolito is the sole elect character among the damned.

Middleton's chronicle-tragedy *Hengist, King of Kent* (1620) uses similar characterization to that in *Women Beware*. Here too, at most of the 'decision-points,' sins are committed without any mental conflict, and the two moments of conscience are comically brief: when the assassins kill Constantius, 'they seeme to be over come with pittye Butt lookeing upon the gold kills him as hee turns his back' (2.2.0.8–10);[56] and when Vortiger and Hersus are about to abduct Castiza, she begs them to spare her, provoking the following response:

> *Hers*: [*aside*] this almost mooves
> *Vort*: [*aside*] by this light heele be taken
> *Hers*: [*aside*] Ile wrastle downe all pittye   (3.2.94–5)

In both cases, the characters' mental conflicts are represented as a brief moment of sanity that is so short as to emphasize its powerlessness; it makes their 'pittye' look worthless against their other desires. This is a stark contrast with *All's Lost*, which draws out the extreme anguish of its characters; Rowley represents the desire for good as a powerful emotion, even if it fails to be as powerful as passion.

Like the characters in the other Middleton tragedies, those in *Hengist* gain awareness of damnation only after they have committed their crimes. For example, Vortiger begins to realize his fate only at the end of the play:

> are these the noblest fruites and fairest
> requitalls from workes of our owne raiseing[?]
> me thinks the murder of Constantius
> speaks to me in the voice ont.   (4.4.113–16)

It must be acknowledged that two moments in *The Second Maiden's Tragedy* (1611) recall more strongly the inner conflicts suffered by Rowley's characters. When Govianus prepares to kill the Tyrant, he falters:

> A religious trembling shakes me by the hand
> and bidds me put by such unhallowed busines[;]
> but reveng calls fort, and it must go forward (5.2.91–3)[57]

Like Margaretta and Antonio in *All's Lost*, Govianus backs away from the consequences of his actions but then resolves to 'go forward' regardless of damnation. And in the subplot, Votarius suffers inward conflict as he pauses in his seduction of Anselmus's wife:

> heart, I growe fond my self; twas well she wakt me
> before the dead sleep of Adultery tooke me[;]
> twas stealing on me[;] up yo^u honest thoughtes
> and keep watch for yor master (1.2.225–8)

The Second Maiden's Tragedy has sometimes been perceived as different in tone from Middleton's other tragedies,[58] and this greater emphasis on inward conflict may be one reason why. Middleton was evidently capable of experimenting with his methods of characterization, and we should therefore be wary of totalizing accounts of his dramaturgy. Nonetheless, the practice that I have highlighted is a feature of most of his tragedies, and in my analysis of *The Changeling*, we will see that the play's differences in characterization correspond with its division of authorship.

Collaboration and Choice in *The Changeling*

The early modern theological and psychological concepts discussed thus far are fundamental to an appreciation of *The Changeling* (1622), a play that is self-consciously about changes within the human mind. Although the *dramatis personae* of the 1653 quarto labels Antonio 'the Changeling' because the word was used to refer to idiots, the word could also refer to an inconstant, changeable person, and in this sense the title may apply to many of the characters; indeed, at the end of the play, the characters itemize the moral changes that each has undergone.[59] As we have seen, in post-Reformation England the nature of such changes was a matter for debate. In Calvinist theology the subject's moral state is unchangeable without God's will, but in non-Calvinist theologies, in which grace can be earned or lost, the body and mind are inherently mutable; the potential for change is present in everyone. To understand Middleton's and Rowley's representations of change in this play, we must therefore ask whether the characters are represented as choosing to commit evil or as essentially damned from the start.

Much criticism of *The Changeling* has argued for the latter reading by showing that the play depicts the revelation or discovery of evil within characters who had appeared to be good. A number of valuable studies have demonstrated that the play's thematic structure, characterization, and stagecraft are built around an image of secrets being uncovered within the characters' minds. Alsemero's private closet (4.1), the castle walls that hide secrets within (1.1.167–9), and the madmen that lurk behind the walls of the madhouse all contribute toward a recurring image of disturbing secrets hidden behind a facade. This imagery culminates with the revelation of Beatrice's crimes and with Alsemero's desire to remove the 'vizor / O're that cunning face' and 'seek out truth within' her (5.3.46–7, 36). Once 'discovered,' evil is banished when Beatrice acknowledges her crimes and begs to be thrown into the sewer (149–53). The play can therefore be thought of as building toward a cathartic dramatization of the unmasking and expulsion of evil.[60]

However, the unmasking of evil means different things depending on one's theological assumptions. A non-Calvinist perspective would see the discovery of the crimes of Beatrice and DeFlores as a simple case of 'whodunnit': an uncovering of the truth about what happened and the administering of appropriate punishment to the malefactors. Calvinists, in contrast, would see it as the discovery of whether the characters are damned or elected. John Stachniewski has shown that the doctrine of double predestination generated a pre-Freudian concept of the unconscious: since individuals could not know with certainty whether they were damned or elect, the potential for evil was imagined as a 'secret' element within a human's soul that he or she was unaware of. The true horror of the Middletonian tragedy is thus not only the crimes that the sinners commit, but also the realization of the 'hidden logic' that was governing their actions all along.[61] Other critics of *The Changeling* have made similar points, although not always with reference to theology, arguing that the play depicts unconscious sin: the characters – in particular Beatrice – are 'blind,' behaving without any awareness that their thoughts and actions are governed by evil.[62] As we have seen, such ideas are common in Middleton's dramaturgy when he represents reprobates performing sinful acts automatically, without hesitation.

However, reading *The Changeling* as a collaboration shows that the scenes written by Rowley are still indebted to the traditional theological schema used in *All's Lost*. Authorship studies of *The Changeling* agree that Rowley wrote all of the comic subplot, as well as the opening and closing scenes of the main plot, while Middleton wrote the central scenes of the main plot. In what follows, I focus on Rowley's contribution to the tragic main plot (the subplot too is strongly reminiscent of *All's Lost* in its dramatization of characters fighting their passions, but its structure, which concludes with the 'curing' of the characters, is that of comedy, not tragedy, and hence I discuss it only briefly here). As described in the previous chapter, my analysis of the main plot assumes that the dramatists were working from a plan of the story and characters. The events of the play were thus predetermined, but, I will argue, during the process of writing the dramatists' individual preferences coloured the way those events were written. In other words, my interest is not in what *happens* in the play so much as the language with which the dramatists chose to *represent* these events. The 'decision points' in *The Changeling* appear to reflect a divergence between the writers that complicates the audience's experience of the characters.

Rowley's opening scene contains much that is recognizably similar to the ideas and characterization in *All's Lost by Lust*. The most striking parallel is between Alsemero's behaviour and that of Antonio and Margaretta: Alsemero goes through a long and difficult decision-making process, in which he finally makes the knowing choice to place himself in danger of committing a sin. Furthermore, Rowley uses a variety of techniques to emphasize Alsemero's active culpability in making his decision.

The play begins with a speech in which Alsemero attempts to reinterpret the events of the previous day in a positive light. He has met a beautiful woman but is disturbed by the ominous fact that they met during a church service:

> Twas in the Temple where I first beheld her,
> And now agen the same[;] what *Omen* yet
> Follows of that? None but imaginary,
> Why should my hopes [of] fate be timerous?   (1.1.1–4)[63]

Alsemero's hopes of fate should indeed be timorous, because the church was considered an unsuitable place for flirting; the play's source, John Reynolds's *The Triumphs of God's Revenge*, rails against the practice of treating a church like a brothel.[64] However, Alsemero overcomes his misgivings by turning the omen into a positive sign: 'The Church hath first begun our interview / And that's the place must joyn us into one, / So there's beginning and perfection too' (10–12). This is somewhat similar to the self-deceit of the Duke in *Women Beware Women*, and Alsemero has indeed been described as a typically Middletonian sinner, oblivious of his sinfulness except in 'unconscious stirrings';[65] that is, unaware that he is suppressing his doubts. Joost Daalder writes that Alsemero 'cannot admit to himself that he is propelled by sex' and therefore 'has to convince himself that his devotion to Beatrice is religious and pure.'[66] However, there is no reason to describe Alsemero's reinterpretation of the omen as unconscious; Alsemero knows that his hopes of fate should be 'timerous' because he knows that a church meeting is a worrying omen; it is this that has prompted him to find a more a positive interpretation. This is also true when Alsemero insists on his normality to Jasperino by saying that he is well, 'Unless there be some hidden malady / Within me, that I understand not' (23–4). There is no reason to believe, as Michael Neill does, that Alsemero is unaware of what this 'malady' might be;[67] at this point, he is deliberately deceiving Jasperino about his feelings rather than unconsciously doing so. Daalder dismisses the possibility that Alsemero is conscious of his lust, saying that 'if he had been, no doubt lawful devotion would have been triumphant, or if not he would at least have acted on sexual impulse with some understanding of its nature.'[68] But this *conscious* sinning is exactly what we would expect from Rowley: *All's Lost* features characterization of exactly the kind that Daalder finds so implausible.

Furthermore, as the scene progresses, Alsemero fails to suppress his knowledge. He learns that Beatrice is already engaged to be married, and that he will thus not be able to marry her.[69] At first he makes the decision to back away, and we see reason taking over:

> I must now part, and never meet agen
> With any joy on earth; Sir, your pardon,
> My affairs call on me.   (202–4)

But when Beatrice's genial father invites him to stay in the castle, Alsemero is unable to tear himself away. Instead of fleeing, he finds himself walking toward the castle in the full knowledge that what he is doing could lead him into a damnable situation. Rowley marks this change of mind with the language familiar from *All's Lost*:

> How shall I dare to venture in his castle,
> When he discharges murderers at the gate?
> But I must on, for back I cannot goe. (226–8)

As with Antonio and Margaretta in *All's Lost*, Rowley uses the image of a character walking into a situation that he knows will damn him. Alsemero consciously rejects both the omens and his own judgment as he enters the castle. His characterization therefore bears the stamp of Rowley's method of representing 'decision points.'

Rowley emphasizes Alsemero's agency even further by toning down the predestinarian imagery in Reynolds's source text. In *The Changeling*, Alsemero observes a second omen in the movements of the weathervane: 'Even now I observ'd / The temples Vane to turn full in my face, / I know 'tis against me' (19–21). Jasperino is baffled by this comment, since the wind is perfect for leaving Alicante, but of course Alsemero does not want to leave. This reverses the situation in Reynolds's story, in which the wind *prevents* Alsemero from leaving Alicante.[70] Reynolds attributes the contrary wind to 'the providence of God' which 'doth crosse him [Alsemero] in his intended purposes,'[71] implying that Alsemero is predestined to stay in Alicante and become a sinner. In Rowley's version, however, the wind offers Alsemero an opportunity to escape the city; when he deliberately ignores this opportunity and describes the wind as an opposing force, he is implicitly operating against the will of God.[72]

In Alsemero, therefore, we can see Rowley repeating the focus on the characters' responsibility for their actions that is evident in *All's Lost*. This method can also be detected in the representation of Beatrice and DeFlores. In much criticism of *The Changeling*, Beatrice-Joanna is described as blind or unthinking, incapable of understanding the consequences of her actions until after they have been committed;[73] and as we have seen, such characterization is typical of Middleton. But although Beatrice is certainly represented this way in the central scenes (culminating in 3.4, in which DeFlores confronts her with her identity as a sinner), Rowley depicts her suffering an inner conflict in the first scene. Her switch of affection from Alonzo to Alsemero is accompanied by an awareness that it is dangerous; she says, 'I shall change my Saint, *I fear me*, I find / A giddy turning in me' (158–9; my italics), a hint of turmoil that betrays an inner conflict. Furthermore, it is Beatrice who focuses the audience's attention onto the competing faculties of the mind:

> Be better advis'd, sir:
> Our eyes are Centinels unto our judgements,
> And should give certain judgement what they see;
> But they are rash sometimes, and tell us wonders
> Of common things, which when our judgements find,
> They can then check the eyes, and cal them blind. (71–6)

Her statement is strongly reminiscent of those tracts that describe the operation of 'right reason.' Thomas Wright wrote, 'Passions and sense are determined to one thing, and as soon as they perceive their object, sense presently receives it, and the passions love or hate it: but reason, after she perceiveth her object, she stands in deliberation, whether it be convenient she should accept it, or refuse it.'[74] Beatrice's speech separates the bodily senses and passions from the faculty called 'judgement,' which seems to be the same as 'right reason'; it is also reminiscent of Julianus's 'understanding faculties' (*All's Lost*, 4.1.78), which he describes as distinct from his passions. In articulating the idea of judgment, both Beatrice and Alsemero are shown to understand the ideas of self-analysis and rational consideration, and implicitly this is what causes the misgivings and inner fears that both express, despite their overt conviction that their eyes and judgment now meet (77–9, 85).

In the first scene, then, Rowley repeats some of the ideas and techniques that he used in *All's Lost*: he focuses the audience's attention on the mental conflict of the characters as they decide to commit a sin, incorporating theories about the process by which this works, and represents them as moving toward potentially sinful actions with an awareness that they are sinful. All of this changes when Middleton takes over the story. But before I discuss Middleton's contribution, it is first necessary to look at Rowley's closing scene. The way in which Rowley concludes the story can help to illustrate how his conception of the characters may have differed from Middleton's.

The ending of *The Changeling* is famously discordant: after the violent deaths of Beatrice and DeFlores, the characters from the comic subplot explain how they have changed for the better in a conclusion that celebrates the potential for moral change: Isabella tells her husband that he is a 'jealous Coxcomb' who needs to change (5.3.209–12), and Alibius promises to 'change now / Into a better husband' (213–14). Similarly, the main plot ends with Alsemero assuming the role of moral spokesman, announcing that 'justice hath so right / The guilty hit, that innocence is quit / By proclamation, and may joy agen' (185–7). While this sequence has justifiably been read as ironic, reading it from a Rowleyan perspective suggests that Alsemero's position as moral spokesman may have been intended to be taken at face value. Alsemero is used in a similar way to Julianus in *All's Lost*: he represents someone who wishes to restrain his passions rather than succumb to them. The difference, however, is that Alsemero succeeds in maintaining his reason at the critical moment.

In the final scene of *The Changeling*, Rowley reiterates some of the imagery that he had used in the first so as to draw a moral conclusion. The audience is reminded of the omens that haunted Alsemero at the beginning of the play:

> Oh the place it self ere since
> Has crying been for vengeance, the Temple
> Where blood and beauty first unlawfully
> Fir'd their devotion, and quencht the right one,
> 'Twas in my fears at first, 'twill have it now   (5.3.72–6)

Alsemero recognizes that his initial fears about the omen of the church were justified: the liaison between himself and Beatrice had been doomed and he had tried to suppress the warnings. But it is important to remember that the dramatists have constructed the plot so that Alsemero has remained free from the taint of sin. In the final scene, faced with a 'decision point' at which he must choose his response to Beatrice's crimes, Alsemero is represented as restraining his passions rather than allowing them to take over as he had done previously. When he learns the truth about Beatrice, he does not fly into a rage but instead says calmly,

> It must ask pawse
> What I must do in this[;] mean time you shall
> Be my prisoner onely, enter my Closet.
> Ile be your Keeper yet.   (84–7)

Readers and audiences often criticize Alsemero for his avoidance of 'meaningful action' here,[75] but his words are strikingly reminiscent of those uttered by Julianus when he advocates 'sitting' on a problem before unleashing one's passions. Unlike Julianus, Alsemero's attempt at self-control is successful, for by pausing, he escapes condemnation himself and is able to watch as the evil characters destroy each other, in a didactic dramatization of the self-destructiveness of evil.[76]

By reading these scenes via the psychological assumptions of *All's Lost*, it is possible to see that Rowley portrays Alsemero as a moral exemplar in the same way as he does Isabella in the subplot: the character progressively battles with his or her conscience, lapses into passion, but keeps a hold on reason at the conclusion.[77] Alsemero can therefore be seen as occupying the moral high ground, and his closing speech thus accords with the subplot characters' promises to change for the better in the play's closing moments.

Of course, few readers and theatregoers experience the scene this way; many critics describe Alsemero's final speeches as hypocritical and complacent. In response to Alsemero's insistence that because the guilty have been punished, all memory of the events must be 'blotted out' so that the surviving, innocent characters will not be dishonoured (182–7), Michael Neill describes his attitude as 'smug self-approval' that encourages 'suppression of the truth.' Peter Morrison calls the survivors 'zombies' who 'quickly regroup, suffering no more than a momentary, horrifying glimpse into the consequences of their own alienation.'[78] What is 'the truth' that Neill and Morrison observe Alsemero suppressing? Is it the truth that the evil discovered in Beatrice lies within all the characters, despite their appropriation of moral righteousness? I think such a 'truth' is implied by the scene, but it is not caused by anything in Rowley's writing. Instead, it is the characterization used by Middleton in the play's central scenes that creates the complexity of the final scene.

Close collaboration between the writers is initially apparent at the beginning of Middleton's first scene, because he picks up some of the imagery of 1.1; in particular, Beatrice repeats the central idea of her earlier speech when she says, 'Me thinks I love now with the eyes of judgement. / And see the way to merit, clearly see it' (2.1.13–14). But if Middleton initially takes a cue from Rowley's already written opening scene to smooth the transition,[79] his distinctive ethos soon colours his representation of the characters set in motion by Rowley.

None of the characters in Middleton's scenes suffers mental conflicts during their respective 'decision points.' When Alsemero has an illicit meeting with Beatrice in 2.2, his qualms have vanished completely: Middleton represents him as decisive and single-minded, offering to duel with Alonzo 'instantly' (28). Similarly, Beatrice's decision to murder Alonzo is made as soon as the idea occurs to her; she demonstrates no mental conflict or awareness that this will be sinful on her part. 'Blood-guiltiness becomes a fouler visage' (2.2.40) she says, assuming that the guilt and responsibility will lie solely with DeFlores. For his part, De-Flores is equally thoughtless. Overcome with happiness at receiving favourable attention from Beatrice, he agrees to the murder without hesitation: 'His ends upon him, he shal be seen no more' (2.2.136). And Diaphanta, whom Beatrice solicits to sleep with Alsemero on her wedding night, is represented similarly. There is no hesitation on her part, and she agrees eagerly:

> [*Aside*] The brides place,
> And with a thousand Duckets; I'me for a Justice now,
> I bring a portion with me, I scorn small fools. (4.1.128–30)

At each of these points there is the opportunity for Middleton to depict the characters debating with their conscience over whether to commit the crimes. Each time, he avoids that opportunity, presenting us instead with instant, amoral decision-making. As in his other tragedies, he depicts the characters as if sin is their natural disposition.

Similarly, as in Middleton's other tragedies, it is only after the crimes have been committed that the question of damnation arises. This moment is dramatized with exceptional power in scene 3.4, when De-Flores reminds Beatrice that she is a sinner just like him. Beatrice, horrified, demands that he remember her aristocratic birth, forged in God's 'Creation' (133); but DeFlores tells her that she is 'the deeds creature' (140): her moral state is revealed by her actions, not her lineage, and 'Creation' has thus made her DeFlores's moral equal. As John Stachniewski points out, this is a classic example of Calvinist writing: Beatrice realizes with certainty that she is a reprobate soul, damned from the beginning, when she asks, 'Was my creation in the womb so curst[?]' (168). Thus for Middleton's Beatrice, conscience arrives only when it is too late: 'Vengeance begins; / Murder I see is followed by more sins' (166–7).

Similarly, DeFlores's mental anguish arrives only after his crimes, when Alonzo's ghost haunts him. Although he dismisses the spirit as 'a mist of conscience' (5.1.60), the memory disturbs him so much that he is paralysed when Piracquo's brother draws a sword on him:

> I cannot strike, I see his brothers wounds
> Fresh bleeding in his eye, as in a Crystall.   (5.2.32–3)

The contrast between these scenes and Rowley's is clear: Middleton seems uninterested in representing the to-and-fro of inner debate that is prevalent in Rowley's drama. When audiences watch the play without an awareness of the details of the collaboration, the juxtaposition of these two styles may thus create a discordant experience of the characters' moral states.

The dramaturgical effects of this discordance are considerable. Martha Tuck Rozett may be correct when she argues that 'the act of choosing has always been an important element in tragedy'[80] and that if a character's choice is seen as inevitable, dramatic tension is lost. Middleton's plays have been criticized in just these terms: Schoenbaum, for example, complains that *Women Beware Women* conveys more 'clinical insight' than genuine emotional power.[81] Schoenbaum's assessment is unfair; theatrical performances of Middleton's plays have found a great deal of emotional tension in them. However, it is certainly a different type of tension to that which would have been generated in a performance of *All's Lost by Lust*. Rowley's opening scene for *The Changeling* creates tension by focusing on the decisions of individuals. When Middleton takes over, tension ceases to be centred on individual agency and is created instead from confrontations *between* characters with opposing desires (the intense dialogues between Beatrice and DeFlores in 2.1, 2.2, and 3.4 are the most memorable). In contrast to Rowley's scenes, Middleton's do not raise doubts about the characters' determination to enact their desires; the doubts are about which characters will be triumphant when their desires collide. The tension between Beatrice and DeFlores in 3.4, for example, is created by the opposition between DeFlores's implacable desire and Beatrice's angry, uncomprehending resistance. It does not reside in doubts over whether one of them will change, but over which of these powerful, determined characters will overcome the other.

The change from Rowley's style to Middleton's therefore has the effect of altering the audience's perceptions of the characters. Its most important effect is on the representation of Alsemero, whose character dwindles in Middleton's hands as he changes from a state of complex mental turmoil to a one of apparent emotionlessness. Middleton's style creates excellent tension between characters who are powerful, like Beatrice and DeFlores, but in Alsemero's scenes Beatrice always has the upper hand, and when this is combined with the disappearance of his inner conflicts, the character's impact is diminished.

This effect of the collaboration helps us understand why the return of Alsemero's reason in 5.3 fails to seem fully admirable in the theatre. But Middleton's Calvinist dramaturgy also has a second effect on Alsemero's characterization: he introduces details that create doubts about the character's moral state, and Rowley's conclusion fails to resolve these doubts. This process begins in 4.1, after the wedding, when Beatrice discovers the book of *Secrets in Nature* in Alsemero's closet. Rowley's first scene had depicted Alsemero as having been impervious to female charms before his encounter with Beatrice: Jasperino reminds him that 'your mother / Nor best friends, who have set snares of beauty, / [Aye] and choyce ones too, could never trap you that way' (1.1.37–9), and is startled when Alsemero greets Beatrice: 'How now! The Laws of the *Medes* are chang'd sure, salute a woman[?] he kisses too: wonderfull! where learnt he this? & does it perfectly too; in my conscience he nere rehearst it before' (57–61). Rowley had portrayed Alsemero as a 'Stoick' (36), whose imperviousness to passion unexpectedly crumbles for the first time in his life. But when Beatrice discovers the virginity test within Alsemero's closet, the audience's image of his past is revised. The fact that Alsemero possesses such a test is not in itself inherently dubious; Dale Randall and Deborah G. Burks have shown that there were cultural reasons for Jacobean gentlemen to feel a need for such devices.[82] The discordance is caused by Middleton's choice of words: he represents Alsemero as an old hand at the game. Alsemero tells Jasperino, 'it ne're mist, sir, / Upon a virgin' (4.2.140–1), demonstrating an apparent familiarity with the test's success rate, a familiarity confirmed by the note that he has written above the instructions: 'A merry slight, *but true* experiment' (4.1.45; my italics). And when Beatrice asks Diaphanta if she knows of her husband's whereabouts, the latter assumes that he will be with other women before his marriage vows are taken:

> ... let him compass,
> Whole Parks and Forrests, as great Rangers doe[;]
> At roosting time a little lodge can hold' em.
> Earth-conquering *Alexander*, that thought the world
> Too narrow for him, in the end had but his pit-hole. (4.1.60–5)

Diaphanta's puns imply that Alsemero is a philanderer;[83] they are reminiscent of Alibius in the subplot, who 'cannot always be at home'

(1.2.33) and whose desire to 'look out' (35) is implicitly a sexual one. Middleton thus complicates Alsemero's character with suggestions that his Stoic past is fraudulent, concealing a secret sexual life.

Yet when Rowley takes over in the last scene, it is once more suggested that Alsemero has had no experience with women; he says, 'Did my fate wait for this unhappy stroke / At my first sight of woman?' (5.3.12–13). The line is spoken in soliloquy, a mode of address conventionally used to impart truthful expressions of the character's feelings, but the audience cannot accept this comment as a simple truth after watching Middleton's scenes. This means that when Alsemero describes the mask falling from Beatrice's face to reveal her moral ugliness (3–6), he looks like a hypocrite, because Middleton's scenes have suggested that he too is wearing a mask. The possibility that 'hidden maladies' lurk within Alsemero's mind has been created, and is neither confirmed nor denied. Furthermore, since Alsemero's comments about his 'first sight of woman' are spoken in soliloquy, the discontinuity even creates the peculiar, and highly disturbing, suggestion that Alsemero may be *unaware* of the contents of his own mental 'closet.'

This apparently inadvertent contradiction in Alsemero's characterization makes his assumption of the role of moral spokesman unacceptable to audience members who notice it, because it gives Alsemero an inner core of lust that is neither 'discovered' nor punished. Thus, while the structure of Rowley's final scene represents Alsemero as a man whose knowledge has caused him to change for the better by developing self-control over his passions, the lack of closure of the ideas Middleton has introduced makes Alsemero look like a 'changeling' in the folkloric sense: a malevolent fairy-child lurking behind a fair exterior.[84]

Middleton's attribution of hidden qualities to Alsemero is in keeping with Calvinist psychology. In Rowley's traditionalist psychological schema, it is perfectly possible for Alsemero to be ruled by passion temporarily. But in the schema implied by Middleton's tragedies, evil people must be inherently evil at their essence, and it is therefore natural for Middleton to represent Alsemero as having a hidden core of evil. This conflict between two attitudes to moral change is what causes the moral complexity, and is one of the reasons why critics have often assumed that the final scene must be intended as ironic. When Neill describes Alsemero's demand for evil to be forgotten as 'suppression of the truth,' the 'truth' he refers to is the truth about the darkness within all the characters. But as we have seen, in Rowley's mode of characterization truth is found in self-recognition and the individual's ability to make rational choices. The collision of these different interpretations of truth is one reason why the conclusion of *The Changeling* remains both upbeat and disturbing: neither Calvinism nor Pelagianism alone is sufficient to explain it.

Divided Authors

Even if he was unable to define how, Arthur Symons was right that *The Changeling*'s characters change under the pens of its two authors. Despite the play's careful construction, Middleton's and Rowley's approaches to tragedy remain profoundly different. Apparently proceeding from very different theological perspectives, their representation of tragic protagonists in the process of making moral choices is demonstrably divergent. This difference prevents them from effacing their collaboration within *The Changeling*. Indeed, it hints at a fundamental disagreement about the role of tragedy itself. Rowley's work on the play emphasizes the potential of human agency to prevent the enactment of sin, so that the play culminates in a didactic moral that emphasizes human potential for change. Middleton's scenes frustrate that moral with an essentialist representation of the characters' moral states. Of course, this discrepancy might be part of the authors' collaborative design. But the close correspondence of the different methods of characterization with the scenes believed to be by each author suggests that the play is a patchwork, not a perfectly interwoven text.

Rowley's assumptions result in his work appearing less bleak in its implications than Middleton's, at least to modern readers. In one of the earliest studies of Middleton and Rowley as a collaborative team, Pauline G. Wiggin concluded that Middleton was a 'realist' while Rowley was a 'romantic.' Middleton, Wiggin claimed, had a cynical view of humanity whereas Rowley believed in 'the essential dignity and beauty of human nature.'[85] It is difficult to agree with the latter claim after reading the bloodbath that is *All's Lost by Lust*, but we can certainly agree with Wiggin if we say that *All's Lost* and Rowley's scenes in *The Changeling* derive their dramatic power from their representation of the characters' ever-present potential for change, even if that potential is rarely realized. Reading the plays via post-Reformation theology enables us to use a more appropriate terminology than Wiggin's terms.

The popularity of *The Changeling* on page and stage demonstrates that the failure to achieve unity or coherence between authorial voices does not inherently entail theatrical failure. The discoherence between the authors makes the characters fascinating in their complexity, and even if some of its effects are inadvertent, they still have the potential to thrill and disturb. Daalder is right to say that those who do not view the play 'with the fact of dual authorship in mind will experience it as though it was the product of one unified sensibility,'[86] but 'dissecting' the play can reveal a wealth of information, both about the play and about the assumptions held by its writers. One need not stop there, however. I have discussed *The Changeling* as if it were purely the product of playwrights, but there were other forms of collaboration in the early modern playhouse. In the next chapter I introduce the persona of Rowley the actor, whose presence on stage would have made abundantly clear the impossibility of separating the dramaturgical choices of playwrights from their polyvocal theatrical circumstances.

Chapter Three

The Actor as Collaborator: *Wit at Several Weapons* and the Incorporation of Personae

The preface to Middleton and Rowley's masque *The World Tossed at Tennis* permits a brief glimpse of an aspect of the early modern theatre that is almost lost to us. The masque was performed by Prince Charles's Men at a public theatre in 1619 or 1620, perhaps as a result of its court performance being cancelled. Rowley, who was also the company's regular clown actor, played the role of Simplicity, a comical embodiment of human nature unspoilt by civilization.[1] In the preface to the printed text, published in 1620, Rowley, signing himself 'Simplicitie,' writes of the character in the third person: 'though he be now in a Masque, yet is his face apparent inough' (Epistle, 26–7).[2] Rowley's pun indicates that he expects his readers to be surprised by Simplicity's presence in a courtly entertainment but nevertheless to recognize him: a masque cannot mask a famous clown. Rowley is thus not only referring to the character of Simplicity that appears in this text but also to those qualities of the character that are continuous with Rowley's previous clown roles. In other words, he is referring to his own stage persona, which regular attenders of performances by Prince Charles's Men would have known well. The preface can thus be seen as one of the exercises in self-promotion described by Nora Johnson, in which clown actors of the period carried over their popular personae into printed forms that 'promised buyers both the pleasures of the stage and an experience of [the actor's] personal talents.'[3] Some of the qualities that Rowley's audience would have recognized can still be traced in playtexts today: his physical appearance, for example, is suggested by abundant references to his obesity.[4] The existence of this distinctive stage persona had great significance for the results of Rowley's collaborations with Middleton, and complicates the model of dramatic collaboration that I have used thus far.

That significance can be seen in *A Game at Chess* (1624), a play that could be regarded as Middleton and Rowley's last collaboration, because even though Middleton wrote the entire text, part of his work would have been to find a way to incorporate Rowley's stage persona. We know this because the earliest surviving text of the play contains no clown role, whereas the subsequent texts all contain a comic character called the Fat Bishop, a caricature of the apostate Bishop Marco Antonio de Dominis. The likely reason for this change is that having had the play accepted by the King's Men, Middleton was obliged to add a role for Rowley, who was by then performing with that company.[5] The characteristics of the Fat Bishop are thus not only the product of Middleton's satirical imagination and of de Dominis's public image but also of Rowley's characteristics as an actor: there needed to be a fat, clownish character in the play. Rowley's talents and limitations were thus a constraint upon Middleton's choices.

Middleton's experience must have been a common one: many early modern dramatists wrote plays for specific acting companies and would have had particular actors in mind when creating characters.[6] Part of the playwriting process would have involved 'shaping each written part to a specific player, creating lines that explicitly matched an actor's size, vocal range, and mannerisms.'[7] Clown actors like Rowley were the most extreme examples of actors whose characteristics were strong enough to affect what a playwright could write. In an important study, David Wiles shows that most adult playing companies employed a clown actor, and 'writers had an obligation to cater for his distinctive talents.'[8] For example, Wiles demonstrates clear differences between the sets of characters created for Will Kemp and Robert Armin during their respective periods as clown actor in Shakespeare's playing company. Attributing these differences to the distinctive qualities of the actors – their physical appearances and their idiosyncratic talents – Wiles argues that the well-established clown actor appeared to the company's regular audience as a constant element, not as a series of separate characters, and thus functioned as a 'sign' that the playwright was obliged to use.[9] This 'sign' is the actor's persona: the image that is created by an audience member's familiarity with his or her previous roles, and which colours the audience's expectations of productions in which he or she appears.[10]

Since an actor's distinctive talents and specialities were constraints on what the character could or could not do, the relationship between playwright and actor was a complex form of collaboration. In some descriptions of this relationship, the actor is dominant over the frustrated playwright: for example, the writing of clown roles is satirized as a tiresome obligation in the Cambridge University comedy *The Pilgrimage to Parnassus* (ca. 1599), in which a clown is dragged onstage with a rope, left alone to improvise some irrelevant low comedy, and then dragged off again; his only reason for being there, it is explained, is that 'a playe cannot be without a clowne[.] Clownes have bene thrust into playes by head & shoulders, ever since Kempe could make a scurvey face.'[11] At least once, a Middleton-Rowley play featured just such an insertion of superfluous fooling: the 1617 text of *A Fair Quarrel* was reissued 'with new additions of M^r. *Chaughs* and *Trimtrams* Roaring, and the Bauds Song,' presumably because the clown scenes already present had proven popular; while the new scene has thematic unity with the rest of the play, it is detachable from the plot and is very much thrust in 'by head and shoulders.'[12]

However, actors were not entirely dominant in this form of collaboration: the playwright's text could in turn be a constraint on the actors if it required them to use their talents in specific ways. For example, since the Fat Bishop was a caricature of a well-known real person, de Dominis, the audience would not have seen the character entirely as William Rowley returning to do his turn. In addition, Middleton gave the Fat Bishop blank verse dialogue very different from the colloquial prose that a clown would normally speak. The collaboration is thus extremely complex: Middleton the playwright imposed constraints onto Rowley's persona by creating a specially designed 'character' for him, while the nature of that character was also constrained by Rowley's persona; and furthermore, the collaboration continued into performance, since Rowley's choices as actor could affect the audience's interpretation of the playwright's text.

Middleton's creation of the Fat Bishop can thus be thought of as a collaboration with Rowley in that it required a negotiation between two personalities even if the two men did not literally communicate about it. Whatever Middleton's feelings about the need to incorporate Rowley, the combination of their work produced one of the play's most popular characters: the Fat Bishop appears on the title page of the quarto publications and the character received attention in several contemporary responses.[13] But this collaboration also resulted in a change to the play's meaning. In the allegory of *A Game at Chess*, the chess pieces represent real political figures: for example, the White King is an idealized depiction of King James, while the Black Knight is a caricature of the Spanish ambassador. Cleverly constructed though it is, the play is not morally complex; Roussel Sargent summarizes its political subtleties as follows:

> Middleton, in his writing of [*A Game at Chess*] demonstrates the narrow dogmatism, the irrational bias, and the extravagant oversimplifications likely to arise at a time of national crisis … By making the Spaniards the black pieces, Middleton has already conditioned our response: we know that they are evil, just as we know that the white pieces must be good. The symbolism is simple and obvious, but so is Middleton's argument; basically all he is saying is that England is good and is being threatened by Spain, which is evil.[14]

Gary Taylor counters this reading somewhat, noting that the distinctions between the 'houses' 'are not always clear': characters on both sides dissemble, pretending to be other than they are.[15] But this dissembling does not alter the fundamental identity of the characters as either White or Black. It is only the Fat Bishop who complicates the play's binarism: labelled with neither colour in speech prefixes and stage directions, he is merely 'Fat,' defined by his greed, not by his political allegiance. De Dominis, on whom the Fat Bishop is based, was an Italian archbishop in London who had published a famous recantation of his Catholicism but who then returned to Rome in 1623 and recanted his recantation.[16] In the play, the Fat Bishop is initially depicted as a propagandist for the White side, writing 'Invectives / agaynst the Blackhouse,' his former employers (2.2.13–14). However, his motives for having converting to the White side are not holy: he left the Black side for a suitably clownish reason:

> of all things I commend the Wh[ite] house best
> for plentie and Varietie of Victualls[.]
> when I was one of the black Side profest
> my flesh fell halfe a Cubit[;] time to turne
> when my owne Ribs revolted. (2.2.23–7)

But the Fat Bishop becomes dissatisfied with the White house; he wants better access to prostitutes and is greedy for promotion (2.2.35–45; 3.1.6–18). When the Black Knight appears with the promise of a high-ranking bishopric, the Fat Bishop converts back to the Black house, reasoning thus:

> it is but penning
> another Recantation, and inventing

> 2 or 3 bitter Bookes agaynst the white house
> and then I'me in a tother side agen[,]
> as firme as ere I was, as fatt and flourishing.   (3.1.52-6)

To be 'fatt and flourishing' is all the Fat Bishop's aim. Unlike the other characters, who are driven by zeal, he 'feede[s] uppon the Fat of one Kingdome, / and rayle[s] uppon another with the Juice on't' (2.2.19-20).

Because the character is so unprincipled, T.H. Howard-Hill argues that his inclusion 'attenuates rather than reinforces the political impact of the play.'[17] Howard-Hill notes that Middleton created the Fat Bishop in part by transferring lines to him from the Black Bishop (who represents the Father-General of the Jesuits). By giving these lines to the Fat Bishop and adding some comic references to the character's gluttony, Middleton minimized the suggestion in the first draft of a close bond between the Black Knight (who represents the real-life Spanish ambassador, Gondomar) and the Father-General; Howard-Hill thus argues that the replacement of the Black Bishop with Rowley's 'self-aggrandizing buffoon' curtails Middleton's anti-Catholic political point.[18] This may be so, but the introduction of the Fat Bishop also makes the play more complex. In the first draft, all the characters are locked into their unshakeable identities, either as evil Catholics or as virtuous Protestants. But the Fat Bishop switches easily between sides: he has no faith at all, only a clownish desire for food, sex, and comfort. As such, he seems an embodiment of those pragmatists who are happy to adopt whatever faith happens to be the dominant one, and he undermines the play's Protestant didacticism with his comically simple survivalism. Whether Middleton appreciated or was frustrated by this result of the incorporation of Rowley's persona cannot, of course, be known.

Nora Johnson writes that the presence of clown actors as 'independent theatrical professionals' who play themselves rather than individualized characters has caused some scholars to describe these actors as the antithesis of the playwright; the clown actor, it is argued, undermines 'the fantasy of textual control that we generally imagine as belonging to authors.'[19] However, Johnson questions any absolute division between authors and actors, pointing out that the recognizable actor is, in some ways, rather like an author. The names and images of the great stage clowns were reproduced in print and in other media in what was clearly a form of early modern celebrity.[20] Rowley's fame did not match that of Richard Tarlton and the myriad ways in which his name was traded on, but he seems to have been known well enough for his distinctive physique to appear in the illustration on the title page of *The World Tossed at Tennis*.[21] Johnson argues that this appetite for 'individual figures who could, as individuals, promise theatrical pleasure' means that an actor might be perceived by the audience as a source of the text's meaning if he is 'an irreplaceable source of wit and of pleasure that can only be considered his own.'[22]

The figure of the playwright-clown adds a further complication, combining as it does literary authorship with the theatrical authority of the clown. Johnson focuses on Robert Armin to explore these ideas, but Rowley's situation was more complex than Armin's because Rowley was a prolific playwright, more so than any other playwright-clown of the period.[23] Rowley's long career meant that he was regularly in the position of performing roles that he had written himself, within narrative structures that he had partly created (even in collaboratively written plays, he normally appears to have been the writer responsible for the clown's part).[24] Furthermore, as we have seen in previous chapters, Rowley's position as sharer in Prince Charles's Men gave him a greater position of authority than that of most actors and writers. Rowley's degree of 'textual control' may have varied according to his situation – it may have declined when he joined the King's Men in 1623, since there is no evidence that he was a sharer there until 1625[25] – but it would have been at its strongest when performing roles that he had written to perform himself for Prince Charles's Men between 1609 and 1622.

For these reasons, understanding Rowley's stage persona is vital to understanding his collaborations with Middleton. Fortunately, the careers of clown actors can be traced with relative ease because the clown role is easily recognizable in early modern playtexts. It is thus possible to reconstruct in part what a London playgoer of the 1610s and '20s might have found 'apparent enough' in Rowley's performances. At least fourteen roles in extant plays can be shown to have been written for Rowley; some were written by himself, others by Middleton, and still others by John Fletcher and Phillip Massinger. There is direct evidence for four of Rowley's roles: Jaques in Rowley's own *All's Lost by Lust* (1618–20), Plumporridge in Middleton's *The Inner Temple Masque* (1619), Simplicity in *The World Tossed at Tennis* (1619–20), and the Fat Bishop in *A Game at Chess* (1624).[26] The first three were performed by Prince Charles's Men; the last was performed by the King's Men. Because his company affiliations are known, other Rowley roles can be identified in the clown roles of those companies' plays for which the dates of composition are known. For the Prince's Men, Rowley can thus be presumed to have played Roger in *A New Wonder: A Woman Never Vexed* (ca. 1611–15), Pompey Doodle in *Wit at Several Weapons* (ca. 1613–15), Chough in *A Fair Quarrel* (1616), Barnaby in *A Shoemaker a Gentleman* (ca. 1618–20), Gnothos in *The Old Law* (1618–19), Cuddy Banks in *The Witch of Edmonton* (1621), and the Clown in *The Birth of Merlin* (1622).[27] For the King's Men, he would have played Bustofa in *The Maid in the Mill* (1623), Cacafogo in *Rule a Wife and Have a Wife* (1624), Tony in *A Wife for a Month* (1624), and Belgarde in *The Unnatural Combat* (1624–5).[28] As confirmatory evidence, references to the clown's obesity appear in the texts of many of these plays.[29]

In what follows, I will demonstrate that the texts of these roles display striking continuities. First, Rowley uses a persona based on guileless plain-speaking in play after play, and puts it to a variety of different purposes. Second, the roles differ according to the author: other playwrights represent Rowley's persona as a figure that needs to be punished, but in his self-written roles, Rowley himself encourages the audience to agree with some of the ideas put forward by the clown. Finally, Rowley has a distinctive method of achieving the latter effect: he repeatedly structures his clown subplots in such a way that the final scene contrasts the clown positively with another character. After discussing the variations to which Rowley could push his persona, I will illustrate his typical method of structuring clown plots with the aid of *All's Lost by Lust*. I will then discuss the difficulties faced by Middleton and Rowley in incorporating Rowleyan clowns into Middleton's satirical form of comedy, and how they made it work in their first collaboration, *Wit at Several Weapons*.

Rowley's Persona under Different Playwrights

Clowns in early modern drama can have a variety of dramatic functions: there are 'holy fools' who behave with innocent goodness and there are amoral selfish gluttons; there are mindless idiots and there are witty court fools. What unites these figures is their function as an emblem of 'natural man,' where 'nature' corresponds to the lower bodily stratum, as described by Mikhail Bakhtin.[30] Hence, the name 'Simplicity' in *The World Tossed at Tennis* is appropriate for such a character. The fool emblematizes nature because he is unable to repress the expression of his instinctive desires and is interested only in the most immediate needs of a living thing; thus, Nicholas Breton wrote of the fool in 1616, 'his exercises are commonly divided into foure parts, Eating and Drinking, Sleeping and Laughing,'[31] and one could add to this list the fool's sexual desires, signified by his enlarged codpiece and 'bauble.' The Fat Bishop's comic prioritizing of his corporeal desires over his religious zeal is thus a perfect example of the clown figure.

As a fat man, Rowley was particularly well suited to personifying 'nature' in this sense. However, the signification of his obesity could vary. Bakhtin has shown that in folk culture the material dimension of human existence was often celebrated as an image of vitality, so that the obese body of the natural man represented 'the incarnation of the people's utopia and feasting'; similarly, François Laroque shows that it could suggest the renewal of vitality after Lent, paralleling the body of a pregnant woman and symbolizing 'renewed abundance and a promise of births to come.'[32] However, Bakhtin also writes that the obese character can sometimes be seen as the antithesis of popular merriment: as he puts it, 'the soul of the people as a whole cannot coexist with the private, limited, greedy body.'[33] There could be no better example than the Fat Bishop, who, when he is thrust into the 'Bagg' with the other Black chess pieces, squashes his former comrades, crying, 'the Bishop must have roome, hee Will have roome, / and roome to lye at pleasure[!]' (5.3.193–4).

The greed of the Fat Bishop was only one of several ways in which Rowley's clownish persona could be used. Owing to their association with plebeian festivity, clowns could also emblematize the popular voice and the topsy-turvy reversals of the dominant order enacted at carnival times; they frequently scoff at the distinctions between social classes in a manner reminiscent of the medieval Lords of Misrule.[34] Accordingly, Rowley frequently played plebeians who get a chance to raise their social status via marriage (in *A New Wonder*, *Wit at Several Weapons*, *All's Lost by Lust*, *The Birth of Merlin*, and *The Maid in the Mill*), or higher-status characters who behave vulgarly (such as the Cornish gentleman Chough in *A Fair Quarrel*, and the Fat Bishop). This function, too, could have varied connotations: modern critics have debated the extent to which the clown's questioning of class divisions is subversive or merely a 'safety valve' that neutralizes transgressive ideas by placing them in the mouth of a fool; there is no simple answer to this question, and some clown roles appear more subversive than others.[35]

As a clown, Rowley thus had the potential to be holy or selfish, an emblem of carnivalesque vitality or of carnivalesque excess, a harmless safety valve or an anti-establishment rebel. As Ronald Knowles points out, one reason for the difficulty of interpreting clowns on the page is the absence of the actor: his 'compact with the audience to make them laugh to the best of his ability' might clash with his duty to fulfil the written role,[36] so that a role written to encourage laughter *at* the clown could be warped by a skilled performer to produce a different effect. However, Rowley's position as author and clown gives an unusually clear window into one clown's attitude toward the function of his role.

Reading all of Rowley's clown roles, regardless of the playwright, it is clear that his stage persona consistently emphasized one aspect of the natural man's simplicity: guilelessness. The idea that the clown utters plain truth because his 'natural' state makes him incapable of deceit is of course a traditional one: Robert Burton wrote, 'They are no dissemblers, liers, hypocrites, for fooles and mad men tell commonly truth.'[37] However, Rowley's version of the clown has its own quirks: whereas a common feature of Will Kemp's roles (regardless of the playwright) is the Dogberry-esque malapropism,[38] Rowley's humour stems from the clown's bluntness, not from his incompetent mistaking. Rowley is also unusual in his repeated emphasis on the clown's artless inability to lie, which differs from the artful truth-telling of Robert Armin's courtly fools. Rowley's guileless clown appears in many forms – plebeians, noblemen, and even allegorical figures – but whatever the situation, his plainness always accords with Enid Welsford's comment that fools and clowns tend to be 'unabashed' in their behaviour.[39] Hence, the comic fun of the Fat Bishop stems in part from his flagrant greed: when persuaded to return to the Black House, he does not pretend to have a religious conversion: he simply tells the Black Knight that 'this was the Chayre of Ease I ever aymde at[;] / Ile make a Bonfire of my Bookes immediatelie[!]' (3.1.48–9).

This plain speaking is a sign of the Bishop's wickedness, and the five roles written for Rowley by others similarly treat his persona as an object of derision: the clown is comically wicked and often punished at the end of the play. The Fat Bishop is hurled with the other Black pieces into the bag that 'like Hell opens / to take her due' (5.3.179–80). In Fletcher's *Rule a Wife and Have a Wife*, the grasping usurer Cacafogo spends the final scene drunk in a cellar (represented by the space below the stage, from which devils traditionally emerged), from which he utters drunken roars so devil-like that they terrify the wicked Duke into repentance; Cacafogo is then banished with the words, 'When he is sober let him out to raile, / Or hang himselfe, there will be no losse of him' (5.5.133–4). Plumporridge in Middleton's *Inner Temple Masque* is a grotesque emblem of festive greed, who exits symbolically when New Year enters (142). The other two clown characters are not banished but are still represented as unwanted or irrelevant: Belgarde in Massinger's *Unnatural Combat* is a lower-class soldier who resents the upper classes but 'learns to know his place,'[40] and in Fletcher's *A Wife for a Month*, Tony is a 'knavish foole' (according to the *dramatis personae*) who utters cynical commentaries, contributing nothing to the plot.

In these roles, Middleton, Fletcher, and Massinger use Rowley's blunt persona to represent devilish greed, transitory festivity, uppity commoners, and misanthropy, and the endings of these plays do not invite the audience to sympathize with the clown's perspective. Strikingly, the least offensive of these clowns, Plumporridge – who merely behaves with festive vulgarity and then exits without a fanfare – appears in the only one of these roles written for Prince Charles's Men; the others were written when Rowley was in his less powerful position at the King's Men. It appears from these roles that the less control Rowley had, the more the clown was denigrated.

This is not to say that Rowley's self-written roles go to the opposite extreme. The only example of a 'holy fool' among them is Simplicity in *The World Tossed at Tennis* (the writing of this role appears, unusually, to have been divided between Rowley and Middleton).[41] *World Tossed* depicts the birth of 'custom' in the world, and Simplicity represents the innocent first state of humanity. A character representing Deceit introduces corruption to the world, but Simplicity is incapable of deceit, having only enough guile to remain impervious to temptation: 'All the rest / Is innocence about him, truth and bluntness' (470–1). This holy innocence is a version of guilelessness that is very different from Middleton's normal approach, but is also unusual even for Rowley.

Instead, Rowley's other self-written roles occupy a middle ground between these extremes. These clowns express antisocial attitudes and their 'natural' state is depicted as excessive and grotesque, but Rowley always provides them with a climactic scene that justifies the validity of the opinions that they have expressed during the play, typically by contrasting them with a similar character who is even worse. Rowley's tragedy *All's Lost by Lust*, which features a typically plain-spoken, plebeian clown, is a useful example of the way he commonly structured these plotlines.

The Rowleyan Clown in *All's Lost by Lust*

In *All's Lost by Lust*, the clown, Jaques,[42] appears in the context of a passionate tragedy. Like all Rowley's clowns, he is guileless: he is called 'open / Plaine, and rusticall' (3.2.17–18), where 'open' refers to his inability to hide his thoughts or to be trusted with secrets – as one character warns, 'What ever your purpose is, let it not appear to him' (19). This openness is used to undercut the poetic speech of the higher-ranking main characters.

The play's main plot concerns a rapist king and its subplot a bigamous nobleman; both characters are overwhelmed by lust and express their intense emotions in agonized poetic speeches. Jaques appears in the bigamy subplot, and his actions have what Bakhtin calls a 'degrading' effect by reducing high culture to its material level, highlighting the grotesque physicality that it attempts to efface with elevated language.[43] As the subplot tells its story of an unequal marriage between a nobleman and a peasant woman that ends in bigamy and murder, the clown's mockery of the elevated language in which the nobleman articulates his emotions highlights the way the high-ranking characters justify their lusts as more noble than those of the other characters.

Jaques is the brother of Margaretta, the orange-seller who marries the nobleman Antonio. He first appears as Margaretta's family debates whether she should accept Antonio's offer of marriage. Her father warns about the hazards of unequal marriages, but Jaques cares only for himself, revelling in the prospect of becoming a 'lord's brother.' The comedy derives from Jaques's inability to contain his excitement:

> *Mar.* [*to Antonio, indicating her parents*]
> Heres all the barre;
> When these have given consent I am your owne.
> *Ant.* [*to the parents*]
> It shall be done in this acknowledgement.
> Father and mother let me but call you so.
> *Jaq.*
> And brother eke also[!]
> *Ant.*
> Yes, brother too,
> [*Kissing Margaretta*] By this I claime them all, [*to the parents*] your daughter makes
> Me your sonne, and yours.
> *Jaq.*
> And my brother[!]
> *Ant.*
> Ile not forget that neither.
> *Jaq.*
> If you do, I will forget to call your Lady Sister.   (1.3.73–80)

Jaques's guilelessness is obvious: he does not disguise his selfishness by claiming that the marriage will be good for his sister but expresses himself bluntly. In the rest of the play, Rowley uses Jaques's shamelessness to show how the other characters employ rhetoric to conceal their own clown-like desires.

Antonio's subsequent bigamous marriage to the noblewoman Dionyzia is considered by both the aristocrats and the peasants to be an inevitable result of his unequal marriage to Margaretta; however, each group blames the other. Antonio's confidante Lazarello encourages his friend to think of Margaretta as an embarrassment whose rude speech will 'staine' Antonio's 'worth' (2.6.19–21), unlike Dionyzia, who would praise Antonio eloquently, like 'music gracing the solemnity' (26). Conversely, the peasants distance themselves from the rakish sexuality that they believe to be inherent in aristocratic men: Margaretta's father compares noblemen with the inconstant moon (1.3.27–9), and Margaretta herself learns that 'Base ones made big by beauty are but slaves[;] / Their Lords nere truly bed but in their graves' (3.2.14–15). Both social groups partition the classes into distinct, separate worlds and recoil from integration because of the others' perceived vulgarity.

The appearance in scene 3.2 of a vulgar clown dressed in lordly attire is therefore a powerful image: Jaques, now a 'lord's brother' and presumably dressed accordingly,[44] brings a letter from Margaretta to Antonio. As we have seen, Jaques's absurd appearance could inspire mocking laughter at the aspirations of the plebeians, but Rowley instead directs the laughter at the aristocrat. Jaques sees Antonio wooing Dionyzia, and Antonio is terrified that he will tell Margaretta, but Jaques considers himself a man of the world and instead spouts a series of proverbs about male infidelity. The humour comes from Antonio's embarrassment and Jaques's seemingly endless supply of proverbs:

> *Jaq.* Come, I know flesh and bloud will be sporting. And I were a married man my selfe, I would not alwayes be at home. I woud hawke, and hunt, and ride[;] there are divers members in one body[;] there are flesh dayes, and there are fish dayes[;] a man must not always eate one sort of meat.
> *Ant.* I see you are a wag brother.
> *Jaq.* Always let a married man get his owne children at home if he can[;] if he have a bit abroad for procreation or so –
> *Ant.* Well good night brother, I pray hold a good opinion of me.
> *Jaq.* O Sir, I can winke with one eye like a gunner.   (3.3.135–46)

Jaques interprets Antonio's behaviour in the plainest way, assuming that they are both clowns, interested only in gratifying their base desires. Bakhtin writes that 'laughter degrades and materialises,'[45] and that is what Jaques does to Antonio as he articulates the gross materiality beneath the nobleman's refined rhetoric.

As soon as Jaques has left, Antonio launches back into blank verse anguish:

> Oh my afflicted soule, wert thou capable
> Of separation, thou woudst now be rent
> Into a thousand peeces. (151–3)

However, Jaques's interpretation of Antonio's actions may affect the audience's experience of these speeches and prepares for the subsequent sequence in which, torn between his 'conscience' and his 'affection' (175–8), Antonio decides not to reject Dionyzia but to slander Margaretta's reputation in order to divorce her. By placing the conversation with Jaques immediately before this sequence, Rowley reminds the audience of the baser emotions underlying Antonio's tragic rhetoric and encourages the audience to see in Antonio a layer of affectation that covers a 'natural' layer. Thus Jaques's own appearance – a 'natural' clown in the clothes of a gentleman – is a mirror of Antonio, not a foil.

Jaques's intervention denies the logic behind Lazarello's arguments against unequal marriages and also accords with Margaretta's words when she decides to murder Antonio in revenge. Margaretta's actions are not represented as characteristic of a peasant: instead, she claims to be taking on the qualities of an aristocrat, saying, 'Spite of the low condition of my birth, / High spirits may be lodg'd in humble earth' (3.2.88–9), and after she has done the deed, announces, 'My birth was base, but my revenge flew high' (5.5.67). The passionate anger that leads to revenge and tragedy is associated with the aristocracy, not with social descent.

Unlike Massinger's play *The Unnatural Combat*, in which Rowley's clown is punished for his social transgressions, the structure of *All's Lost* supports Jaques's view of the world: the aristocratic repudiation of plainness is mocked without a corresponding mockery of the assumption that lords are all rakes. Furthermore, Rowley does not punish the clown but ends his story with a scene that pairs him with a worse character. After Margaretta murders Antonio (as she thinks), Jaques enters alone, cursing his sister for overthrowing their 'honourable house' (5.3.11). There he encounters Lothario, a nobleman from the main plot who is the comically vulgar pander to the rapist King Roderick. The characters mirror each other perfectly, because this role too was written for an obese actor: the text continually emphasizes Lothario's heavy flesh.[46] The stage image thus consists of two fat comic actors wearing lordly attire, and their laments echo each other:

> *Lo.* I was a Lord, altho a bawdy Lord.
> *Jaq.* I was a Lords brother, altho a bawdy Lords brother.
> *Lo.* O Lechery, how hast thou puft mee up and undone me.
> *Jaq.* O Lechery, thou hast battend me awhile, and then spoild me. (5.3.15–18)

Lothario has made a noose and asks Jaques to be his executioner. Jaques is initially concerned that this may compromise his newfound gentility: 'I have liv'd a Lords brother, and would be loath to die a hangman' (28), but when he remembers that hangmen inherit the possessions of their victims, he accepts with another demonstration of blunt amorality:

> [*Aside*] Hum? my brother is dead, and there is no way to raise our house agen but by ready money, or credit; [']The hangman many times mounts above his betters.['] [*To Lothario*] well I will hang [i.e., hang you], but my conscience beares me witnesse[:] tis not for any good will I beare unto thee, nor for any wrong that I know thou hast committed; but innocently for thy lands, thy leases, thy clothes, and thy money. And so come along with me to the next tree, where thou shalt hang till thou art dead, and stink above ground. (58–66)

The scene encapsulates the materiality of the bigamy plotline. Lothario, though he regrets his sins, clings to the abstract idea of nobility: 'I have liv'd a Lord, and I would be loath to dye an executioner' (8–9). Jaques, meanwhile, decides that social status is merely a matter of inherited clothes and money. This degrading of gentility continues as Lothario promises to follow Jaques 'With all my heart, my guts, my lights, my liver, and my lungs' (67), emphasizing the physical body that has motivated the lusts and passions of all the characters.

The contrast between the two characters is illustrated by Jaques's use of the word 'innocently' to describe his actions: Jaques has no understanding of morality. In their echoing laments, Lothario curses himself and repents, while Jaques curses his sister and mourns the misfortune that the other characters' lusts have 'battened' him with. Because the other characters continually fight the clown-like lusts inside their own identities, they are responsible for their actions. Jaques is not, for he is a clown through and through.

In *All's Lost*, then, the 'open, / Plaine, and rusticall' clown is an emblem of the lusts that infuse the other characters. However, the clown is placed into the story in order to satirically undercut the eloquent speeches uttered by the serious characters, in such a way that the passionate speeches that justify sinful behaviour are coded as both aristocratic and evil. For this reason, there seems to be an underlying radicalism in the bigamy plot, which goes some way toward contradicting the conservatism of the main plot, in which the usurper of a rapist monarch ultimately repents being 'a traytor to my lawfull King' (5.5.140). There are signs that Rowley structured the main plot in such a way as to avoid the censorship problems that might result from overtly advocating the usurpation of a king.[47] The subplot, and its final insistence that clownish vulgarity lies within everyone, may thus be structured to imply an attack on lasciviousness in high places that the main plot could not.

The Structure of Rowley's Clown Plots

The structure of the clown plot in *All's Lost by Lust*, in which the guileless 'natural' clown is ultimately vindicated via contrast with another character, is echoed in many of Rowley's other self-written roles for his company. In *The Witch of Edmonton*, Cuddy Banks is paralleled with the protagonists of the play's two tragic plotlines, and is, like them, subject to temptation and persuasion from the Dog, a canine devil.[48] Throughout much of the play, Cuddy is gullible and easily tempted: he plots with the witch and the Dog to win the affections of a young woman, rewards the Dog with stolen goods, and is complicit in the framing of his rivals, Warbeck and Somerton. However, as in *All's Lost*, Rowley gives his clown a climactic scene that explicitly sets him off against another character. In this case, he is contrasted with the Dog, whom Cuddy engages in a Faustian interview. Rowley stresses the differences between the clown and the devil when Cuddy says, 'certainly *Tom*, I begin to pity thee' (5.1.150), expressing bewilderment at the Dog's behaviour:

> *Clow.* Were it not possible for thee to become an honest Dog yet? 'tis a base life that you lead, *Tom*, to serve Witches, to kill innocent Children, to kill harmless Cattle, to stroy Corn and Fruit, &c. 'twere better yet to be a Butcher, and kill for your self.
> *Dog.* Why? these are all my delights, my pleasures, fool. (152–6)

The effect of this passage is to demonstrate an important difference between the devil's amorality and the clown's. Cuddy is not interested in evil for its own sake; for him, it is merely a means to achieve comfort and satisfaction with worldly pleasures. Cuddy suggests to the Dog,

> [You could] serve in some Noble Mans, Knights or Gentlemans Kitchin, if you could brook the wheel, and turn the spit, your labour could not be much; when they have Rost-meat, that's but once or twice in the week at most, here you might lick [your] own Toes very well[;] Or if you could translate your self into a Ladies Arming-puppy, there you might lick sweet lips, and do many pretty Offices. (165–71)

This is a canine version of the land of Cockaigne: an easy life in a kitchen full of food or a life snuggled in the arms of a lady. These visions of infinite food and sensual pleasure are utopian for the greedy, lazy, lusty clown. But they are incomprehensible to the Dog, whose 'delights' and 'pleasures' (156) consist in destroying those of others, as he had explained earlier in the play:

> Those that are joys denied, must take delight
> In sins and mischiefs; 'tis the Devil's right.   (3.1.147–8)

The scene therefore has the effect of emphasizing the difference between the Dog, who is actively sadistic and indeed prepared to undergo discomfort in order to cause suffering in others, and Cuddy, who does not commit crimes for the sake of being cruel but rather because he desires more comfort. This difference explains why it is not incongruous for Cuddy to beat the Dog 'out of the bounds of *Edmonton*' (5.1.191–2) in the play's climax. When Cuddy tells the Dog, 'to morrow we go in Procession, and after thou shalt never come in againe' (192–3), Rowley is linking the clown with a folk festival, the Rogation ceremony, in which parishioners would mark the perimeters of the parish in a symbolic banishment of evil spirits before indulging in communal feasting.[49] The final stage direction reads, '*Exeunt Y[oung] Banks, Dog barking*' (197), which may indicate that Cuddy is physically beating the Dog off the stage, as promised. In both *All's Lost by Lust* and *The Witch of Edmonton*, then, the clown forms a vulgar parallel with the play's main protagonists, but his attitudes are justified or valorized in a climactic scene that contrasts him with a far more despicable character.

This strategy is also apparent in plays that Rowley co-wrote with Middleton. Michael E. Mooney has described how the adventures of the clownish Chough and Trimtram in *A Fair Quarrel*, who earnestly train at a 'school' for roaring boys, parallel in comic form the story of the main plot characters, Captain Ager and the Colonel, whose adherence to the code of duelling leads them almost to the brink of death. The parallel implicitly suggests that the outrageous swearing of the roaring boys, while vulgar, is more benign than aristocratic duelling, since the participants 'fight' only with meaningless insults and then 'conclude in wine' (4.1.190–1).[50] As with Cuddy in *The Witch of Edmonton*, Chough and Trimtram receive a moment of comparison in *A Fair Quarrel*'s climax: their inability to lie contributes toward the play's comic denouement when they vent forth a slanderous accusation against Chough's intended fiancée using the language of roaring. Despite the pandemonium that it initially causes, their outburst ultimately brings about the play's happy ending. The Captain and the Colonel achieve *their* happy ending by giving up duelling in favour of generosity and forgiveness, but Chough and Trimtram do not give up roaring; instead, they are invited to participate in the play's climactic nuptial ceremony, and Chough announces, 'Ile dine and dance, and roare at the wedding' (5.1.387). Roaring is embraced at the end of the play while duelling is not, and the vulgar clown is vindicated once more.

Similarly, in *A Shoemaker a Gentleman*, set during the Roman persecution of Christians in Britain, Barnaby, the clownish shoemaker, is initially a coward who puts self-preservation ahead of being a soldier or a proud Christian (3.2.9–23; 4.2.52–63), but during the play's climax he becomes a brave defender of the memory of the martyred Sir Hugh and a martial defender of Britain from invasion (4.2.189–269; 5.1.43–59). An attenuated version of this pattern also appears in Rowley's earliest known self-written role, in *A New Wonder*: the clown Roger's comic dislike for the various characters who hang around his wealthy mistress is vindicated in his last scene as he is permitted to banish two dissolute gentlemen from the house (4.3.99–102), although this takes place in the fourth act, lacking the finality of the other plays. Of the other self-written roles, only *The Birth of Merlin* lacks this recurrent structure – the clown simply fades away in the fifth act – but there is evidence that this part of the play may have been reorganized by a later reviser.[51] Rowley's final self-written role, Bustofa in *The Maid in the Mill*, features only a bland comparison between Bustofa's sister Florimell (who has been revealed as a foundling) and Bustofa himself (who wishes he was one), a comparison that is not presented as anything other than comically absurd – but this role was written for the King's Men, when Rowley may have had less control over the purposes to which his persona was put.

Among the roles that Rowley wrote for other actors, some include the structure that I have described and others do not. For example, Compass, the clown in *A Cure for a Cuckold*, which Rowley co-wrote for Prince Charles's company after he had left it, has a climactic moment in which his forgiving nature contrasts with the obsessive jealousy that drives the main plot characters.[52] In contrast, Lollio in *The Changeling*, written for Lady Elizabeth's Men while Rowley was acting with Prince Charles's, lacks the structure: while his role is certainly significant to the play's themes (parallels are drawn between him and De-Flores when both demand a sexual reward from the women they serve; see chapter 1), Lollio disappears in the fifth act and there is no suggestion that his point of view is in any way 'vindicated' by the comparison. Perhaps Rowley wrote this role for an actor with a different, less charming persona.

As this survey suggests, Rowley's roles were not clumsily inserted or irrelevant: he made them significant to the play's themes through parallels with the serious main plots and through meaningful contrasts in the clown's final scene. Shakespeare's Hamlet, who complained about undisciplined clowns who 'set on some quantitie of barren Spectators to laugh ... though in the meane time, some necessary Question of the Play be then to be considered' (3.2.41–3), might well have approved of Rowley's work. Indeed, Rowley goes further in that his clown roles are often designed to *pose* necessary questions as well. The recurrent structure that he utilized is almost a riposte to his fellow writers, at whose hands his persona was portrayed only as an object of disgust. Rowley's clown roles never deny the clown's stupidity, greed, and vulgarity, but they insist on the importance of the clownish perspective in articulating the play's ideas. In addition, they often express the clown's plebeian suspicion of the social hierarchy without defusing those ideas by making the clown a mere foil or safety valve.

For these reasons, Rowley's roles have a distinctiveness and a sense of writerly control that can only be called authorial. It is thus fascinating to study the interaction between Rowley's persona and Thomas Middleton's equally distinctive writing. Before he began collaborating with Rowley in or around 1614, Middleton had specialized in satirical city comedies written for the children's companies. These companies did not employ specialized clown actors and tended to avoid humour associated with the tradition of the jigging clowns like Tarlton and Kemp.[53] As Wiles suggests, this may in part be due to the social elitism and neoclassical aesthetic of the children's company comedies.[54] But it may also be a result of the nature of satirical comedy. In the city comedies of the children's companies, satire on contemporary morality and class politics is achieved by depicting characters whose amorality is overt and goes unpunished at the end. In such a play, a traditional clown has no clear purpose: if the clown's function in *All's Lost* was to literalize the vulgar desires that underlie those of the noble characters, then satirical comedies do this directly. This meant that when Middleton and Rowley combined their talents in writing satirical comedies, they had to find a way of enabling Rowley's clown to retain a function.

The Old Law shows that it was possible for them to fail: the failure stems from the play's premise, which makes the Rowleyan clown unnecessary. At the beginning of the play, the Duke of Epire declares that the elderly must be executed once they reach a certain age, and his edict produces strong reactions from the city's youth. While the ensuing play's generic structure is technically that of romance – its central story is the fight of the virtuous Cleanthes to save his father from death – it is dominated by comic satire about the gleeful reactions of the other Epirean youths. Since the law has been announced by the Duke himself, the youths do not need to mince their words as they express avaricious delight at the ensuing deaths of their parents. Simonides, for example, impatiently awaits his father Creon's death in this manner:

> *Duke.* Old *Creon*, you have been expected long.
> Sure y'are above fourscore.
> *Sim.* [*Interrupting*] Upon my life
> Not four and twenty houres my lord, I search'd
> The Church Booke yesterdaie[;] does your Grace think
> I'de let my Father wrong the Law my Lord?
> Twere pitty a'my life then, no, your Act
> Shall not receive a minutes wrong by him
> While I live sir, and hee's so just himselfe too
> I know he would [not] offer't[;] heere he stands.   (2.1.78–86)

The comedy in this passage comes from the outrageous bluntness of Simonides as he demands the swift despatch of his father. He and the other courtiers are blatantly clown-like or 'natural' in their behaviour: free from any fear of reprisals, they express their feelings plainly, without restraint.[55]

This means that Rowley's character, Gnothos the clown,[56] is an amusing but redundant figure. Gnothos invades the church register in order to adjust his wife's date of birth and is comically blunt in informing her of her ensuing death (3.1.315–45). His brazen lack of any attempt to disguise what he is doing is funny, but since the characters in the main plot share this quality, Gnothos adds nothing new to the play (indeed, his adjustment of the parish register is merely an elaboration of Simonides's earlier comment about checking the church-book), and his function is simply to provide a role for Rowley. Rowley does manage to give himself a 'comparison moment' in act 5: as the other characters grovel before the Vincentio-like Duke, who has revealed his law to be a hoax aimed at testing the morality of his subjects, Gnothos bursts in, accompanied by his old wife and his new future wife, to celebrate a simultaneous funeral and wedding. Appalled to learn that the law was only a test, Gnothos is the only character to defy the Duke, protesting, 'Heaven blesse, and mend your Lawes, that they do not gull your poore Country men [in this] fashion!' (5.1.533–5).[57] If Jeffrey Masten is right that the play exposes fractures in the ideology of absolutism,[58] this outburst of frustration at the monarch's whims has some thematic significance that could perhaps only be safely uttered by a clown. It does not, however, relate to anything the clown has done previously in the play.

But if the clown in *The Old Law* is rendered almost redundant by the play's satirical nature, in *Wit at Several Weapons* Middleton and Rowley found a way to use Rowley's persona within a satire, adjusting his signification to give him an important structural and tonal function and in the process giving the play a different structure than is conventional for a Middletonian satire.

Middleton, Rowley, and the Clown: *Wit at Several Weapons*

Wit at Several Weapons was first published within the Beaumont and Fletcher folio of 1647, but stylistic analysis and external evidence confirm that the text as we have it was written by Middleton and Rowley. The consensus is that even if the play was based on a Fletcherian original, it seems to be a wholesale revision that left little or no trace of the original author's style.[59] However, it is worth noting that the history of Rowley's playing company provided a likely route for a Fletcher play to come into his hands. Around 1614, Prince Charles's Men merged with Lady Elizabeth's Men, who had themselves recently merged with the former Children of the Queen's Revels. As a result, some or all of the Queen's Revels playbooks ultimately became the property of the company of Prince Charles.[60] Since Fletcher frequently wrote for the Queen's Revels during his early career,[61] a likely explanation of the play's conflicting evidence for authorship is that Fletcher wrote the original version for the Queen's Revels, and then, when the playbook found its way to Prince Charles's Men around 1614, Middleton and Rowley adapted the play for its new venue. This would certainly fit with the proposed dates for Middleton and Rowley's work on the play, around 1613–15.[62]

If this hypothesis of the play's genesis is correct, the playwrights would have needed to create a role for Rowley. That role is easily recognizable in the play's clown, a servant called Pompey Doodle.[63] Pompey may conceivably be an expansion of a character that already existed, but close analysis of the text suggests that he could have been inserted into a pre-existing play that did not include him, just as the Fat Bishop would later be inserted into *A Game at Chess*.

Wit at Several Weapons is an intrigue comedy in which an assortment of tricksters engage in scams to bamboozle their credulous relatives. Pompey is a gullible servant who is fooled into believing a young gentlewoman, the Niece, has fallen in love with him; he thus dramatically resigns from the service of his master, Sir Gregory, only to learn that he has been fooled. Almost all of his story could be removed from the play without affecting the other plotlines; indeed, the Niece's method of tormenting Pompey – ordering him to wait for her alone in the countryside, far away from the other characters – seems designed to keep the clown isolated from the rest of the story. Scene 2.3, in which Pompey resigns his service, is entirely self-contained. The sequence in scene 4.1 in which Pompey tells Cunningham that the Niece has not yet contacted him (299–366) is also easily detachable, since Cunningham's soliloquy before Pompey's entrance would make an acceptable ending to the scene (this could explain, too, the scene's stylistic texture: although the authorship attributers give this entire scene to Middleton, the section involving Pompey contains none of the stylistic features cited as 'conclusive evidence for Middleton,' and it could thus have been inserted by Rowley).[64] In scene 5.1, as Pompey watches Cunningham gulling Sir Gregory, his presence makes no difference to the scene and the lines concerning him could easily have been inserted.[65] Similarly, Pompey's climactic disappointment in 5.2 (216–94) is one single, detachable chunk. The earlier scenes are less easily removable, as the clown is more integrated into the story. In scene 2.2, Cunningham makes the Niece jealous by flattering her Guardianness; the Niece thus pretends to flirt with Pompey in order to make Cunningham jealous. This ploy succeeds, as Cunningham angrily rejects the Guardianness and stalks off, leaving the Niece to commiserate with the Guardianness. Pompey's presence is thus important to the scene. However, this sequence, too, could be an addition: if the lines referring to Pompey (98–197, 208–48, and 258–9) were dropped, Cunningham's motivation for suddenly abandoning the Guardianness would simply be his alarm at the Niece's entrance rather than jealousy; the elegant stage image of the two tricksters wooing their two gulls would thus be lost but the fundamentals of the plot would remain. In 3.1, Pompey himself is not present, but Cunningham torments Gregory with descriptions of the Niece's attraction to the clown in order to trick him into giving up a scarf that the Niece had given him (250–302); if there was no Pompey in the original version, this short sequence must have been rewritten rather than inserted, as the scarf-gulling is important to the scene overall. In summary, if Pompey was inserted into the story of *Wit at Several Weapons* to provide a new plotline for Rowley to perform in, the process would not have been difficult, as it could have been achieved primarily through insertions and minimal rewriting.

As with *The Old Law*, there is no immediate need in *Wit at Several Weapons* for a clown to literalize the desires that underpin those of the main plot characters. Rather like the Duke's edict in *The Old Law*, the Old Knight's demand that his son Wittypate prove his wit liberates the tricksters from moral restraints. The play's satirical nature stems from the fact that its main plot has 'no ethical dimension whatsoever':[66] the tricksters have no consciences and are not punished for their trickery; instead, their happy ending emerges from their successful acquisition of wealth and spouses by deceit. However, unlike in *The Old Law*, Middleton and Rowley found a function for the clown in *Wit at Several Weapons*, giving him a form of simplicity that makes him the antithesis of the other characters – he is not only gullible (like Sir Gregory) but also emotionally sensitive.

Pompey's first scene introduces him as a typical iteration of Rowley's persona of guileless simplicity, as he displays comically inappropriate grotesquery and blunt speech. As the Niece tries to make Cunningham jealous by wooing the clown, she praises Pompey's 'pretty rowling eye' (2.2.161),[67] and the clown proudly demonstrates his ability to roll his eyes all the way back: 'I can turne up the white and the black too, and need be' (2.2.162–3). Having used Pompey for her purposes, the Niece is subsequently unable to shake him off. Eventually, she tells the love-struck clown that their relationship must remain secret and that he must not come until she calls him. This is a mistake since, like all of Rowley's clowns, Pompey is incapable of deceit. As soon as he encounters Sir Gregory, Pompey triumphantly resigns his position and reveals both his secret and his resentment of his master:

> This I give you to understand[:] That another man may have as good an eye, as amorous a nose, as faire a stampt beard, and be as proper a man as a Knight, (I name no parties) a Servingman may be as good as a Sir, a *Pompey* as a *Gregory*, a *Doodle* as a *Fop*; so Servingman *Pompey Doodle* may be respected as well with Ladies (though I name no parties) as Sir *Gregory Fop*; so farewell. (2.3.46–53)

Rowley appears to be setting up a carnivalesque topsy-turvy comedy here: the clown hopes to marry a lady and become a nobleman, and the servingman hopes to cheat his master of his bride.[68] Instead, something unusual happens: the clown is motivated by love more than greed, and his festive spirit is crushed.

By act 4, Pompey is still waiting for his 'mistress' to contact him. He has 'kept out a Towne these two daies, a purpose to be sent for' (4.1.346–7), and to pass the time has undertaken 'solemne walks / 'Twixt *Paddington* and *Pancridge*' (321–2).[69] He tells Cunningham that if he happens to see a coach that has been sent for him, 'direct him and his horses toward the new River by *Islington*, there they shall have me looking upon the Pipes, and whistling' (360–2). An image is created of the lonely clown walking solemnly in the fields as he waits for a summons that will never come. This pathos is developed further in the next act, in which Pompey is 'almost starv'd with love, and cold, and one thing or other' (5.1.38–9). Emphasizing Pompey's physical discomfort, Rowley quashes any sense of festive fun: when the clown tries to cheer himself up by eating, he finds that ''Tis a strange thing, I have no taste in any thing' (52).

This dampening of the clown's festive qualities is unusual: Renaissance clowns are almost always irrepressible, and when disappointed in love 'bounce back' without mournful behaviour. Shakespeare's Bottom, after losing Titania, rapidly returns to his gung-ho personality, and the same is usually true of Rowley's love-struck clowns.[70] In contrast, even though Pompey laughs (while munching on plums with restored appetite) at Sir Gregory being gulled, he loses his humour again when he thinks about his love:

Oh Knight, that thou should'st be gull'd so; ha, ha, it does me good at heart,
But oh Lady, thou tak'st downe my merry part.   (5.1.261–2)

In the conclusion to the play, Pompey realizes that he has been gulled and invades the happy ending, in which the witty tricksters are congratulating themselves, to confront the Niece (now married to Cunningham). 'I do heare strange stories,' he announces, 'are Ladies things obnoxious?' (5.2.221). But the Niece torments him further, claiming that he is the guilty party for ignoring all her messages to him. Pompey protests his innocence, but the others compound his misery by pretending that the Niece has married Cunningham only in response to Pompey's rejection. The clown curses his ill fortune and says, 'I could almost cry for anger' (282); he then imagines the lady pining for him and exits dejectedly, in a scene reminiscent of the departure of Malvolio (several verbal parallels suggest that *Twelfth Night* was a direct influence on *Wit*).[71] Rowley leaves Pompey's fate less ambiguous than Malvolio's: the Niece feels guilty and asks Sir Gregory to give Pompey his job back. The social order is thus restored, but the result of the sequence is a significant complication to the usual ending of a satirical city comedy, because Pompey's debased romantic love is more poignant than the love expressed by the tricksters for each other. Sir Gregory marries Mirabell with the sole aim of spiting the Niece's father, and the Niece's love for Cunningham is untrustworthy because of her ability to deceive (206–11). Entering immediately after these expressions of unromantic, suspicious, and financially motivated marriage, Pompey offers by contrast an image of simple, if foolish, devotion.

Stage clowns are usually uninterested in romantic love, and Rowley's alteration of the clown's usual behaviour adds to the play's satirical effect. Walter Cohen writes that satirical plays typically stage happy endings in such a way that it is clearly ironic, thereby highlighting 'the disjunction between the social assumptions and resolution of the plot, on the one hand, and the implicit moral judgement by the author, on the other.'[72] At the conclusion of *Wit at Several Weapons*, the tricksters have achieved their desires by deception and fraud, and the 'social assumption' of the plot is that this form of 'wit' is the only route to success in London (a point made by the Old Knight at the beginning of the play). If the play is interpreted as condemning that fact rather than celebrating it, Pompey's exit adds to that effect. I have compared it to the exit of Malvolio, but there is an important difference. Malvolio is a Lenten killjoy who battles with Sir Toby Belch, the emblem of Carnival excess, and is defeated,[73] while Pompey is a symbol of Carnival, and at the end of *Wit at Several Weapons* it is Carnival that has been defeated. The grotesque, boundary-hopping clown is returned to his social position with his appetite quashed. And yet the sympathy that is generated by his treatment contributes to the 'implicit moral judgement': 'wit,' Rowley suggests, may be a quality of Lent rather than Carnival.

Both Jaques and Pompey behave with guileless simplicity, but the two clowns create different effects within their respective generic contexts. In *All's Lost*, the satirical impact comes from the contrast between the clown's blunt sexuality and the poetic speech of the main characters; in *Wit at Several Weapons*, the contrast is between the clown's clumsy but heartfelt love and the cynicism of the other characters. Rowley's stage persona of 'simplicity' could clearly be adapted to give his clowns an important role in a play's structure, whatever its genre; yet the persona of guilelessness remains a constant in his work, whether he is comically amoral or innocent and sentimental. *Wit at Several Weapons* also illustrates Rowley's preference for valorizing the clown's perspective at the climax of the play, emphasizing its thematic or moral importance.

The Clown's Perspective

My analysis of *The Changeling* shows that collaborations, even theatrically successful ones, may not simply be harmonic blends of their writers' work but may still contain discoherences that reveal the multiple and clashing perspectives that created them. However, in *Wit at Several Weapons*, the discoherence is not within the play itself. Certainly there is a clash of tones, as the cold-hearted glee of the tricksters is interrupted and suddenly questioned by the invasion of the pathetic clown. Yet the clown's outburst at the end of the play clearly has a deliberate structural function, as it uses Rowley's persona of simplicity not only for laughs but also to condemn a world in which guile and deceit are the only way to succeed, a condemnation that the play's other characters, whether victims or victors, are incapable of uttering. As such, *Wit at Several Weapons* is an example of the careful integration of Rowley's persona into a style of theatre that is more commonly associated with Middleton.

The discoherence between the collaborators can be seen only when the play is compared with those that they wrote individually. As we have seen, when Middleton was writing without a collaborator, he was far less sympathetic to the clown's perspective at the end of the play. In *A Game at Chess*, the Fat Bishop may ask 'necessary questions' in his role as the one character who is flexible about religious ideologies, but his position is in no way supported at the end of the play. And when Middleton was writing plays for other companies with different clown actors, he retained that disdain for the clownish perspective: one need think only of the revolting Ward in *Women Beware Women* or the idiotic Mayor of Queenborough in *Hengist, King of Kent* to see that Middleton did not carry through Rowley's approach to clown plots in his other work. It is possible, then, that in the collaborative plays *Wit at Several Weapons*, *A Fair Quarrel*, *The World Tossed at Tennis*, and, in a more limited way, *The Old Law*, we are seeing the dominance of Rowley's preferences over Middleton's; left to his own devices, Middleton might have preferred to do something different with Rowley's persona in those plays. Indeed, it is possible that Middleton is making an in-joke about the additional clown scene in *A Fair Quarrel* when a character in *Hengist* says, 'pox of your new additions, they spoile all the plays that ever they Come in' (5.1.325–6).

Yet even if Middleton and Rowley did not agree on the role of the clown in drama, this does not affect the power of the final scene of *Wit at Several Weapons*. Just as the rub between Middleton's Calvinism and Rowley's more traditional metaphysics is theatrically effective in *The Changeling*, so too the collision between the sentimental clown and the cynical satire in *Wit at Several Weapons* could potentially be thrilling theatre, as the resulting play is more vibrant than an entirely sentimental or an entirely cynical comedy would have been. This apparent clash between two different approaches to comedy is explored further in the next chapter, which examines more closely the notion of Middleton the satirist and Rowley the romantic by comparing their theatrical backgrounds and suggesting that in *A Fair Quarrel*, they managed to effect a reconciliation between their different styles.

Chapter Four

Collaborators and Playing Companies: Class and Genre in *A Fair Quarrel*

> That's the fat foole of the Curtin,
>   and the leane foole of the Bull:
> Since *Shanke* did leave to sing his rimes,
>   he is counted but a gull.
> The players of the Banke side,
>   the round Globe and the Swan,
> Will teach you idle trickes of love,
>   But the Bull will play the man.[1]

In these lines from his *Dish of Lentten Stuffe* (1612), the ballad-maker W. Turner describes some of the distinctions between the people and the places of the Jacobean theatre. Turner knows that the tales of love on offer at the Bankside theatres contrast with the more manly plays of the Red Bull in Clerkenwell; that the actor John Shanke is noted for his singing; and that the fools of the Curtain and the Red Bull look very different (the 'fat foole of the Curtin' is probably William Rowley, who was certainly performing at the Curtain playhouse by at least 1613 with the playing company that would become known as Prince Charles's Men).[2] The ballad is written for a theatregoing audience that recognizes individual actors and individual playhouses as providing particular kinds of entertainment, and hence as having distinct identities. Turner's vivid array of recognizable figures is a useful introduction to the approach of this chapter, in which I attempt to locate Middleton and Rowley's *A Fair Quarrel* within the context of the playing company that performed it in 1616.

Perhaps more than any of Middleton and Rowley's plays, the London comedy *A Fair Quarrel* has been subject to widely differing interpretations. There is a considerable body of criticism on the play, but there is disagreement among readers over the degree to which its generic structure is romantic or satirical. This critical debate has been muddied by a tendency to study the play only in the context of Middleton's canon. Ignoring Rowley's presence is especially problematic for this play, because its authors had earlier specialized in different comic genres: Middleton's writing was dominated by satirical comedies, often for the private theatres, whereas Rowley tended to write romantic comedies for the public theatres. In this chapter I will argue that the genre of *A Fair Quarrel* can be better understood by looking at it in the context of both Middleton's and Rowley's careers. However, as my reference to private and public theatres suggests, the playwrights are not the only factors to be considered in a discussion of a play's genre: playhouses and playing companies could be associated with particular kinds of drama, and playwrights were required to write for the tastes and expectations of particular audiences. Studying *A Fair Quarrel* as a product of Prince Charles's Men, I will suggest that the play has an unusual structure that utilizes both satire and romance, allowing the two authors to work in their specialist areas for a company that was in a transitional phase between the public and private theatres. This approach can help us to understand why the play has provoked such divergent interpretations.

The earliest critical studies of *A Fair Quarrel* focused almost entirely on what is normally called the play's 'main plot,' which depicts young Captain Ager trying to obey the duelling code while his mother tries to prevent him. Subsequent studies began to devote equal attention to the other two plotlines (normally labelled the 'subplot,' about the secretly pregnant Jane's encounter with a blackmailing physician, and the 'clown plot,' about the foolish Chough's desire to be a roaring boy). These studies revealed *A Fair Quarrel* to be an intricately constructed play about codes of honour and the difference between reputation and true virtue; structural and verbal parallels between the plots encourage the audience to compare and contrast their characters, each of whom are faced with dilemmas relating to masculine honour and the duelling code or to feminine honour and the code of chastity.[3] Despite this shift of critical emphasis, many studies of the play's form still regard the subplot, which is focused on citizens, as less important or less serious than Captain Ager's story, which is set among the gentry. This view is beginning to be challenged, however: Suzanne Gossett in particular questions the validity of the label 'subplot' for Jane's story, arguing that 'the citizens need not be minor' and that Jane, rather than Ager, can be seen as the play's moral centre.[4] The class identity of the characters is, I believe, more significant to this argument than has been recognized, because *A Fair Quarrel*, in its depiction of the interactions between citizens and gentry, is rather more sympathetic toward the values that it attributes to citizens than those it attributes to the gentry.

My interpretation of the play centres on its generic structure, variously interpreted by some critics as satirical and by others as romantic. I will argue that the play is in fact an unusual hybrid that stages two forms of comic resolution in parallel, contrasting a climax that is harmonic and inclusive with another that is awkward and socially exclusive to the gentry. This hybrid quality has been obscured, I suggest, by a critical tendency to interpret the subplot through the lens of Middleton's cynical city comedies, even though most of it was written by Rowley, whose romantic comedies often celebrate the citizenry.

The genres that Middleton and Rowley favoured were not entirely a matter of personal preference, of course; the work they produced was closely related to the requirements of the playing companies for which they wrote. Just as the presence of the recognizable actor can be seen as an additional author-like figure who exercises influence upon the dramatic text, so too can the 'house styles' of playing companies be examined for their influence, as several recent studies have argued: Mary Bly, for example, maintains that the plays of the Whitefriars company 'display a similar texture due to the deliberate intent to capture a particular market,' and that its playwrights needed to adhere to this style.[5] The contemporary debates about social mobility underlie the narratives and characters of all London comedies,[6] but there are considerable differences in the political stances of the playwrights and companies. In *A Fair Quarrel*, I believe, we can see Middleton and Rowley negotiating a way to combine the genres they specialized in and to follow the mandate of a particular company without either of them losing their integrity.

Middleton and the Factious Comedy

A Fair Quarrel is usually classified as a tragicomedy that 'reveals the strong influence of Beaumont and Fletcher's tragicomic dramaturgy' but which differs in being set in contemporary London and in depicting a wide spectrum of social ranks.[7] As such, it retains similarities with the city comedies that Middleton had long specialized in, and indeed some critics consider the tone of Middletonian tragicomedy in general to be closer to those early plays than to Beaumont and Fletcher's style.[8] This issue is complicated further, as I will later argue, by Middleton's collaboration with Rowley, as the play also has similarities with that author's work.

Given these complications, a useful way of approaching the play's genre is via the terminology used by Walter Cohen and Lawrence Manley in their analyses of London comedies, as it cuts across the distinctions between the early modern comic subgenres, categorizing plays instead according to their representation of class divisions.[9] Explaining his approach, Manley notes the prologue and epilogue of the second edition of *Mucedorus* (1610), which contrast plays that seek to 'gaine the love of all estates' with those composed of 'darke sentences, / Pleasing to factious braines'; in other words, plays written to be enjoyed by all ranks, as opposed to 'factious' plays that encourage division, not harmony.[10] Manley and Cohen both articulate this distinction by dividing London comedies into 'romances' and 'satires.' Romance plays are those in which the social ranks learn to regard each other as emotional and moral equals. Often, as in Thomas Dekker's *The Shoemaker's Holiday*, they show tensions between citizens and gentlemen being resolved: rivalry is transformed into friendship, forgiveness, and order,[11] and the plays end with an inclusive ethos that expels 'the demon of social conflict,' celebrating the common humanity of Londoners without contesting the hierarchical order.[12]

Middleton occasionally wrote romances such as this for Prince Henry's Men, who performed at the public Fortune theatre. In *The Honest Whore, Part 1* (1604, with Dekker), the comically patient citizen Candido, having suffered torments at the hands of gentleman tricksters, is ultimately rewarded by the Duke for his quiet suffering. *The Roaring Girl* (1611, with Dekker) and *No Wit, No Help Like a Woman's* (1611) also have endings that emphasize social cohesion and acceptance. Despite the radicalism of its gender politics, the class politics of *The Roaring Girl* are romantic, as it concludes with 'an orgy of bonding ... between the merchant husbands and the aristocratic gallants,'[13] and with a gentleman accepting the common humanity of the underclass transvestite heroine (9.311–54; 11.242–50). *No Wit* also ends in harmony, with a citizen woman helping a gentlewoman regain her lost estate and then marrying a gentleman (9.620–90) without any suggestion that the latter 'is demeaning himself by marrying a merchant's widow.'[14] However, these public theatre comedies are rarities among Middleton's early output, and in addition the first two were collaborations with Dekker. Most of Middleton's pre-Rowley work belongs to the other vein of comedy and was written for private theatre companies.

Manley argues that 'much of the history of city comedy is a history of dissent against romance dynamics.'[15] That dissent is expressed through the parody of romance in satirical plays such as *Eastward Ho* and *A Chaste Maid in Cheapside* that expose 'the partisan interests of self and class which underlie the apparently romantic triumph of virtue over exploitation.'[16] Because the endings of these plays dramatize the continued presence of class rivalry rather than its defeat, they have greater potential than the romances for social criticism; as Cohen puts it, 'since the objects of the satire are not permanently vanquished ... satiric form thus provides an ideal vehicle for a playwright convinced both of the necessity of attack and the improbability of reform.'[17] Of course, there remains a traditionalist quality to most satirical plays because they typically dramatize class rivalry by mocking the citizens, who are perceived to be threatening the dominant class's position of superiority.[18] Middleton's early comedies for the children's companies at the private theatres are satirical in this sense; as Louis B. Wright observes, 'Although the upper classes do not entirely escape his ridicule ... in practically all of Middleton's plays [for the private theatres], only unpleasant qualities are attributed to citizens.'[19] *Michaelmas Term* (Children of Paul's, 1604–6) is perhaps the best example of a play that revels in the 'deadlye enmitye' (1.2.111) between citizens and gentry: it depicts the defeat of the grotesque Quomodo, a monstrous caricature of the upstart citizen, by the gentry characters, and there is no sense of reconciliation at the end, as Quomodo is simply informed by a judge, 'Thou art thine owne affliction' (5.3.163). Similarly, in *A Trick to Catch the Old One* (Children of Paul's, 1604–7), the prodigal gentleman Witgood defeats the usurers Lucre and Hoard. Critics generally feel that *Trick* has a milder sense of class rivalry than *Michaelmas*: Margot Heinemann notes that one of the usurers (Lucre) is a gentleman, and C.L. Barber argues that the emphasis is on the equivalence of the gentleman-turned-usurer and the usurer who aspires to be a gentleman.[20] Still, at the end of the play, the emphasis is very much on Witgood and Lucre's joint delight at watching the citizen Hoard being gulled, so that a sense of gentlemanly togetherness remains. While the play ends with a brief invitation to a communal dinner by the humbled Hoard, most critics do not take this perfunctory harmony any more seriously than they do the versified moralizing of Witgood and Jane, which is usually interpreted as a parody of simplistic romance narratives.[21] Among Middleton's lesser-known city comedies, *The Puritan* (Children of Paul's, 1606) ends with a citizen widow and her daughter being admonished by an unnamed virtuous nobleman against their stereotypical attraction to grasping, upwardly mobile citizens; they are then married off to rather dubious gentleman suitors and 'the only consoling thought for the women is that they have swapped the tricksters for real courtiers.'[22] Theodore B. Leinwand finds this ending 'fully complicitous with conservative and unimaginative ideology,' as the citizen characters are 'exposed, admonished, and accommodated by members of the gentry and nobility who thrive on stereotypes of the city.'[23] Similarly, in *Your Five Gallants* (Blackfriars Boys, 1607), social-climbing upstart citizens are defeated by the true gentleman, Fitsgrave.[24]

The sense of class rivalry is thus strong at the ends of Middleton's comedies. Of course, some satirical plays, Middleton's included, mock the gentry as well, but they tend to be structured to expose a lack of virtue from the top to the bottom of the hierarchy, subjecting *all* classes to equal ridicule rather than highlighting the gentry in particular. Middleton was moving toward this in *A Trick to Catch the Old One*, and it can be seen more clearly in *A Mad World My Masters* (Children of Paul's, 1605–6), in which the citizen is duped but the gallant trickster is also punished, even as Middleton continues to revel in the stereotype of the 'stupid or usorious citizen and his climbing or adulterous wife.'[25] His most spectacular example, however, was a public theatre play: *A Chaste Maid in Cheapside* (1613), written for Lady Elizabeth's Men at the Swan. That company appears to have experimented briefly with public theatre satires, since it also staged Jonson's *Bartholomew Fair* at the Hope in 1614. Both plays are written for a large cast and use its size to create a panoramic view of London life; the aim may have been to avoid offending particular groups by insulting everybody. Alongside its all-encompassing satire, *Chaste Maid* contains what is perhaps the classic example of a parodic romance ending. It stages the return from the grave of the two virtuous lovers and the miraculous conversion of the villainous gentleman, Sir Walter Whorehound, but it undercuts the climactic group celebration of the citizen and gentry characters with reminders of the exploitative London life that carries on around them. There is no sense that the social tensions the play depicts will end.[26]

At the time he began working with Rowley (around 1614), Middleton had begun to experiment with the Fletcherian tragicomic mode, although his first attempt, *No Wit, No Help Like a Woman's* (1611) is generally considered awkward.[27] His encounter with Rowley may have been a significant step in this transition, since Rowley came from a completely different background, and his early work forms a striking contrast with Middleton's early comedies.

Rowley and Romance

Rowley's social status is unknown. He was sometimes described as a gentleman, but unlike Middleton, there is no clear evidence that he was.[28] There are no records of Rowley at the universities or Inns of Court, which suggests that he did not have a gentleman's education, and he himself called his writing 'low-bred' in style.[29] Even if he was a gentleman, his career as a stage clown would suggest that he identified more with lower-class popular culture than did Middleton. Rowley first appears in the historical record in 1607, writing public theatre plays for Queen Anne's Men at the Curtain, and, later, the Red Bull. His first comedy was *Fortune by Land and Sea* (1607–9), written with Thomas Heywood. A moralistic tale set in the reign of Elizabeth, it tells of two families: the Forrests are decayed gentry who have become the tenants of their social inferiors, the Hardings (lines 1185–97). Young Harding wins a fortune by land, thanks to his diligence and patience when he is forced to become a servant to the father who had disinherited him. Young Forrest wins a fortune by sea when he helps a merchant vessel battle pirates (the pirates are impressed, saying, 'We did not look for such a valiant spirit / In any Merchants breast' [lines 1591–2]). Young Forrest's exploits coincidentally aid Young Harding's fortunes, and the play's climax celebrates harmony between the ranks, as Young Forrest marries the citizen Anne, echoing Young Harding's marriage to Forrest's sister. As such, *Fortune* exemplifies Alfred Harbage's point that when faced with the private theatre attacks on citizens, the public theatres did not respond with 'a counterattack upon the gentry' but rather with 'a defense' of the citizens and an emphasis on social harmony.[30]

After writing for the Queen's Men, Rowley joined a newly formed company, Prince Charles's Men, in 1609.[31] This company, too, operated in the northern public theatres, apparently occupying the Curtain by at least 1613.[32] The Curtain seems to have been associated with a lower-class milieu, as in 1613 the Florentine ambassador called it 'an infamous place in which no good citizen or gentleman would show his face.'[33] The only play that may survive from Prince Charles's Men's first four years is Rowley's *A New Wonder: A Woman Never Vexed* (ca. 1611–15),[34] which shows the company performing a popular romance that celebrates the citizens. The play is based on the legends, recorded in Stow's *Survey of London*, of the erecting of St Mary's Hospital by Walter Brunus (called Bruyne in the play) and the improving of Ludgate Prison by Mayor Stephen Foster and his wife, Agnes. As such, the play belongs to a subgenre that idealizes famous London merchants of the past as heroically generous and unworldly. In *The Shoemaker's Holiday*, Dekker rewrote the story of Simon Eyre to make him genial and honest, while in Heywood's *If You Know Not Me You Know Nobody Part 2*, the generosity of Gresham and Old Hobson is so exaggerated that '"the spirit of capitalism" is simply not present.'[35] These merchants are represented as content to remain in the social rank to which they were born, without aspiring to gentle status. The plays are romances, in Manley's and Cohen's terms, because they attempt to show that wealthy merchants need not be threatening to the social order; the plays generate 'a fantasy [of citizen life] that suppresses precisely the social tensions that characterize mature city comedies.'[36]

In *A New Wonder*, Rowley depicts a ruthlessly acquisitive merchant, Old Foster, who plans to use his wealth to climb the social ladder, imagining that when he has made his fortune, 'Titles will faster come, / Than we shall wish to have them' (3.1.233–4). But Foster is contrasted with Bruyne, who replies, 'Faith I desire none' (235), and is the opposite of Old Foster: he is selflessly generous and his continual donations to charity culminate in the erection of St Mary's Hospital. He lacks social ambition, being content to remain in his own social group[37] and avoid 'Publicke Blazon of my estate' (3.3.2).[38] Old Foster's ambition is punished when his ships sink and he is sent to the debtor's prison; there, he learns the error of his ways and becomes more charitable. The play's romance structure therefore justifies the citizen-merchant while upholding the status quo. At the end of the play, as Foster and Bruyne are praised by the King, the play echoes the traditionalist politics of Dekker's and Heywood's earlier plays, as the spectacular entrance of the King, his lords, and the aldermen in their scarlet robes creates a powerful image of the traditional hierarchy. Announcing that he will join the citizens at their celebratory feast (5.2.235–6), the King declares that the play ends with

The liveliest harmony that ere I heard:
All instruments compar'd to these sweet tunes,
Are dull and harsh. (231–3)

With this conclusion, the play appears at first glance to exemplify Harbage's claim that the public theatre playwrights 'were speaking not for a class but for the whole community, and they persisted in portraying gentleness in the gentry, and nobleness in the nobility.'[39] However, Rowley's vision of London is not entirely free from class friction. Conspicuously absent from the final tableau are the two unsuitable suitors of Bruyne's daughter Jane, Sir Godfrey Speedwell and Master Innocent Lambskin. These characters are gentlemen whose poverty is so desperate that they are seeking a low-ranking wife. Bruyne finds this topsy-turvy situation amusing:

> Gentlemen, y'are welcome …
> Here's your merchandize, this is your prise,
> If you can mix your names and gentle bloods
> With the poore Daughter of a Cittizen.
> I make the passage free, to greete and court,
> Traffique the mart of love, clap hands and strike
> The bargaine through, (she pleas'd) and I shall like.   (3.1.1–9)

The play does not satirize gentleman, however, so much as bought gentlemen. Sir Godfrey says his 'wealth and wit' have brought him 'the paraphrase of Knighthood' (3.1.47–8), while Lambskin's wealth has purchased him 'the paraphrase of gentility,' but as the latter innocently explains, 'my father was a Starch-maker, and my Mother a Laundresse; so being partners, they did occupy long together before they were marryed; then was I borne' (3.1.66–8). Ultimately, the citizens humiliate and expel the parvenu gentlemen. Realizing that his daughter finds both men repulsive, Bruyne dismisses them, and is delighted when she chooses to marry the citizen Robert Foster instead. This appals the suitors, who cannot believe that Jane could prefer a man of lower status: 'S'foote, let's shew our selves Gallants, or Gallymaw-fryes; shall we be out-brav'd by a Cockney[?]' (4.1.97–8). Their humiliation increases when Robert strikes Lambskin, who gasps, 'has struck me, and we are Gentlemen[!]' (109–10). Stephen Foster puts them in their place, describing them as 'muddy Groomes' (125) and announcing that Robert is 'a Gentleman / As good as either of you both' (115–16). He then puts the boot in by revealing that the two men are heavily in debt to his wife. The contemporary belief that society was changing is epitomized here in the fact that Robert the citizen can provide a better living for Jane than can the two noblemen, who are in financial thrall to their social inferiors. Stephen tells Jane,

... they are but such
As seeke to build their rotten state on you,
And with your Wealth to underprop their weaknesse.   (153–5)

Left penniless, the 'gentlemen' are finally banished by the clown, the character of lowest status, who says of Lambskin, 'this leane Gentleman lookes as if he had no lining in's guts, I could take him by the leg and hurle him into the dog-house' (4.3.100–2). By expelling the buyers of gentility, Rowley uses them as foils for the unashamed merchant citizens, celebrating their values of hard work and generosity while upholding the traditional hierarchy.

As I have noted in the previous chapter, Rowley's forays into satirical drama began when he met Middleton. But before studying those plays, it is worth noting that he continued to write London romances for Prince Charles's Men throughout his career. *A Cure for a Cuckold* (with Webster and Heywood, 1624) has a perfect example of a romance ending, featuring forgiveness and harmony among characters from the gentry and the citizens, as well as a sailor from the slums of Blackwall. More overt in its engagement with issues of class is *A Shoemaker a Gentleman*, possibly written around 1618.[40] Although that play is set in ancient Britain rather than Jacobean London, it depicts a community of shoemakers whose hierarchy of shopkeeper, journeyman, and apprentice is like that of contemporary London. Just as *A New Wonder* and *Fortune* do, *A Shoemaker* promotes the merits of the citizen class even as it simultaneously reinstates the traditional hierarchy. When the disguised princes Crispinus and Crispianus arrive at the Shoemaker's shop, they mistakenly greet the shoemakers as gentlemen. The Shoemaker replies, 'Gentlemen[?] We are good fellowes[,] no Gent[lemen]. Yet if gentlenes make Gentility we are Gentlemen' (1.2.55–6).[41] Punning on different meanings of the word 'gentle,' the Shoemaker proposes 'gentility' to be a quality of anyone who behaves virtuously. This levelling notion is articulated in more detail when the Roman princess Leodice falls in love with Crispinus while he is disguised as a shoemaker. Her love inspires her to decide that men are born equal, and she problematizes the distinction between nobleman and commoner by reminding the audience of interbreeding between social ranks and the arbitrary conferring of gentility by kings:

Whence springs that fount
That runs all Royalty[?] tis the Sea it selfe[;]
The lesser Rivolets and running Brookes
Are those of Common sence, yet all doe mixe

> And run in one another[.] What are Titles[?]
> Honors bestow'd *ad Regis plàcitum*[;]
> Should my Father make that shoo-maker a Lord,
> Then were he Noble, yet where's his bloud refine[?]
> Tush tush, greatnesse is like a glistering stone,
> More pretious in the esteeme than in the vertue ...   (2.1.51–60)

Elsewhere, Leodice lists the many men 'made great / That were ignoble borne' (2.3.9–10), including the play's emperor, Dioclesian, who was a scrivener's son, and Leodice's own grandfather, who was a smith (11–25).[42] The ranks are blurred still further when the dying Sir Hugh awards the shoemakers the right to call themselves 'the Gentle Craft' (4.2.155–8).

Martin Butler may be correct to see an element of popular radicalism in such passages; noting the revivals of similar plays in the years leading up to the Civil War, he suggests that 'the apprentices who invaded parliament in July 1647 and expelled the Independent MPs would not have understood plays like ... *A Shoemaker a Gentleman* merely as extravagant fantasies.'[43] But Butler acknowledges that such plays invariably locate the potential for social transformation in popular, reformed monarchs rather than in the establishment of an egalitarian society.[44] Sure enough, in *A Shoemaker*, the pleas for social equality are defused by the audience's knowledge that the two heroic 'shoemakers' are princes in disguise; their heroism is ultimately a product of their breeding. When Crispinus reveals his true identity to Leodice, he tells her, 'Love would not so have forc'd you to an errour' (2.3.195), and the Shoemaker's Wife says, 'I ever thought they were some worshipfull mans sonnes, they were such mannerly boyes still' (4.1.254–6). Furthermore, the artisans of the 'Gentle Craft' are not permitted to be heroic in aristocratic terms (by marrying princesses or defeating noblemen in battle). Instead, as in *Fortune by Land and Sea*, their virtue comes from charity, friendliness, and what Laura Stevenson calls 'diligence,' a quality that consists of obedience to one's masters and not refusing work beneath one's dignity.[45] In the play's ending, the social ranks agree on their common humanity but remain contentedly separate in their social duties and behaviour. Stevenson shows that such undercutting of levelling ideas is commonplace in popular literature; writers shied away from scenes with 'serious social implications' for fear of overturning traditional divisions.[46]

As with Middleton, it is likely that Rowley's tendency to write in a particular genre was in part due to the preferences of the theatres in which he was working. It may thus be significant that Middleton and Rowley began collaborating at a time when their respective theatres were experimenting with changes to their repertory. As we have seen, Middleton had been experimenting with new forms of satirical comedy for Lady Elizabeth's Men; Manley explains the 'strange, hybrid' form of *Chaste Maid* as 'the adaptation of London's popular adult companies to private theatre modes and styles'[47] (although it was actually the reverse, since the plays were performed by a company that began in the private theatres).[48] Then, in 1614, Prince Charles's Men merged with Lady Elizabeth's in an attempt to acquire a lucrative private theatre at Porter's Hall. In this process, they probably gained a number of playbooks originating with the Children of the Queen's Revels, many of which were satirical city comedies, including the anti-citizen satire *The Dutch Courtesan*.[49] However, the Porter's Hall project failed and the company spent about a year at the public Hope playhouse in Bankside, followed by the Red Bull for three years.

As I argued in chapter 3, Middleton and Rowley's first collaboration, *Wit at Several Weapons*, was a satirical comedy written at this time, perhaps as an adaptation of a Fletcher play. It is impossible to know what kind of audience they wrote it for – was it a private audience at Porter's Hall, the public theatre audience for which *Chaste Maid* was written, or the more conventional public theatre audience of *A New Wonder*? But this intrigue comedy about witty gallants might not have been completely incongruous among the older plays of Prince Charles's Men. I have noted that the introduction of a sentimental clown was one way in which Middleton and Rowley tried to adjust the play's genre for a new venue, but there are further ways in which the play seems aimed at a public theatre audience. *Wit at Several Weapons* revolves around the escapades of a trickster-gallant, Wittypate, and his 'blocking figure' father, Sir Perfidious Oldcraft (called the 'Old Knight' in speech prefixes). Unusually, the Old Knight is a gentleman who engages fully in the mercantile world. Scorning the other gentry, he believes that the accumulation of wealth by worldly means is the only way to live:

> Give me a man that lives by his wits say I,
> And never left a Groat, there's the true Gallant.   (1.1.62–3)

For the Old Knight, 'wit' is more important than blood; he is unconcerned about the continuance of the aristocratic 'breed,' being content to see his wards debased into apprenticeship:

> When I grew somewhat pursie, I grew then
> In mens opinions too, and confidences,
> They put things call'd Executorships upon me,
> The charge of Orphans, little sencelesse creatures,
> Whom in their Childe-hoods I bound forth to Feltmakers,
> To make 'em lose and work away their Gentry,
> Disguise their tender natures with hard custome.   (64–70)

The ambiguous status of gentlemen who became apprentices was a topic of discussion in the period; *The City's Advocate* (1629) by Edmund Bolton argued that engagement with trade does not eradicate a gentleman's noble status.[50] But for the Old Knight, ancestry is simply irrelevant; he refuses to allow his heir, Wittypate, an inheritance until he has proven his ability to make money with his wit.

It is at first difficult to see where the audience's sympathies might lie. The Old Knight's 'wit' has nothing in common with that of the generous and unworldly merchants of the romance genre. He is ruthlessly cunning and specializes in using the immorality of others to further his financial gain:

> I knew which Lady had a minde to fall,
> Which Gentlewoman new divorc'st, which Trades-man breaking,
> The price of every sinner to a haire,
> And where to raise each price; which were the Tearmers
> That would give Velvet Petty-coates, Tissue Gownes,
> Which Peeces, Angells, Suppers, and Halfe crownes;
> I knew how to match and make my market,
> Could give intelligence where the Pox lay ledger,
> And then to see the Letchers shift a point,
> 'Twas sport and profit too.   (48–57)

The Old Knight behaves like a merchant from the satirical plays of the boys' companies, profiting from the vices of London. What makes him unusual is that he is an ancient-established gentleman, not a citizen (he can study the Oldcraft family history in Stow, Holinshed, and the *Polychronicon*; see 4.1.11–13). *Wit at Several Weapons* articulates anxiety about social mobility and blurring of distinctions, but the blame for it is directed onto gentry figures rather than citizens.

In addition to the Old Knight, the other characters in the play can also be read as caricatures of gentry types. Sir Gregory Fop is a credulous country gentleman whose intellect is inversely proportional to the size of his inheritance. He is the type of man the Old Knight most disapproves of, a member of the 'witless' idle gentry. Cunningham is an impoverished younger brother (1.1.262) who is a parasite on Sir Gregory (109–11). Wittypate is a conventional trickster-hero who successfully fleeces his older relative in order to prove his 'wit.' Similar to these male tricksters are the Niece and Mirabell, who both use trickery to attract rich husbands. Sir Ruinous Gentry and his wife are impoverished aristocrats who have lost their estate and have been forced to make money by deception. Finally, there are two university men: Priscian, the poor scholar who has had to turn to crime: and his opposite number, Credulous Oldcraft, *'a shallow-brain'd Scholar.'*[51]

Wit at Several Weapons is a rogue's gallery of the state of the gentry in Middleton and Rowley's time. It consists almost entirely of unflattering portraits of the gentry, representing them either as idiots or as shamelessly cynical and avaricious. These portraits reflect a new world in which inherited money is being replaced by wealth won by trade. On occasion, the play eloquently captures the anguish felt by the gentry in this topsy-turvy world. Lady Ruinous mourns,

> I am well methinkes,
> And can live quiet with my fate sometimes,
> Untill I looke into the world agen,
> Then I begin to rave at my stars bitternesse,
> To see how many muckhills plac'd above me;
> Peasants and Droyles, Caroches full of Dunghills,
> Whose very birth stinkes in a generous nostrill,
> Glistring by night like Glow-wormes through the High-streets,
> Hurried by Torch-light in the Foot-mans hands
> That shew like running Fire-drakes through the City,
> And I put to my shifts and wits to live. (2.1.14–24)

Lady Ruinous's speech might generate some sympathy for her, but this kind of pathos is not dwelt on, and the rest of the play is fast-paced amoral comedy that builds to a decidedly unromantic conclusion. Wittypate and the other characters engage in various projects to gull the Old Knight, who, in the final sequence, applauds their expertise in cheating and bestows money on them all in a speech that parodies the virtuous, hospice-building merchants like Bruyne: 'love me as I love wit; / When I dye, / Ile build an Almes-house for decay'd wits' (5.2.331–3).

The play's final tableau, in which the tricksters celebrate the triumph of their wit, is thus highly satirical in Cohen's and Manley's term in that it suggests the triumph of exploitation. As I have suggested in the previous chapter, this triumph is emphasized by the humiliation of Pompey the clown, whose social difference from the other characters is emphasized throughout, so that the play ends not in harmony between the classes but in the humiliation of an innocent, trusting clown by the cunning gentry tricksters, who unite in marriage at the end.

In depicting the Old Knight's forays into mercantilism alongside Sir Ruinous's decay, *Wit at Several Weapons* creates an image of a changing world in which the gentry are adapting to new ways. There is therefore an implicit nostalgia for a previous age in which the upper classes behaved differently. But despite the conventionality of the complaints, the play's method remains unusual in suggesting that the gentry, not the citizens, are to blame for society's transformation. Fredric Jameson describes generic adaptations that work by conspicuously removing an important feature of the genre, and uses as his example 'a double plot system of which we have been given only the secondary line, the comic or low-class subplot.'[52] *Wit at Several Weapons* works the opposite way: by not staging a traditional citizen subplot, it places the blame for avarice, callousness, and even uncharitable mercantilism onto the gentry because the citizens are not present to attract any condemnation. It is therefore possible to see how *A New Wonder* and *Wit at Several Weapons* could coexist within the same public playhouse repertory, even though their methods of transmitting their messages are extremely different.

Wit at Several Weapons represents one way in which Middleton and Rowley may have attempted to blend their very different specialities in order to produce satire that would be palatable to public theatre audiences. *A Fair Quarrel* attempts the same thing but in a far more complex way, and brings the citizens back into the picture. It too engages with the clashes between the values associated with the gentry and those of the citizens, but in so doing, it not only suggests the moral superiority of citizens over the contemporary gentry through satire; it also does so via a sophisticated new way of combining satire and romance.

The Double Ending of *A Fair Quarrel*

'Sister[!]' announces the merchant Russell in the opening scene of *A Fair Quarrel*, as into his house walks '*the Lady Ager, with two servants*' (1.1.24–

5). This is an odd moment, for two reasons. First, it is strange that the dramatists go to the trouble of making these characters siblings, since they do not speak to one another after their brief conversation here and subsequently participate in separate plotlines. The simplest explanation, proposed by Richard Levin in his classic account of the play's structure, is that a family connection between the characters enables the play's three plotlines (Lady Ager's attempt to prevent her son from duelling; Russell's attempt to force his daughter Jane to marry a rich fool; and the clownish adventures of Jane's unwanted suitor, Chough) to begin in the same location: Russell's house.[53] Furthermore, Suzanne Gossett has noted that brother-sister relationships are a recurring theme in the play, so that Lady Ager's and Russell's kinship heralds the two more significant pairs that appear later in the play.[54] Yet there is a second oddity, which Levin even calls an 'improbability': Russell is a citizen, while his sister belongs to the gentry.[55] Gossett rightly argues that this class difference is not so improbable: we can presume Lady Ager to have acquired her title and status by marrying a gentleman, a common occurrence at the time (and indeed precisely what Russell wants his daughter to do).[56] But Gossett attaches no further significance to Lady Ager's upward mobility, even though the dramatists pointedly draw attention to it: the lady enters with two servants who perform no dramatic function other than to emphasize her wealth and status. I believe that most studies of the play have overlooked the significance of the class identity of the characters to the play's structure. Key to this argument is Lady Ager's halfway status between the citizen and gentry worlds, which is essential to the play's structure and to its unique position among London comedies.

The main plot of *A Fair Quarrel* is concerned in part with the duelling code, a topic of principal concern to the gentry. The protagonist, the honour-obsessed Captain Ager, has clearly been studying the duelling handbooks that Middleton would later describe in his 1618 pamphlet *The Peacemaker* as books 'that teach young Gentlemen, when they are beforehand, and when behind-hand, and thereby incense and incite them to the *Duell*' (463–6).[57] Middleton's choice of words illustrates that duelling was an activity regarded as specific to the gentry, and the honour the male characters in this play aspire to is thus class-specific. C.L. Barber has shown that when referring to male conduct, the word 'duelling' was 'used only of the gentry, or of people who claim[ed] gentry'; indeed, it was part of their self-definition, a way of 'mark[ing] themselves off from the rest of society, and especially from the professional and commercial classes.'[58]

The notion of duelling as a concept that separates the gentry from the citizens is already apparent in the opening scene, in which Russell is amazed by the verbal sparring between Ager and his friend the Colonel, which repeatedly threatens to break out into a duel. Russell protests, 'Can words beget swords and bring um forth, ha? / Come[,] they are abortive propagations' (1.1.95–6), and he calls their clashes futile: 'all this is weighing fire, vaine & fruitles, / The further it runnes into argument / The further plung'd' (112–14). In an aside, Russell shares his incredulity with the audience, dismissing the sparring of the 'noble youths' as compensation for sexual disappointment: 'Belike some wench has crost 'em, and now they know not what to doe with their blood' (50–1).

But whose position does the play support: the fiery soldiers or the scoffing merchant? The hierarchical status of Ager and the very notion of aristocratic honour as idealistic and elevated above the norm has encouraged many critics to see Ager as the play's moral exemplar. Certainly, Ager behaves as an assiduous reader of the popular courtesy books and duelling manuals, which taught that any grave insult should be answered with a duel; as Joseph Swetnam put it, 'At one time or another a mans reputation may be so nearly touched, that it cannot stand with his credit to pocket it up, although it be made upon drinke,' and a man should thus 'answer a good quarrell, not onely with words but with deeds.'[59] In particular, critics have read Ager as a man determined to follow to the letter the contemporary notion that 'it was no fortitude to shew vallour in a quarrell, *except* there were a just and worthy ground of the quarrell.'[60] Ager, having been confronted with the insult 'son of a whore,' decides to confirm his mother's chastity before he defends her. Some critics have admired this action, as well as Ager's subsequent agonizing over the ramifications when Lady Ager tells him that he is illegitimate, because it suggests that he wishes to fight only a 'fair quarrel' in defence of the truth, and that he values true virtue over the mere reputation sought by his opponent.[61]

The attitudes idealized in duelling manuals were under assault at the time from King James himself, however.[62] Middleton's *The Peacemaker*, quoted above, is a key text in this assault, as James personally licensed it himself, and it was published as if it were written by him.[63] The pamphlet represents an intensification of James's opposition to duelling, rejecting the earlier 'fair quarrel' argument that had excused duels fought on 'just and worthy ground[s].'⁶⁴ It laments that 'so much Noble and Gentle bloud shall be spilt upon such Follies' (481–2) and argues that gentlemen should steadfastly ignore attacks on their reputation. Reputation, it says, 'is but another mans Opinion, and Opinion is no substance for thee to consist of. For how canst thou consist of a thing that is without thee? Which may be any mans at an instant, as well as thine; and when thou hast it, it is but a breath' (537–41). The pamphlet advises against duelling, arguing that true virtue is independent of one's reputation, and therefore 'whatsoever Injuries are attempted against a wise man, returne without effect, and are to him but as Cold or Heat, Raine or Haile, the Weather of the World' (405–8). This royal hostility toward duelling is echoed in the drama of the period, in which there is a marked shift to an anti-duelling perspective during the second decade of the seventeenth century.⁶⁵ For these reasons, it is not inherently obvious that Captain Ager's behaviour must be seen as exemplary; indeed, since the title page of *A Fair Quarrel* says it was 'acted before the King,' it is conceivable that James chose Middleton to write *The Peacemaker* because the play's ethics seemed to accord with his own beliefs.⁶⁶

A number of critics thus describe the character of Captain Ager as a mockery of the 'fair quarrel' ideology rather than a celebration of it. The textual justification for this is Ager's contradictory behaviour upon his arrival at the duelling field, having learned (as he thinks) that his mother was an adulteress and that the slander he had planned to defend is all too true. Ager refuses to fight, as it would be dishonourable to defend a falsehood. However, neither does he admit that the insult was true. Instead, he conceals his shame and utters an impassioned speech that anticipates the premise of *The Peacemaker*,⁶⁷ advocating Christian forgiveness and describing duelling as a pathway to hell:

> Why should man,
> For a poore hasty syllable or two,
> (And vented onely in forgetfull fury)
> Cheine all the hopes and riches of his soule
> To the revenge of that, dye, lost for ever?
> For he that makes his last peace with his Maker
> In anger, anger is his peace eternally.   (3.1.81–7)

But having urged Christian pacifism, Ager immediately abandons it when the Colonel calls him a coward; he joyfully launches into battle, having now been given a cause that he *can* defend (109–15). Ager's action here follows the letter of the duelling code, but his sudden adoption and then rejection of pacifism (emphasized by the bewildered second, who exclaims, 'Impossible, coward do more [than] bastard?' [119]) makes him appear insincere and also highlights the duelling code's incompatibility with Christianity.[68]

Ager's eccentric behaviour continues when his mother reveals that she had lied in the hope of preventing the duel and is not an adulteress after all. She is shocked when Ager responds by praying for the wounded Colonel's recovery, so that he can fight him again to prove the first insult false (4.3.40–90); even the admiring Fredson Bowers admits that this is excessive, going beyond the strictures of the duelling manuals.[69] When these excesses are noted alongside the anti-duelling attitudes current at the time, it thus seems plausible that Ager's behaviour was created by the playwrights to show a self-deluded man valuing the pursuit of honour over Christian virtue, and to show that the duelling code encourages such behaviour.

Furthermore, the honour codes of gentlemen remain problematic even in the plotline's happy ending, which begins when the dying Colonel recants his insults and offers gifts to Ager in recompense. As Anita Pacheco notes, Ager and the Colonel abandon their battle to the death but replace it with a battle of generosity (which Pacheco notes is 'the upper-class virtue *par excellence* ... a traditional mark of prestige, a demonstration of exalted rank and virtue').[70] The Colonel opines that 'he that forgives largest & sighes strongest / Is a tride Soldier, a true man in deed' (4.2.54–5), and when Ager receives the Colonel's generous will and his sister's hand in marriage, he describes his former enemy's repentance in competitive terms: '[He's] such a conquering way i'th' blest things[;] / Whoever overcomes, he only wins' (4.3.123–4). The possibility of being 'conquered' by the Colonel's generosity motivates Ager's response in the concluding scene: 'No way to give requit-all[?]' he exclaims, feeling that the Colonel has 'shame[d] me lastingly' (5.1.420–1), and magnanimously returns the will that the Colonel had bequeathed to him. Only when the Colonel responds by returning the will with the addition of a manorial estate is Ager pushed 'past [his] answers,' and falls into the Colonel's arms to 'be silent ever' (441–3). Even in friendship, the characters remain engaged in acts of one-upmanship, still provoked by the desire for reputation and the avoidance of shame.

The rest of the play poses similar questions about other kinds of honour, but although the other characters encounter similar dilemmas to those faced by Ager, they respond differently. Unlike her son, Lady Ager decides that it is worthwhile to lose her own reputation for chastity in order in order to keep him from duelling. In the subplot, Jane is forced to choose between keeping a false reputation or enduring shame in front of her father, and she chooses the latter. Chough, meanwhile, earnestly seeks a comically meaningless reputation for 'roaring.' These thematic parallels have long been noted, but the class differences built into this structure have not been fully recognized in criticism. Russell's scepticism about duelling can be related to the way citizens like Jane, her helper Anne, Lady Ager, and ultimately even Russell himself, are represented as having a flexible attitude toward honour and a willingness to endure shame that is more admirable than the attitudes of the gentry, as represented by Ager and his comic counterpart, Chough.[71]

Critical responses to the play's representation of citizens have often taken their lead from the ebulliently cynical Russell, who, as we have already seen, is unimpressed by the code of honour that Ager and the Colonel are prepared to die for. He is equally pragmatic about the codes of female honour: although he is concerned to protect his daughter's chastity, envisioning it as 'a meere cubbord of glasses, / The least shake breakes, or crakes em' (1.1.8–9), he considers its purpose only to help 'cast her upon riches' (10); for him, honour is something to be purchased, as he tells Jane: 'Honour and attendance, these will bring thee health, / And the way to 'um is to clime by wealth' (424–5). Thus for all the play's critique of the duelling code, Russell's blunt pragmatism is presented as a symptom of his avarice, and there is no reason for the audience to disagree with the Colonel's description of him as 'a blood sucking Churle, / One that was born in a great frost, when charity / Could not stir a finger' (337–9). For this reason, critics who have noted the play's association of the citizens with a sceptical attitude to honour codes have tended to see that scepticism in a negative light, and Russell's commodification of honour as the lens through which to view all of citizen society.[72]

It is certainly the case that if idealism dominates the gentry in the main plot, the subplot's events are motivated by the heartless calculations of Russell and the opportunistic physician. Consequently, some critics have gone so far as to extend this logic to the central dilemma of the subplot, in which, Jane, like Ager, must decide whether to value reputation above truth. Hence, when the secretly married and pregnant Jane is subjected to sexual blackmail by her physician and opts to abandon her chaste reputation rather than actually submit to him,

Brian Parker calls her 'as devious and untruthful as her mercenary father' and her behaviour 'blithely conscienceless'; Arthur Kirsch says her pregnancy results from 'the blindness of lust,' and the physician's blackmail attempt is 'its inevitable retribution'; and John F. McElroy even criticizes her rejection of the physician's sexual demands as 'hysterical abuse.'[73] These responses are eccentric, but even the more sympathetic Levin, noting that Jane rises 'above the cynical commercialism of her world,' writes that 'in the terms given us by the subplot she is the most admirable person there, although these terms, and consequently our admiration, are at a significantly lower level than in the main action,' a response that he attributes to the lack of 'spiritual crises' in her story compared with Ager's.[74]

As other critics have noted, this negative response to Jane is unwarranted, as she does undergo a test of her own ideals and passes it more convincingly than Ager does. The physician's threat to reveal Jane's pregnancy is dangerous to her reputation because she is unwilling to reveal to the world that she is married by a *de praesenti* contract. However, she herself does not consider her marriage to be wrong, saying "twas love did sin' (2.2.64) and calling herself 'the bad mother: *If* it be offence' (3.2.21; italics added). Since a *de praesenti* marriage would not have been thought immoral by many in the audience,[75] these ambiguities enable the playwrights to give Jane's dilemma a degree of danger while still enabling the audience to support her.

For this reason, Jane's decision to reveal her pregnancy and suffer shame and loss of reputation makes her response to the dilemma different both from her father's amoral pragmatism and from Ager's sophistry. As Anita Pacheco puts it, Jane 'upholds the primacy of inner moral worth over a specious code of outward respectability'[76] and is driven by a powerful desire to speak the truth:

I must reveale[;]
My shame will else take tongue, & speake before me.
Tis a necessity impulsive drives me. (2.2.53–5)

Though the physician's sister, Anne, warns her that she should value reputation higher than truth, since 'A good name's deare, / And indeed more esteemed than our actions, / By which wee should deserve it' (3.2.162–4), Jane elects instead to wear 'one spot upon [her] face / To keepe [her] whole body from a leprosie, / Though it were undiscovered ever' (166–8). She defiantly rejects both the blackmailer and the foolish suitor who is plaguing her:

> Ile rather beare the brand of all thats past,
> In Capitall Characters upon my Brow,
> [Than] thinke to be thy whore or marry him. (5.1.23–5)

When the physician threatens to bring her to 'publike pennance,' she replies, 'No matter, I care not, / I shall then have a cleane sheet' (28–9), referring to the white sheets that sexual offenders wore during penance. As such, she echoes in female terms the spirit of *The Peacemaker* when it states that 'whatsoever Injuries are attempted against a wise man, returne without effect' (405–6).[77]

Since Jane is aided by Anne and her struggle is paralleled by Lady Ager (as I will discuss further below), Pacheco rightly states that the female characters in the play are better able to reject, albeit in a limited way, the demands of reputation than are their male counterparts.[78] There is a second pattern observable, however: this escape from honour codes is associated with citizens, too. Lee Bliss hints at this when she describes Jane as having a 'citizen sense of honour' (different from Ager's) that 'balances the satiric treatment of her father's mercantile ethic.'[79] Yet even her father becomes a part of this pattern: Russell may begin the play as an embodiment of unfeeling mercantilism, but at the end of the play he transforms for the better as his pragmatism becomes a positive force. When the physician announces to the assembled company that Jane has had a child out of wedlock (supposedly with him) and is thus 'an honor stayned Bride' (5.1.197), Russell does not disown her, as both she and the physician had expected. Instead, he accepts the situation and is even pleased at the addition to the family:

> *Russ.* [*Aside to Jane*] Come tell truth twixt our selves, heers none but friends[.]
> One spot a fathers love will soone wipe off?
> The truth and [then] trie my love abundant,
> Ile cover it with all the care *I* have
> And yet (perhaps) make up a marriage day.
> *Jane.* Then its true, sir, *I* have [a] child.
> *Russ.* Hast thou?
> Well wipe thine eyes, Ime a Grandfather then,
> If all bastards were banisht, the Citty would be thinne,
> In the thickest terme time. (243–51)

As Pacheco puts it, 'Russell's private emotional bonds ultimately mean more to him than his society's rigid code of female sexual morality.'[80]

This might seem a clumsy reversal that simply effaces Russell's earlier behaviour; after all, he is still plotting to marry Jane to Chough and simply 'cover' the existence of the baby. But the sequence is carefully arranged to punish Russell for his overconfidence in his own 'wit and wealth' (281) and thus to make his final transformation acceptable. When Chough refuses to marry Jane, having learned of the baby, Russell frantically tries to marry her to Fitzallen after all. Fitzallen wins by following Chough's lead in refusing the bride until Russell offers a large dowry as compensation, which Fitzallen gratefully accepts before revealing that the baby is his and he had been married to Jane all along. The money acquired by Jane and Fitzallen thus becomes their reward for fortitude and Russell's punishment for avarice. 'By my troth the old man ha's gul'd himselfe, finely,' says Chough (385), and at this point the thoroughly defeated Russell reveals a Simon Eyre-like side by generously inviting everyone present to a feast, where 'there will mirth / Be the most usefull for digestion' (390–1).

As the subplot thus ends with a friendly feast for a mixed group of citizens and gentlemen, its conclusion can be classified as romance (in Manley's and Cohen's terminology) rather than satirical comedy. Reading the representation of Jane, Anne, and Russell via Rowley's tendencies rather than Middleton's suggests that the play is following Rowley's pattern of celebrating what it depicts as citizen virtue.

If the citizens in the play are represented as recognizing true virtue over reputation, this explains why Lady Ager, the other character in the play who is prepared to sacrifice her reputation, is represented as having been born a citizen. Several critics have described Lady Ager's situation as tragic, in that she seems doomed to failure in whatever choice she makes. She first suffers guilt at abandoning her reputation when she pretends to have been an adulteress in order to persuade her son against defending her chastity on the field; she then suffers fear when she learns that her son fought the duel on another ground instead; and finally suffers horror when she admits to her son that she lied, only to watch him return to fight the duel again on the original grounds.[81] If we consider Lady Ager as a citizen who has married into the gentry, we can see these ironic reversals as the fate of someone who cannot appreciate 'the joyes of a just cause' (2.1.197): she is an outsider who does not understand the mores of the world she now lives in.

Jane, too, has married a gentleman and is potentially embarking upon a similar course to Lady Ager's. But the playwrights do not represent her marriage this way. Her husband, Fitzallen, has shown no interest in duelling, and indeed his only expression of interest in honour codes is fake, affected when he tricks Russell (5.1.338–41). At the climax of the subplot, the emphasis is not on Jane 'marrying up' into an aristocratic world but rather on the impoverished Fitzallen building his marriage to Jane upon Russell's wealth. In contrast, Lady Ager's story is entirely about her struggle with gentry culture. This may explain why, unlike Jane, Lady Ager ends the play in thrall to the code of honour; as Pacheco puts it, she returns 'with a prodigal's contrition to the patriarchal moral order,'[82] cursing herself for risking her reputation, 'Which is so hardly ours, with such paine purchas'd' (3.3.30).

The differences between Jane's social world and Lady Ager's become most obvious at the end of the play. Although the play's conclusion gives Lady Ager what she wants most – her son is not killed and ultimately renews his friendship with the Colonel – the conclusion to the story of the Agers is awkward, a quality that becomes most apparent when it is compared with the more straightforward conclusion to the subplot. The connections between the play's two endings are complex and are best understood by considering the play in the context of the generic structures of London comedies, and by noting Lady Ager's halfway position between two social worlds.

As we have seen, Jane's story ends on an unconditionally happy note and concludes with an image of romantic social harmony, as the citizen family of the Russells bonds with the gentry characters Fitzallen and Chough in love, marriage, and friendship, and the demon of reputation is overcome by Jane's faith in true virtue and by her father's flexibility. It is only when the main plot characters arrive at Russell's house that the play's genre becomes more complex.

A curious quality of this final sequence of the play is its detachability: the main plot characters enter, but they barely interact with the group of characters already onstage. This may be due to the collaborative process; some scholars suspect that the sequence was written by Middleton to conclude an act otherwise written by Rowley.[83] But both men were experienced collaborators and knew how to create a sense of unity when they wanted one (for example, in Rowley, Heywood, and Webster's *A Cure for a Cuckold*, the characters from the subplot enter at the end in a similar way but then banter with the main plot characters throughout the play's final lines). Furthermore, the one moment of interaction between the two groups results only in a greater sense of separation between them:

> [*Ager*]. Uncle, the noble *Colonells* recovered[!]
> *Russ.* Recovered[?]
> Then honor is not dead in all parts Cusse.   (5.1.409–11)

If the subplot has successfully 'killed' honour, Russell seems to be saying that it is still alive and well in the main plot, and we are thus directed to see the main plot's characters as returning the codes of honour to the stage that had previously banished them. Yet the ensuing conclusion to the main plot does not look so admirable when compared to the previous conclusion.

Honour certainly seems to be dead at first. The two duellists forgive each other, apparently renouncing their quests for reputation, the Colonel having realized that he has 'pursude [his] ruine' (3.1.177) and Ager having lamented his own 'vertues slow perfection' (4.3.115). The Colonel has already willed Ager his estate and offered his sister as a bride, restoring the friendship and creating a happy ending for themselves and for Lady Ager. Thus many critics, even those who find Ager's characterization unheroic, read this sequence as straightforward romantic closure that neatly solves the play's problems.[84]

As I have already discussed, however, the 'war of generosity' between Ager and the Colonel raises questions about the extent to which they have abandoned reputation. Furthermore, the marriage that concludes the main plot is a perversion of the subplot's ending. In the subplot, Jane escapes her father's demand that she marry the man of his choice, but the main plot ends with the Colonel forcing his sister to marry Ager despite her protests.[85] Some critics assume that the sister falls in love with Ager as soon as she sees him,[86] but in the text she expresses only resigned subjection, saying 'Ime enjoynd by vow to fall thus low' (4.3.107), sacrificing her feelings so that her brother can have his life both ways: 'In life a soldier[,] death a Christian' (113). Levin is correct when he describes the forced marriage as 'just another counter in [Ager and the Colonel's] contest, carefully subordinated, like the property, to the central issue of male honour,'[87] but Middleton's emphasis on the human feelings that accompany that subordination and his refusal to give the sister the words that might ameliorate it suggest that the sequence is intended as a critique of the subordination of everything to honour codes, just as in the subplot.

The silence of the sister in act 5 matches the silence of Lady Ager, who is given no lines after her outburst at 4.3.84–90 and is a mute presence in act 5. The lack of a firm resolution to her story has variously been criticized as poor writing or justified as casting a deliberate pall over the ending.[88] A.L. and M.L. Kistner perhaps put it best when they say that although the ending can be seen as providing 'easement' of Lady Ager's cares, her silence creates a feeling of irresolution, as her 'emotional traumas are never truly redeemed in the play.'[89] If the duellists are to be seen as still trapped within the honour code, that awkwardness and uncertainty fits with the sceptical tone of the ending. The separateness of the two endings may therefore be a deliberate effect that siphons the characters into two physical spaces on the stage: one in which an inclusive, romantic, and festive comedy finds human solutions to the problems raised; and the other in which a group of gentry characters are not incorporated into that ending, remaining in their own space, a space in which honour codes still dominate, in which the illusion of a romantic ending is undermined by unspoken feelings, and in which the only citizen character among them has been persuaded into accepting the damaging ideas that her fellow citizens have abandoned.

A Fair Quarrel is therefore an unusual generic hybrid. Taken by itself, the main plot's conclusion need not be interpreted as a critique of its characters. It is only when the sequence is performed immediately after a straightforwardly romantic conclusion that its awkwardnesses and ironies are brought out. Yet unlike other city comedies, the romantic ending of the subplot is not undercut by the main plot's ending; instead, two generic endings are enacted side by side. For this reason, the play in its entirety must be thought of as satirical in that it is 'factious': it contrasts the attitudes of two social groups, and critiques one of them more than the other. That critique requires, however, an uncomplicated romantic climax with which to contrast the more awkward ending in order to generate that satirical conclusion. Thus, the two genres and the two authors work together to create a play that combines genres for an unusual political purpose.

Duelling Genres

It seems, then, that the reason the dramatists made Russell and Lady Ager in *A Fair Quarrel* siblings even though they have little contact with each other is that their lack of contact is precisely the play's point. Lady Ager has moved from one social world to another, and Middleton and Rowley highlight the differences between those worlds, ultimately showing how the gentry's honour codes leave Lady Ager trapped, unlike the inclusive ending that the citizens Russell and Jane are able to create.

The play's conclusion, in which the attitudes attributed to the citizen characters are idealized above those of the gentry, is highly unusual. As we have seen, even in the plays of Prince Charles's Men, the celebration of citizens tends to be accompanied by a celebration of the traditional social hierarchy. Michael Mooney imagines that *A Fair Quarrel* was written for a largely citizen audience; claiming that it was performed at the Curtain playhouse in Shoreditch, he envisages the public theatre audience scoffing at the play's parody of private theatre tragicomedy.[90] But in fact the play was not written for the Curtain, and its original venue is uncertain.[91] Its unusual attitude may stem more from the fact that its attack on the gentry's moral code was backed by King James's own condemnations, hence the proud advertisement of the play's court performance on the quarto's title page. *A Fair Quarrel* was thus able to be unusually critical because it was in tune with the monarch, whose supposed voice lamented in *The Peacemaker* 'that Folly and Vaine-glory should cast so thicke a mist before the eye of Gentry!' and hoped 'that Gentlemen would learne to esteeme themselves at a just price[!] how dearely they are bought, how most precious their Redemption!' (469–70, 494–7).

Studying *A Fair Quarrel* as a collaboration rather than simply as a Middleton play reveals the ways in which both authors were playing to their different strengths: paradoxically, the play's unity emerges directly from the disjointed nature of its conclusion. Simply seeing the play as constructed by a unified voice called 'Middleton-and-Rowley' is misleading: the play's ideas and structure can only be appreciated by recognizing that it was written by playwrights whose styles developed in different social contexts and whose resulting friction was creatively used in this play.

What this study also reveals, however, is the significance of the different institutions that the dramatists were working in: Prince Charles's Men for Rowley, and the children's companies and Lady Elizabeth's Men for Middleton. The playwrights were not necessarily writing for themselves but rather for their target audience. It is thus possible – if difficult to prove given the fragmentary evidence – that theatregoers of the time may have associated these different companies with different kinds of plays and different social attitudes; they may have expected, for example, a 'Prince Charles's Men play' to be unusually positive toward the citizens. In this way, like playwrights and like actors, the playing company becomes a kind of author figure, a limiting constraint through which a play might be interpreted, an entity assumed to be in part responsible for creating the drama. In the final chapter, I will show how the author-like nature of actors, playing companies, and their patrons can illuminate even those plays in which the roles of the playwrights in the creation of the text are indeterminate.

Chapter Five

A Presence in the Crowd: Multiple Authorship and the Individual Voice in *The Spanish Gypsy* and *The Old Law*

Perhaps appropriately for a play co-written by four dramatists, *The Spanish Gypsy* (1623) includes a comic scene that illustrates well the complexities of theatrical collaboration. Don Fernando, a nobleman of Madrid, has asked a troupe of gypsy performers to stage a play of his own devising. Enquiring into the number of the actors, he is told by the clownish Sancho that there are nine of them. 'You are ten[,] sure[?]' asks the puzzled Fernando, indicating a member of the troupe whom Sancho seems to have missed. 'That's our Poet,' explains Sancho's sidekick, Soto, 'he stands for a Cipher' (4.2.29–33). By labelling the troupe's playwright a 'cipher' (that is, a zero), Soto may simply be explaining that the poet does not act, but he also seems to be joking about the insignificance of playwrights once their stories enter the realm of performance. Fernando, however, corrects Soto: 'Ciphers make numbers,' he insists (34), referring to the fact that a zero added to a number makes it ten times bigger. Having become a playwright himself, Fernando understandably believes that dramatists make a performance far more substantial, although he does not discount the actors either: he is describing a collaborative enterprise in which the writing and acting together creates a single 'number.'

Despite his insistence on the importance of playwrights, Fernando's play is more dependant upon the actors than an early modern English play would have been. Fernando has not written dialogue, as Middleton and Rowley would have done, but is instead relying on the gypsies' skills in *commedia dell'arte*:

> there is a way
> Which the *Italians*, and the *Frenchmen* use;

> That is, on a word given, or some slight Plot,
> The Actors will extempore fashion out
> Sceanes neate and witty. (39–43)[1]

Handing the gypsies a written plot, Fernando explains the story he has devised, apportions roles among the actors, and even dragoons the poet into performing the leading role of the prodigal son Lorenzo. Based on his plot outline, the actors will improvise dialogue and will thus play a more creative role than they would have done in the English theatre, using their individual skills to flesh out the mere skeleton that is Fernando's plot. Thus at the beginning of Fernando's play, Sancho, playing Lorenzo's servant Hialdo, is asked to explain his master's whereabouts, and he replies not with a simple answer but with a comic monologue of his own invention about his master's outrageous behaviour (4.3.39–46). Neither Fernando nor Sancho can be called the singular 'author' of this moment. And yet Fernando is not entirely hands-off in his expectations of the actors: he exercises some authority when he tells the actors to interpret the roles in certain ways, instructing the poet to play Lorenzo as 'a very rake-hell, a debosh'd fellow' (4.2.68).

Already the authorship of Fernando's play is complex, with multiple, sometimes competing sources for the plotting, dialogue, and performances. But there is an additional complication. The poet cast as Lorenzo by Fernando is in fact Fernando's own tear-away son, Roderigo, who has disguised himself as an Italian poet and joined the gypsies in order to hide while he repents his sins. Roderigo is wearing a visor to disguise himself, but – to add more complexity – his father has already recognized him. Indeed, Fernando has designed the play precisely in order to make his son perform the role of the roaring prodigal and thus learn his error and fate, even while he believes himself safely disguised. And then a further complication emerges: reluctantly preparing for the role of Lorenzo, Roderigo realizes that his father has seen through his disguise. 'Why does my Father put this trick on mee?' he asks in soliloquy; 'Spies hee mee through my Vizard?' (100–1). He resolves to vent his anger in performance: 'No matter in what straine your Play must runne, / But I shall fit you for a roring Sonne' (107–8).

When Roderigo emerges onstage in the role of Lorenzo, the resultant performance is thus almost absurdly multilayered. A debauched young man who tries to hide his behaviour from his father is performing a character created by his father that is too close to the truth for his liking; he has been given leave to improvise his dialogue but has been instructed to follow a specific interpretation, and yet he has also decided to perform his own independent version of that interpretation while still simultaneously pretending to his co-players that he is an Italian poet.

Of course, if we step back from the fiction of the play, such questions of authorial control become somewhat simpler. The actors in Lady Elizabeth's Men who performed the gypsy players were not really improvising but were speaking lines written for them by professional dramatists. Even so, as we will see, the identity of those dramatists is sometimes difficult to determine in any given scene. And to return to the playing company, we must remember that the characters were performed by well-known actors who may have put their own interpretations onto the roles. This scene from *The Spanish Gypsy* seems a perfect illustration of the folly of attempting to identify individual voices (whether those of actors or playwrights) within a dramatic text.

Despite this, in my preceding analyses of *The Changeling*, *Wit at Several Weapons*, and *A Fair Quarrel*, I have attempted to identify the recognizable voices of playwrights, actors, and playing companies among the throng of other voices that contributed to the texts. In this final chapter, I turn from the relatively well-understood authorship of those three plays to the far more confusing and indefinite authorship of *The Old Law* (1618–19) and *The Spanish Gypsy* (1623). I argue that despite the greater number of collaborators in those plays, our perception of the presence of the individual contributor can still be of great importance to understanding how the plays were written and experienced.

In discussions of the authorship of disputed or collaborative works, the words 'presence' and 'absence' are common. Studies of *The Spanish Gypsy*, for example, have argued for or against '[John] Ford's presence in at least some scenes,' and for '[Thomas] Dekker's presence' as well as 'the absence of Middleton and Rowley.'[2] In such studies, the word 'presence' refers simply to the linguistic or stylistic evidence that might lead one to plausibly conclude that a particular playwright was primarily responsible for writing a particular section of text. But for the scholar who is using the results of those studies to understand how the collaborative process worked and what effect it had on the play's form, a more mystical sense of the author's presence is never far away: the ghostly 'presence' that might be encountered in a haunted room, the sensation that one can perceive another person's existence, no matter how implausible that might seem. In this book, I have tried to pinpoint those presences. At each of the moments of discoherence that I have observed – the clashing religious perspectives in *The Changeling*, the Rowleyan clown in the midst of the Middletonian satire of *Wit at Several Weapons*, and the double ending of *A Fair Quarrel* – we may identify, if only briefly, the presence of distinct perspectives rather than a smooth, harmonious collaboration.

However, the identification of distinct authorial presences has proven exceptionally difficult for *The Old Law* and *The Spanish Gypsy*. The surviving text of *The Old Law* is so poorly printed that it impedes stylistic analysis, and authorship attributors are unable to make compelling cases for authorial divisions; David J. Lake and MacDonald P. Jackson acknowledge a lack of clear authorial markers in some scenes.[3] What is more, there appears to be a third playwright involved: the title page claims Philip Massinger as co-author, but most studies have rejected this claim, and Gary Taylor has argued that Thomas Heywood fits the stylistic profile better.[4]

The Spanish Gypsy is even more complex. The 1653 quarto states Middleton and Rowley to be the authors, and the play appears among others by Middleton and/or Rowley in a 1639 playlist that seems to be grouped by author. Gary Taylor calls this 'exceptionally strong' external evidence of authorship,[5] but scholars have still questioned the attribution, finding the play, or at least parts of it, to be stylistically different from a normal Middleton-Rowley collaboration. Two alternative authors have been proposed, John Ford and Thomas Dekker, and various studies of the play have either accepted or rejected one or both of these alternatives in a scholarly debate that has persisted for some time.[6] In 2004, Taylor and Jackson used computer-assisted assessment of verbal parallels, analysis of metrical statistics and the amount of interrogative repetitions, and an examination of the use of the source material to conclude that 'the distribution of the linguistic evidence falls into alternating patterns that suggests the collaboration of all four writers.'[7] Such a collaboration is plausible, given that Dekker, Ford, and Rowley had already written *The Witch of Edmonton* together in 1621 and would engage in a four-way collaboration with John Webster on the lost play *The Late Murder in Whitechapel, or Keep the Widow Waking* in 1624. However, identifying the authors does not necessarily help with understanding how they divided the play, as Taylor believes the 'alternating patterns' of the authors to be unusually complex. Stressing that 'there is no guarantee that one author wrote an entire scene,'[8] he shows that the playwrights instead divided the play into 'French scenes' and other short sections. He notes, for example, individual speeches that might have been inserted by one playwright into the work of another.[9]

Taylor provides a breakdown of this division but acknowledges many uncertainties, including the difficulty of distinguishing Dekker's writing from Rowley's, and cautions that 'either Rowley or Middleton might have contributed jokes, speeches or passages to the prose of Sancho and Soto, even in scenes written primarily by Dekker,'[10] in part because 'Rowley might well have written or rewritten material for his own role [of Sancho], even in scenes basically composed by someone else.'[11] (To add my own complication, I am not so sure that Rowley *did* perform Sancho, as I will explain later; he probably wrote it for performance by another actor.)

These tortuous, uncertain descriptions of the origins of these plays might seem off-putting to the critic interested in distinguishing distinct voices within collaborative drama. However, they may serve as a reminder that focusing entirely on *authorial* presences risks missing the variety of other ways in which early modern audiences grouped or made connections between plays. I have already suggested in chapter 3 that studying a clown actor's stage persona can help us find connections between the plays in which he or she performed, and in chapter 4 I argued that playing companies like Prince Charles's Men might have had distinctive identities that can be recognized by studying their plays. In this final chapter, I will suggest some ways in which other kinds of presences – specifically those of non-clown actors and patrons – may be detected within the texts if we draw connections between plays related to them. These presences are author-like in the sense that they reflect distinct personalities or personas that existed before the text and shaped what the playwrights could or could not do. As such, they too were forms of collaborators, in the sense that the playwrights had to engage with their personalities, whether literally or figuratively, when constructing plays. This concluding chapter, then, remains focused on observing discoherence within plays: it is about moments in which the audience's awareness of a distinct personality that contributed to the drama is significant to our understanding of the text.

I will begin with a study of *The Spanish Gypsy*, a play partially about theatre, in which we can recognize the distinctive presence of a boy actor whose name is unknown but who appears to have had a persona distinctive enough that the authors not only had to accommodate him, but also seem to have organized parts of the play around his skills and designed it to maximize the audience's delight at his presence. By studying the traces of this actor in the text, I will show that he seems also to have influenced the characterization of Isabella in *The Changeling*.

Having shown how an audience's expectations of an actor's presence can influence a play's structure, I will then turn to another figure likely to be in the minds of early modern audience members: the patron of the company. The presence of Prince Charles, I will argue, looms over *The World Tossed at Tennis* and *The Old Law*, two plays performed by his company. I will show that remarkable coincidences between his political stances around 1619–20 and the attitudes expressed in those plays suggest that contemporary audiences could have understood Charles to have been an influence on the composition of the texts. Finally, I will briefly return to the *Spanish Gypsy* to consider one strange way in which Rowley the dramatist becomes textually present in a scene that contains a striking number of references to his other plays. Noting that Rowley the actor may not have performed in the play, I conclude by considering the reasons why his absence from the stage is so repeatedly highlighted by his presence in the dialogue.

An Actor's Presence in *The Spanish Gypsy* and *The Changeling*

The Spanish Gypsy seems to have been linked with *The Changeling* in the minds of its publishers. The plays were both published in 1653 by the same stationer, Humphrey Moseley, who attributed them to the same authors and included an advertisement for *Gypsy* at the end of the *Changeling* text. The text of *Gypsy* even mistakenly claims 'The Scene' to be '*Allegant*' (Alicante) just as *The Changeling*'s is.[12] Perhaps the publisher drew this connection between the plays because he knew that they were written within a year of each other by Middleton and Rowley for the same playing company (even if the publisher either did not know or care about Dekker and Ford's contribution to one of them).[13] However, an additional reason for linking the two plays is that *The Spanish Gypsy* contains a speech that seems to allude to *The Changeling*. This speech occurs when the Gypsy Father, leader of the troupe of travelling gypsy actors, is discussing how his daughter, Pretiosa, ought to behave in front of the spectators who are thronging to see them. 'Be to thy selfe / [Thyself],'[14] he says, 'And not a changeling.' Pretiosa replies,

> How! I not a Changeling[?]
> Yes, Father, I will play the changeling,
> I'le change my selfe into a thousand shapes
> To court our brave Spectators; I'le change my postures
> Into a thousand different variations,

> To draw even Ladies eyes to follow mine;
> I'le change my voyce into a thousand tones
> To chaine attention[.] Not a changeling[,] Father[?]
> None but my selfe shall play the changeling.   (2.1.104–13)

Her father replies simply, 'Do what thou wilt *Pretiosa*' (114). While the passage is ostensibly about Pretiosa's view of herself as the consummate performer, its choice of words is obviously designed to remind the audience of the play that many of them would recently have seen within the same theatre, perhaps even in repertory with this one. But why did the authors choose to do this?

Various explanations have been offered, but each is problematic. A.H. Bullen suggested that when Pretiosa says, 'None but my selfe shall play the changeling,' the joke may indicate that 'the actor who took the part of [Pretiosa] had previously played Antonio in *The Changeling*.'[15] Certainly, Antonio is listed as 'the Changeling' in the *dramatis personae* of the quarto text of that play. However, it is unlikely that a boy actor would have been cast as a male, gallant lover, however foolish, while he was still being cast in female roles in other plays. G.E. Bentley proposed that the speech was 'a device to give a boy actor a chance to mimic the comedian of the play of that name' in order to provide 'effective advertising both for the comedian and for the boy actor before the audience the Lady Elizabeth's Men were cultivating at the Cockpit.'[16] This too seems unlikely, as there would be no need for a boy actor to advertise the comedian who would be performing in *The Spanish Gypsy* alongside him as Sancho or Soto (who appear onstage only a few lines later). Furthermore, Pretiosa's speech does not use the word 'changeling' to refer to the comic idiocy of Antonio's role but rather to a seductive, mercurial performer. The assumption that Antonio is the object of the allusion may thus be mistaken; given *The Changeling*'s thematic focus on change, the word 'changeling' is applicable to most of its characters.[17] Douglas Bruster offers the more plausible explanation that 'the actor who played Pretiosa also played Beatrice-Joanna' in *The Changeling*; in other words, that the speech alludes to the boy player's *own* performance in the earlier play.[18] This certainly seems more logical. However, Bruster too may have mis-identified the actor's role. Both *The Changeling* and *The Spanish Gypsy* contain two leading female roles, one serious (Beatrice and Clara), the other comic (Isabella and Pretiosa). It is on the face of it more likely that the actor of Pretiosa played Isabella, then, while Beatrice's role would seem more natural for the actor of

Clara. Speculative though this identification is, an array of textual evidence in the two plays appears to support it by recording traces of the popular qualities of the actor of Pretiosa.

The playtext of *The Spanish Gypsy* offers a remarkable amount of information about the required skills and physical attributes of the actor who was to play Pretiosa. In particular, there is an emphasis on his small size, youthfulness, beauty, musical skills, and mischievous wit. In act 1, the gallants excitedly describe Pretiosa before she appears on stage. They call her 'young of years' (1.5.100) but already of legendary beauty: 'Spaine reports of her not without admiration' (102), and she is 'able to set a World at gaze' (111). Her mind is described in terms suggesting mischievousness or sauciness: she is 'the sweetest, / The wittiest rogue' (111–12), and she has 'a shrewd tempting Face, and a notable Tongue' (121). And she is small of stature: she is called a 'toy,' a 'sparke of beauty,' a 'little Ape,' and a 'little Faire,' that is, fairy (107, 110, 115, 120).[19]

After such a description, the performer of Pretiosa has a lot to live up to. But instead of toning down the descriptions once the actor finally appears in act 2, the authors continue to stress these qualities. Pretiosa's youth is commented on when her mother says she is 'twelve and upwards'; Pretiosa insists that she is 'in my teenes[,] assure you' (2.1.84–5), but she is later called a 'pretty Child' (5.3.16). The power of her beauty to draw admirers from afar is put crudely by Sancho when he calls her the woman 'into whose hand every Spaniard desires to put a Distaffe' (2.1.138–9), and she is later called 'a pretty little toy, whom all our Gallants / In *Madrill* flock to looke on' (3.2.79–80). It is implied that the people who 'throng into the Inne, / And call for you [i.e., the gypsy actors] into their private rooms' (2.1.76–7) are primarily there to see Pretiosa; after all, it is specifically the gentlemen who 'swear all the oaths in Spaine / They have seen you, must see you, and will see you' (115–16). Indeed, Pretiosa is able to 'draw even Ladies eyes' (110). Pretiosa proves herself as mischievous as described, since she is both flirtatious and chaste at the same time:

> *Eug.* Nay Child thou wilt be tempted.
> *Pre.* Tempted! tho I am no marke in respect of a huge But, yet I can tell you great bubbers have shot at me, and shot golden Arrowes, but I my selfe gave ayme, thus; [']wide, foure Bowes; short, three and a halfe[!']; they that crack me shall finde me as hard as a Nut of *Galisia*[;] a Parrot I am, but my teeth too tender to crack a wantons Almond. (90–7)

Her diminutive size is commented on endlessly: she is once again a 'little ape' as well as a 'little Monkey,' a 'little Gipsie,' and a 'little Muskcat'; she has a 'pretty little body,' is called 'little one' twice, and is even a 'little Wart of beauty' (2.1.122, 136, 222; 3.1.89, 5.1.89; 5.3.6; 2.1.228–9). She herself prefaces a statement with 'little as I am,' and notes that 'the smallest Clocks are the pretiest things to carry about Gentlemen' (2.1.86, 88–9).

The sheer number of these descriptors creates a remarkable sense of the actor as a presence in this play. Since they generate the impression of a young, small, beautiful, witty, playful, and mercurial character, the dramatists must have expected the performer of the role to be able to convey all these things. These descriptions do not appear to represent the personal obsession of one dramatist: the majority of them appear in 1.5, which Taylor attributes to Middleton, and in 2.1, which he attributes to Dekker. Thus, it seems to be the actor who is generating this language rather than one of the dramatists.

This suggests that there was a particularly distinctive boy actor in Lady Elizabeth's company whose qualities the playwrights felt obliged to mention. Indeed, the qualities are stressed so heavily that the audience seems intended to take pleasure in these descriptions, as if sharing the characters' delight in this little prodigy and agreeing with Clara's comment that this is a 'wonderful lively Creature' (5.1.85).[20] The fact that Pretiosa does not appear in the opening scene of the play's comic subplot may be a way of whetting the audience's appetite for the appearance of the actor, with the descriptions building up excitement before his entrance in act 2. If, as the text seems to suggest, this actor was very popular with the audience at the Phoenix playhouse, the descriptions of the gentlemen who 'throng' to see her (2.1.76) could be a metatheatrical reference to the actor's own popularity. It is not clear which of Pretiosa's qualities make many of her fans 'believe but thou art a Boy / In Womens Cloaths, and to try that conclusion ... throw down Gold in Musses' (2.1.99–102), but this metatheatrical joke emphasizes further the way the play's language draws attention to the charms of a boy actor.

The boy's appeal may have been written so enthusiastically into *Gypsy* because he had already made an impact in *The Changeling*; textual evidence in that play suggests that the role of Isabella was written for an actor very much like that of Pretiosa. Like Pretiosa, Isabella is described before she appears, as she does not enter until act 3. She is 'young' like Pretiosa (1.2.16), and she too is famed for her beauty, to the extent that gallants 'Of quick entising eyes, rich in habits / Of stature and proportion very comely' (54–6) are so entranced that they sneak into her husband's lunatic asylum in order to seduce her. There is also an emphasis on her intelligence: Lollio considers both himself and Alibius to be candidates to live among the fools and madmen, but they should 'let my Mistress alone, she's of neither sort' (60).

When Isabella finally appears, there is only one direct reference to her having a small stature: Lollio calls her 'my little *Lacedemonian*' (3.3.254–5). However, a small size is also implied during her encounter with Fransiscus, the counterfeit madman. Upon seeing Isabella, Fransiscus cries, 'Hail bright *Titania*' (54) and proceeds to describe her using imagery from *A Midsummer Night's Dream*: 'why standst thou idle on these flowry banks? / *Oberon* is dancing with his *Dryades*' (55–6).[21] The fairies in that play are of course tiny (and as we saw, Pretiosa is also described as a 'little Faire'). Indeed, Fransiscus's display of insanity, supposedly that of a man driven mad for love for someone else but in fact produced by a man faking insanity and in love with Isabella, is infused with references to smallness: according to Lollio, 'he ran mad for a Chambermaid, yet she was but a dwarf neither' (52–3), and Fransiscus himself reminds them that 'love, creeps in at a mousehole' (105–6).[22]

Even more striking than the references to size are those to physical energy and mercuriality. Frustrated by captivity, Isabella's response is not to withdraw but to demand action, saying, 'If you / Keep me in a Cage, pray whistle to me, / Let me be doing somthing' (3.3.2–4), an attitude comparable to that of the energetic Pretiosa, less so to the more passive Clara. The scene in which Isabella rejects Antonio's love after he reveals that his madness is a disguise requires the actor to shift rapidly through very different performance styles. Isabella dresses up as a madwoman and leaps onto Antonio in a state of sexual abandonment, presenting him with an image of his own faked madness. First, she mimics Icarus flapping his wings in the sky (4.3.107–8), then she pulls Antonio to the ground and switches into mock-heroic prose about Icarus's plummet, and then breaks into a song ('He's down, he's down ... ,' 111–12), before lurching into pentameter verse (113ff). 'Let us tread the lower Labyrinth' (114), she cries, 'Let me suck out those Billows in thy belly' (116). Having engaged in this wild, sexualized physicality, the actor must then instantly snap out it when Isabella reveals her true identity (133–40). It may well be this sequence that the 'changeling speech' in *The Spanish Gypsy* is recalling, since that speech describes

Pretiosa changing 'into a thousand shapes ... a thousand different variations,' and 'a thousand tones.'

If so, it is easy to see how the role of Pretiosa would be a variation on a theme for this actor. Just as Isabella works herself into a frenzy in the guise of a madwoman and seems almost about to commit adultery within the madhouse, so Pretiosa is eroticized as the exotic gypsy dancer with whom all the gallants are in love. In addition, both characters are in fact chaste and virtuous, and at the end of the plays both demonstrate maturity beyond their years: Isabella instructs her aged husband to change from 'a jealous Coxcomb' who is less intelligent than his inmates (5.3.211), and Pretiosa begs the revenger Luis to spare her father, saying, 'you are too young, too chollerick, / Too passionate' (5.1.105–6).

Even though his name has been lost to us, then, this boy actor seems to have had a remarkable presence within the Phoenix playhouse. If my reading of the roles of Isabella and Pretiosa is correct, the boy had skills that not only enhanced but may even have inspired Isabella's mad scene in *The Changeling*. As such, he was a force that may have needed to be accommodated into other plays by the company. It is intriguing that Dekker's *Match Me in London*, a play re-licensed for performance by Lady Elizabeth's Men in 1623 and perhaps written a year or two earlier, features a similarly lively, witty, and attractive character, Tormiella.[23] Like Isabella and Pretiosa, she is described before she is seen: the first scene consists of her father angrily looking for her and describing her as a pretty young woman besieged by suitors; after this build-up, she enters in the second scene. Tormiella is also the only character in the play to be called 'little': she is 'my little smirking Mistris' (2.1.7), a 'pretty little pocket dag' (4.3.18), and has a 'little face' (5.5.78). If this represents Dekker writing for the same actor again, it suggests that, as with Rowley's clown persona, the actor was both a constraint on the playwrights and an opportunity for creating a lively, complex, and charismatic character.

But it is *The Spanish Gypsy* that utilizes the actor to the full, as we see a subplot that seems designed not only to showcase his talents but even to celebrate him, using metatheatrical language that allows the audience to revel in his presence. His discernible presence illustrates that recognizing individual personalities within a collaborative work may be pleasurable, and *The Spanish Gypsy* seems to be capitalizing on the affection with which this actor was held and the audience's expectation of his presence. But some constraining influences were less benign. In *The Old Law* there are other presences that the audience may well have been aware of and which the playwrights had to accommodate, but who were potentially very dangerous if recognized in the wrong way: these were the company patron, Prince Charles, and his father, King James.

The Patron's Presence in *The World Tossed at Tennis* and *The Old Law*

In the previous chapter, I noted that *A Fair Quarrel*, which was advertised on the title page of its printed quarto editions as a play 'Acted before the King,' seems almost designed to appeal to King James I, including as it does a condemnation of duelling (as well as a satire on tobacco-smoking).[24] I also noted that James seems to have approved of the play, since Middleton wrote a pamphlet on the same subject, perhaps commissioned by James, not long afterward.[25] For a contemporary reader of the play, King James would thus be a presence significant to it, a figure whose implicit approval the quarto texts foreground. But there is another name on the title page, which states that the play was performed by 'the Prince his Highnes Servants,' referring to the company's patron, Prince Charles. There is nothing unusual about naming the company and patron, of course; most title pages of early modern plays do so. However, if the play was being promoted as a play *for* King James, might the name of the company patron have acquired more significance? Might the audience of the performance before the king, and the subsequent readers of the quarto texts, also have experienced it as a play *of* Prince Charles and his company, a play created by the son for his father?

Such a suggestion is not far-fetched, because Charles may well have had some agency in what the company performed under his name. The performance before the king almost certainly took place at court on 28 December 1616.[26] Charles had been invested as Prince of Wales on 3 November 1616, and the editors of the Chamber Accounts note that he seems to have been given an independent account upon his investiture, so that he now paid for dramatic performances himself. Charles, they suggest, 'immediately launched on an ambitious programme of play promotion,'[27] since during the 1616–17 season, Prince Charles's Men performed fourteen plays at court, far more than they had ever done before.[28] It is intriguing that one of several explanations for an apparent confusion in the record of the 28 December performance (the performance before the king appears to have been paid for by Charles) is that Charles was 'making a gift of a play performance to the king as part of his coming of age celebrations.'[29] Might *A Fair Quarrel* have been understood as Charles's carefully packaged present to his father? Was it written to be so?

We cannot know the answer to these questions, but they are usefully provocative because they highlight the contrast between this apparently successful court performance and an event involving the prince's players at court three years later. At some point during the 1619–20 season, before 10 January, one of the four plays performed by Prince Charles's Men caused offence, and if the Venetian ambassador's description is accurate, the offence is understandable: 'The comedians of the prince, in the presence of the king his father, played a drama the other day in which a king with his two sons has one of them put to death, simply upon suspicion that he wanted to deprive him of his crown, and the other son actually did deprive him of it afterwards. This moved the king in an extraordinary manner, both inwardly and outwardly.'[30]

Although the ambassador does not spell it out, James was presumably 'moved' because he perceived an analogy between the fictional royal family and his own. Since James himself had had two sons, one of whom, Henry, had died eight years previously, one explanation for James's anger is that the play appeared to be accusing him of murdering Henry. This accusation was not unheard of: a vitriolic early biography of James, attributed to Anthony Weldon, claimed that Henry's death was 'not without vehement suspicion of Poyson.'[31] Such beliefs would have been fed by James's rivalrous relationship with Henry, who, desiring a more militant and pro-Protestant foreign policy, had 'threatened to establish a reversionary interest which would offer an alternative to the king's court as a focus for politics and policy making.'[32] A second explanation for James's anger is suggested by Martin Butler, who points out that the play could have been seen as a more topical allusion to James's son-in-law, Frederick, the Elector Palatine.[33] James's months of indecision over whether to provide military assistance to help secure Frederick's hold on the Bohemian crown in the face of invasion by the Holy Roman Empire was a subject of great contention at the court and beyond; in January 1620, the Venetian ambassador would write that 'the whole nation' supported Frederick and 'all the kingdom declares its impatience of this prolonged irresolution,'[34] which was putting Frederick's crown, and potentially his life, in danger.

Whether James saw an allusion to Henry or to Frederick, the lost play also contained another offensive implication: that Prince Charles might take revenge by usurping his father. In these circumstances, it is of course significant, as the Venetian ambassador specified, that the play was performed by 'the comedians of the prince.' The notion that the players were somehow being used as the mouthpiece of Prince Charles leads, of course, to an outrageous conclusion, articulated succinctly by Alvin Kernan: 'It would be fascinating to know at what point in the play King James thought that Prince Charles, Hamlet fashion, had used his players to suggest that his father had murdered his elder brother, Prince Henry, as was rumoured at the time, and to alarm him with the possibility that Charles might himself prove more dangerous to his throne in the end.'[35]

It is doubtful whether the situation was as serious as Kernan suggests. The ambassador's report continues, 'In this country however, the comedians have absolute liberty to say whatever they wish against any one soever, so the only demonstration against them will be the words spoken by the king.'[36] Although the ambassador was misinformed about the players' liberties, the anecdote does seem to indicate that the company was not severely disciplined, and since they performed for the king twice in the following year, there must have been no real rancour held toward them.[37] It is possible, of course, that the anger was directed elsewhere: the Master of the Revels, Sir George Buc, could have been criticized for missing this glaring affront, and of course Prince Charles himself, as Kernan suggests, could have been regarded as the guilty party.

Another argument against Kernan's scenario is that Charles was noted for his obedience, and indeed his father was determined that he would not develop Henry's wilfulness.[38] However, the period 1619–20 was in fact a time of conflict between James and Charles, owing to the aforementioned Bohemian crisis: father and son were at odds over the situation of James's daughter, Elizabeth, and her husband, Frederick, the Elector Palatine, regarding the invasion by the Holy Roman Empire. Elizabeth begged her father for military aid,[39] and Charles, too, supported military action. As the crisis began in June 1619, he told his father's ambassador to the Palatinate that he would 'be glade not onlie to assiste him [Frederick] with my countenance, but also with my person, if the King my father will give me leave,'[40] and in council spoke assertively and influentially when persuading James to express support for the Union of Protestant Princes in Germany.[41] In January 1620, when the king was 'promising to do something for him [the Palatine], but not saying what,' the Venetian ambassador recorded Charles commenting that he had 'been hearing, reading, considering, and studying the arguments of the Bohemians, and they appear to me very strong.'[42] It may not be coincidental that Charles made his first accession day tilt in March 1620; Richard Cust notes that 'for a time in 1620 it looked as if Charles might be offering himself' as leader of a lobby in favour of armed intervention.[43] These events help explain why expressions of hostility toward the king from his son might have been a particularly potent subject at the time, and why the notion of Charles using his players to insult his father is not necessarily implausible during this period. Furthermore, Charles's apparent use of his players for these purposes seems to have continued in Middleton and Rowley's masque *The World Tossed at Tennis*. In this text, the presence of Prince Charles as literal or symbolic collaborator becomes highly significant to its meaning.

The World Tossed at Tennis is a self-proclaimed 'Courtly Masque' by Middleton and Rowley. According to the prologue, 'It was intended for a Royall Night' (12), and the title page of the 1620 quarto says it was '*divers times Presented to the* Contentment of many Noble and *Worthy Spectators, By the* Prince *his Servants*.' However, as scholars have long noted, the masque's performance at court may have been cancelled. The Stationer's Register records 'A booke called, A Courtly Masque or the world tossed at Tennis, acted at the Princes Armes, by the Prince his highnes servant[es].'[44] In other words, the masque may have been intended for the court, but there is no evidence that it was staged there; instead, in an unusual move, it appears to have been staged at a public theatre (the identity of which is uncertain).[45] This is why the prologue (presumably written after the cancellation) has to explain to the audience what a masque is: 'we breake the Stages Lawes to day / Of Acts & Sceanes'; and 'There's one houres words, the rest in Songs & Dances' (2–3, 13).[46]

Various reasons have been suggested for the possible cancellation of the masque. The most obvious, suggested by W.J. Lawrence, is the king's anger at the offensive play described above.[47] However, as G.E. Bentley points out, this explanation contradicts the Venetian ambassador's statement that the players were not punished.[48] C.E. McGee has proposed a better explanation, arguing that the content of the masque was offensive to James because it criticized his pacifist response to the situation in Bohemia. McGee notes that one section of the masque involves a scholar and a soldier, who, lamenting their poor condition, are visited by Pallas. Pallas (the goddess who unites militarism with learning) praises the 'complete man' who possesses both skills:

> To thee I am *Minerva*,
> *Pallas* to both, Goddesse of Arts and Armes,
> Of Armes and Arts, for neither have precedence,
> For hee's the complete man partakes of both,
> The soule of Arts joyn'd with the flesh of valour;
> And he alone participates with me.
> Thou art no Souldier unlesse a Scholler,
> Nor thou a Scholler unlesse a Souldier. (161–8)

Under normal circumstances this would be an innocuous moral, but as McGee notes, in 1620 it could have been read as an attack on the scholarly James's failure to support Elizabeth and the Elector Palatine militarily. Not only that, the masque goes further by overtly promoting Charles, not James, as the 'complete man': Pallas announces that 'the Prince of Noblenesse Himselfe, / Proves our *Minerva's* valiant'st, hopefull'st Sonne, / And early in his Spring puts Armor on' (865–7), probably referring to Charles's first tilt on 24 March that year.[49] As such, *World Tossed* is a striking contrast with that year's Christmas masque, *The Masque of the Twelve Months*, which took peace as its theme and which was the first of many Christmas masques to do so until James's death.[50]

Although the masque may not have been performed at court, the published text preserves references to its intended audience, the king, and to Charles's sponsorship of it. The induction features a debate between Charles's three royal palaces about which is the best venue; the conclusion is that Denmark House – which James had given to Charles in September 1619 – is the best for a winter performance. The figure representing Denmark House then welcomes the king and prince:

> [*to King James*] But first, to you my Royall Royall'st ghest,
> And I could wish your Banquet were a Feast:
> How e're your welcome is most bounteous,
> Which, I beseech you[,] take as gracious:
> [*to Prince Charles*] To you, my Owner, Master, and my Lord,
> Let me the second unto you afford,
> And then from you to all: for it is you
> That gives indeed, what I but seeme to doe. (Induction, 72–9)

The words 'it is you / That gives indeed what I but seeme to doe' demonstrate that the masque was sponsored by Charles[51] and was intended to be performed in his house before him and his father. As such, it is worth noting that Charles sent messengers to Shoreditch on 5 and 6 February 1620, one 'wth a mesuage to Roulle [i.e., Rowley] one of his highnes players' and one 'to the Prince his players in shorediche to warne them to attend his highnes';[52] while this may of course be unrelated, Charles was clearly in contact with company members during the period in which *World Tossed* was performed.

If McGee's interpretation of *World Tossed* is correct, the masque looks like a piece of self-promotion by Charles and a swipe at his father's foot-dragging over the Bohemian crisis. McGee thus argues that the cancellation must have occurred because James objected to it before it was staged,[53] but there are alternative possibilities: Charles may have backed away after the king's angry response to the other (unidentified) play, or perhaps he found Middleton and Rowley's work more extreme than he had envisaged.

Either way, the masque's banishment to the public stage meant that James was spared it, but its critique would still have been resonant when staged before the public. McGee imagines an audience 'made up in part of lords and gentry disappointed by the King's irresolute response to the Protestant cause in Europe and in part of Londoners like those who celebrated the coronation of the Elector Palatine with bonfires, raised money for his defence, and joined the forces levied to protect the Palatinate.'[54] For such an audience, the play could have been viewed as political theatre orchestrated by Prince Charles in opposition to the king. Such an audience is speculative, of course, and the spectators imagined by the prologue are not politicized but rather curious to experience a masque; in this context, *World Tossed* would have been what Paul Yachnin labels 'populuxe' theatre, which gives a lower-class audience the feeling of having experienced the lifestyle of aristocrats.[55] Yet this audience, too, might have found the masque condemnatory of the king, even in its most apparently conventional moments. The main action of the masque depicts the end of the Golden Age, the world's 'first and simple state' (412–13) when it was innocent and uncorrupted. A King then arrives to govern it, whereupon the world is threatened by a figure representing Deceit, who tries and fails to corrupt a series of figures representing army officers, naval officers, priests, and lawyers. Having successfully defeated Deceit, the King brings the masque toward its spectacular conclusion: a globe representing the world is passed around the characters before ending up in the King's hands, in what the stage direction calls a '*reverend and noble acknowledgement to the absolute power of Majesty*' (813.5–6). The priest announces,

> *Regis ad exemplum totus componitur orbis* – Which shewes,
> That if the World forme it selfe by the King,
> 'Tis fit the Former should command the thing. (820–2)

This emblem of absolutist monarchy would no doubt have pleased James had he seen it; the Latin tag even quotes *Basilikon Doron*.[56] Yet in the context of the masque as a whole, which contrasts the world's first state with 'the foule Center where it now abides' (413), the sequence can be read as critical of James by inviting comparison between him and his Golden Age predecessor. The masque's King succeeds in maintaining a world free from affectation and deceit, described by the holy fool Simplicity thus:

> Now it lookes like a brave world, indeed, how civilly those faire Ladies goe yonder! by this hand they are neither trimm'd nor truss'd, nor ponyarded: Wonderment! O, yonder's a knot of fine-sharpe-needle-bearded Gallants, but that they wear Stammel Cloakes (me thinks) in stead of Scarle[t]. 'Slid, whats hee that carries out two Custards now under the Porters long nose? oh, hee leaves a bottle of Wine i'th Lodge: and all's pacified, cry mercy. (833–41)

This description of plainly dressed ladies and gallants and generous-spirited custard-stealers might only serve to remind the audience that the opposite was much in evidence in Jacobean society. The same sense of contrast appears when the King says,

> How blest am I in Subjects! here are those
> That make all Kingdomes happy[:] worthy Souldier,
> Faire Churchman, and thou[,] uncorrupted Lawyer. (826–8)

It is difficult to imagine Thomas Middleton keeping a straight face while writing about a world of uncorrupted lawyers, and when the masque was performed outside of the court and within the city of London, these lines may thus have been heard as a critique of the corruption of the present age. Such an interpretation requires the lines to be heard with a degree of irony, of course – but even that possibility is signalled earlier in the masque when the Scholar lists the rhetorical skills learned by an educated tailor:

> By his Needle he understands *Ironia*,
> That with his one eye lookes two wayes at once. (124–5)

Perhaps this section of the masque is written with *Ironia*, making hostile comments on James despite its superficial idealism. As such, if it was indeed written to promote Charles as the 'complete man,' its banishment beyond the court may have achieved its ends in a different way. Even if this message was not intended, *World Tossed* is a piece of writing in which the company's patron is a very powerful presence throughout the text. Whatever influence Charles may have had over its composition, its audience would have had Charles's presence in mind, would have had their attention drawn to it at moments in the text, and would have formed their own interpretations.

If *The Spanish Gypsy* offers an example of the pleasure of recognizing an attractive individual presence within a playtext, the experience of recognizing Prince Charles's presence in *World Tossed* would have been less about pleasure and more about a thrill of danger, as the association with Charles encourages the reading of the performance as a potentially anti-James statement. This frisson may also have been felt at performances of *The Old Law*, a comedy that was probably performed in 1619, close in time to *World Tossed* and the unnamed offensive play,[57] and which appears on a Revels Office document that may list plays being considered for court performance in 1619 or 1620.[58] *The Old Law* takes as its subject matter the frustration felt by sons toward their fathers. As such, whether Prince Charles or his father had any influence over its content or not, their presences must have been felt by the authors and by the audience, and thus can be thought of as collaborators of a kind, constraining the playwrights and the audience's interpretations even as they open up fascinating areas for dramatic exploration.

The Old Law tells the story of the Duke of Epire, who introduces a law requiring all men over the age of eighty to be executed. The announcement inspires delight from the majority of the city's youth: young Simonides says, 'heers a spring for yong plants to flourish, / The old trees must down kept the sun from us, / We shall rise now' (1.1.72–4). The play articulates the impatience felt by young men who believe they can do better than their elderly fathers: as Simonides asks, 'Are there not fellows that lie bed-rid in their offices / That yonger men would walk lustily in?' (1.1.31–2). When called before the Duke, Simonides's father even responds to his impending doom in a way guaranteed to please such a son:

> Tis just I die indeed my Lord, for I confesse
> I'me troublesome to life now, and the State

Can hope for nothing worthy from me now,
Either in force or counsell. (2.1.87–90)

Whether it was staged at the playhouse or at the court, audiences who knew about the tension between James and Charles might have found this story teasingly close to the bone. Charles had, after all, recently experienced the possibility of his father's death: in late March 1619, shortly after the death of Queen Anne, James became seriously ill for over a week, suffering from bladder stones, ulcers, and diarrhoea. Convinced he was about to die, James gave Charles a speech on protecting the Church and taking good counsel.[59] If the unnamed offensive play had been Charles's Hamlet moment, this week was his Prince Hal moment, as he confronted the need to 'walk lustily' into kingship and consider what changes he could make when he did.

In this context, it would have been intriguing for the audience when the Duke's proclamation in *The Old Law* advocated the removal of old men, as their flaws sound very much like those of the king who was being criticized across the country:

> That these men[,] being past their bearing Armes, to aide and defend their Countrey, past their manhood and livelihood, to propagate any further issue to their posterity, and as well past their councells (which overgrown gravity is now run into dotage)[,] to assist their Countrey ... as it may be supposed is tedious to their successive heires, whose times are spent in the good of their Countrey, yet wanting the meanes to maintaine it[,] and are like to grow old before their inheritance (borne to them) come to their necessary use. (1.1.139–50)

The emphasis on the lack of militarism, the lack of further issue, and (perhaps) the tediousness could have reminded the audience of James if the company's patron were in their minds. Indeed, when the old men to be executed are brought onstage, the authors encourage sympathy for them by stressing their patriotic militarism. Creon, in the face of execution, says, 'In my youth / I was a Souldier, no Coward in my age, / I never turned my back upon my foe' (1.1.223–5), and Leonides confronts death as he had done armies: 'What a base coward shall I be to flie / From that enemy which every minute meets me?' (1.1.422–3).

The play's definition of senility also flirts with applicability to King James. A man, according to one of the lawyers, 'begins to be old at fifty' (1.1.195); James was fifty-three in 1619. The playwrights are careful not to go too far: the Duke demands execution only at the age of eighty 'because we judge / Dotage *compleat* then' (2.1.14–15; my italics); of course, the lawyer continues, a son can speed up the process if he can 'bring good sollid proofes / Of his own fathers weaknes and unfitnes,' although only if he lacks 'five / Or ten yeares of his number' (17–20), an age that still leaves James off the hook.

Another subtle dig at James may appear in the peculiar moment at which the clown praises a butler: 'Oracle Butler, Oracle Butler, hee puts downe all the Doctors a'th name[!]' (2.1.274–5). This is a pun on the name of William Butler, a famous physician who had died in January 1618, known for treating Prince Henry in 1612 and King James from 1614 to 1615.[60] Butler had attended Henry's deathbed and was one of those who allegedly suspected poisoning.[61] The otherwise gratuitous pun on Butler's name may thus be another reminder of mortality associated with the royal family.

To an audience seeing the play as 'Prince Charles's,' then, it might have seemed remarkably in tune with its patron's current frustrations with his father. But the playwrights were not suicidal, and the play does not, of course, celebrate parricide. Simonides is the villain of the play; the hero is Cleanthes, who tries to save his father from death. Cleanthes is praised as the perfect son by Leonides:

> Rise[,] thou art all obedience, love and goodness,
> I dare say that which thousand fathers cannot.
> And thats my pretious comfort[;] never son
> Was in the way more of celestiall rising.   (4.2.50–3)

Cleanthes rails on his fellow youths: 'where are your filliall tears, / Your mourning habits and sad hearts become, / That should attend your fathers funeral[?]' (5.1.171–3). The sons, he says, are cheering 'The heaviest crimes that ever made up / Unnaturalness in humanity' (5.1.226–7), and are against 'The common Lawes of reason and of nature' (232). Cleanthes's love for his father stems from that natural law, 'For he that gives us life first, as a father, / Locks all his naturall sufferings in our blood [too]; / The sorrows that he feels, are on our heads' (4.2.197–9). And the young upstarts are described as monstrous by Cleanthes's wife, Hippolita, who says, 'Once in my life time I have seene grave heads / Plac't upon yong mens shoulders' (5.1.53–4).[62] The play is thus not overtly controversial: it celebrates loving relationships between fathers and their dutiful sons.

Even so, *The Old Law* features so much material about the hostility of young men toward their fathers that it could have been disturbing in the political context of 1619, especially when it focuses on concealed hostility. Charles may have been famed for his obedience, like Cleanthes, who calls his father 'Not old enough by many years, / Cause I'de not see him goe an howr before me,' but there may have been a frisson when Simonides assumes Cleanthes is dissembling and replies conspiratorially, 'These very passions I speak to my father, / Come, come, heers none but friends heer; we may speak / Our insides freely' (1.1.85–9). At such moments, Cleanthes might briefly be suspected to be like Charles, who was described by a diplomat as 'suppressing his own feelings' before his father.[63]

Furthermore, the play retains a powerful complexity in that despite the celebration of filial love and obedience, its philosophical content is pointedly opposed to James's patriarchal interpretation of absolutist monarchy. As several scholars have noted, the characters must choose between obeying the 'natural law' of love for their fathers, or the human law of the Duke, which breaks the natural law. James believed that these two things were one and the same; as A.A. Bromham notes, James had expressed the controversial notion that subjects should obey the king before their own parents in his *God and the King* (1616).[64] Thus, when Simonides insists that the Duke's rules must be followed before filial affection, he is using Jamesian logic:

> there is none can be
> A good son and a bad subject, for if Princes
> Be cald the peoples fathers then the subjects
> Are all his sones, and he that flouts the Prince
> Doth disobey his father.
>   ... as our Princes
> Are fathers, so they are our soveraignes too,
> And he that doth rebell against soveraignty
> Doth commit treason in the height of degree.   (5.1.197–201, 205–8)

By giving these morals to the villain, the play is directly criticizing James's privileging of state authority over parental authority.[65]

Here, once again, the play sidesteps controversy, this time by concluding as a conventional romance: the Duke's law is revealed to have been a test of his young subjects, and the supposedly executed fathers are returned to their sons (to the delight of Cleanthes and the horror of Simonides). This climax has been criticized as 'the kind of meaningless turnabout made fashionable by Fletcherian tragicomedy,'[66] and it certainly diffuses the play's satire on absolutism even if it does not quite defuse it. At the play's conclusion, as the wicked sons are duly punished with a new law demanding their 'duty, vertue, and affection' (5.1.303–4), the play seems to present a 'cured' version of James's and Charles's relationship: young men are to be treated with respect, but only if they demonstrate submission to their fathers' wills. As such, by the time it was over, the play might have looked almost like an apology from Charles, a humble acknowledgment of the importance of filial piety. But it is a double-edged apology: for all the moralism of the ending, most of the play is an extended depiction of sons dancing for joy at the impending death of their parents. And there remains a degree of ambiguity: as Cleanthes reads the Duke's new proclamation, it demands 'that no son and heire / Shall be held capable of his inheritance / At the age of one-and-twenty' – a pointed remark when Charles was still two or three years short of this age – but then continues, 'unless he be at that time / As [mature] in obedience, manners and goodnesse' (5.1.293–6).[67]

Is it possible, then, that Prince Charles's players were being used as part of a campaign by the prince to employ theatre to anger his father, or at least to give vent to his own frustrations? Biographers of Charles have noted the differences of opinion between the prince and his father but also his reluctance to express his opinions fully or to contest his father boldly;[68] as Charles Carlton notes, this reticence is illustrated well by the manner with which Charles expressed his aim of fighting to aid the Elector Palatine: 'I will be glade not onlie to assiste him with my countenance, but also with my person, *if the King my father will give me leave.*'[69] While the unnamed play that offended James is thus uncharacteristically direct, the likely cancellation of *World Tossed* and the double-edged nature of *The Old Law* seem more symptomatic of Charles's reluctance to openly contradict his father.

As this analysis suggests, Middleton and Rowley were collaborating with Prince Charles on these plays, regardless of whether that collaboration was a literal one or not. With *World Tossed*, they could have been working to his instructions. With *The Old Law*, this may not have been the case, but they still had to grapple with the presence of Prince Charles, given that his name was hanging over the production in the company's title, and that the audience had the potential to recognize his personality and identity in the play's action. In other words, Prince Charles could, rightly or wrongly, have been seen as an authorial figure: a figure to whom the play's meaning may be attributed, a voice that may be heard within it, and with whom Middleton and Rowley had to collaborate whether they liked it or not. Despite the completely different natures of Prince Charles's presence in *The Old Law* and that of the unknown boy actor in *The Spanish Gypsy*, there is, then, a strong similarity between them. Both are individual and recognizable personalities with whom the audience was familiar, and at precise moments the playwrights make the presence of those personalities felt very strongly. At such moments, we are encountering a moment of discoherence like that of the examples discussed in previous chapters, at which the presence of one of the contributors to the play becomes briefly but powerfully apparent, despite our tendency to assume that playwrights wanted to smooth over the presence of diverse agents within the text.

Epilogue: The Presence of the Absent Author

This chapter has detected in the playtexts two presences that are not playwrights. However, *The Spanish Gypsy* also contains a scene that returns our attention to the collaborating dramatists on whom this book is centred and which helps to summarize the arguments about collaborative drama that I have put forward throughout this study. The scene in question seems, like the others discussed in this chapter, intended to evoke the presence of an individual, but this time it is one of the play's authors, William Rowley. In particular, the scene involves the replaying of some typically Rowleyan catchphrases by the clown character Sancho, even though it is unlikely that Rowley performed that role himself. The curious decision by the authors of *The Spanish Gypsy* to evoke Rowley's presence despite his absence from the stage illustrates well the possibilities and limitations of the approach that I have been using in this book.

Gary Taylor notes that Rowley's writing is difficult to distinguish from Dekker's in *The Spanish Gypsy* and that his contribution to the play cannot be determined with any precision. However, Taylor points out that scene 4.3, in which the gypsies perform their play-within-the-play, contains abundant examples of language connected with Rowley's other work.[70] Even if it cannot be proven that Rowley wrote the scene, an audience familiar with his acting career would have recognized his presence within its language, which seems deliberately to hark back to Rowley's earlier performances through what appear to be catchphrases or recurring stage business. This kind of allusion to Rowley is not unique to *The Spanish Gypsy*. In *A Cure for a Cuckold* (performed by Prince Charles's Men in 1624), the clown Compass, in the midst of a discussion about a prostitute, gratuitously calls her 'A *Tweak*, or *Bronstrops*,' and adds, 'I learnt that name in a Play' (4.1.121). This joke relies on the audience recalling these comic slang terms for prostitutes from Middleton and Rowley's *A Fair Quarrel* (1616), in which they are used several times by Rowley's clown, Chough (4.1.111–21; 4.4.67, 107–11, 150–1, 193; 5.1.155–6, 321, 324, 333). Since Compass was almost certainly not played by Rowley, who had left the company before 1624,[71] the metatheatrical nature of the joke rests in part on the audience being aware of Rowley's authorship of *A Cure for a Cuckold* despite his absence from the stage.

There are several similar allusions in *The Spanish Gypsy*. One of the most obvious occurs when the play-within-the-play's character Lorenzo is threatened by his father with being hanged for piracy. Sancho, playing Lorenzo's servant Hialdo, is afraid that he too will be hanged for his master's crime and exclaims, 'Trim, tram, hang Master hang Man[!]' (4.3.78). Hialdo is adapting a proverb about servants and their masters: 'Trim, tram, like master, like man.'[72] The line is also, however, a joking reference to the character of Trimtram, the servant of Rowley's clown Chough in *A Fair Quarrel*. Indeed, the comic style of Sancho and Soto in *The Spanish Gypsy* is remarkably similar to that of Chough and Trimtram: both double acts consist of an excitable clownish aristocrat accompanied by a servant who is smarter than he is and with whom he tends to engage in lengthy sequences of pun-filled comic dialogue that are rather like tennis matches of wit.[73]

There follows a cluster of further references to Rowley plays. When Lorenzo offers to leave for the West Indies, his father sneers, 'To have thy throate cut for thy quarrelling[?]' (81); coming immediately after the last joke, the word 'quarrelling' would inevitably remind the listeners of *A Fair Quarrel* again; they might even recall one of Trimtram's puns: 'we cut out quarrels, and breake glasses where wee goe' (*Fair Quarrel* 2.2.123–4). Roderigo/Lorenzo then calls Sancho/Hialdo his 'ningle' (82), a word that appears repeatedly for comic effect in *The Witch of Edmonton*, staged two years previously in the same theatre; Rowley's clown, Cuddy Banks, uses it as his nickname for the demonic Dog (*Witch of Edmonton* 3.1.113–41; 3.4.38–65; 4.1.254–8; 5.3.86–95). As if to add another reminder of that play, Sancho replies, 'Wee'l fight Dogge, fight Beare!' (84).

Elsewhere in the scene is a reminder of a recurring piece of stage business in Rowley's plays. In *The Changeling*, the clownish Lollio, keeper of the madhouse, forces the lovesick madman Fransiscus away from Isabella by brandishing his whip. Fransiscus, chastened, says, 'O hold thy hand great *Diomed*, / Thou feedst thy horse well, they shall obey thee; Get up[;] *Bucephalus* kneels' (3.3.61–3). Fransiscus is apparently kneeling, perhaps imitating a horse, while encouraging Lollio to mount him ('Get up'). There is a parallel moment to this in *The Thracian Wonder* (date and company uncertain but most likely late 1610s or early 1620s).[74] Another lovesick madman, Palemon, encounters the clown character of that play. Fired up by the militant speeches of the heroic Radagon, Palemon becomes wild with excitement:

> Ile leap into the Saddle of the Moon,
> And tye two Stars unto my heels, like Spurs;
> Ile make my warlike Lance of a Sun-beam,
> And mounted on some strange *Bucephalus*,
> Thus will I overthrow my Enemy.   (4.2.162–6)

On 'Thus,' he probably accosts the clown violently, since the latter protests, 'This 'tis to keep mad-men company, that has not the wit to know his friends from his foes' (167–8). Palemon is probably trying to mount the clown as if he is a horse, since he demands that the clown 'take the Moon, and place it me upon the Axle-tree, Ile mount on horse back streight' (169–71).[75] Both sequences thus involve a madman and a clown violently struggling, with the madman obsessed with either being or riding an imaginary horse, Bucephalus. This joke reappears in *The Spanish Gypsy*: acting in the play-within-the-play, Sancho/Hialdo, announcing the arrival of the lovesick and tempestuous Roderigo/Lorenzo, says, 'Here comes *Bucephalus*[,] my prauncing Master' (4.3.49–50); presumably the clown is, once again, imitating a horse as he abases himself before his 'master.' Repeated this often, the 'Bucephalus gag' seems like a popular running joke or schtick that grows funnier the more it is repeated.

To make sense of why these intertextual references appear in *The Spanish Gypsy*, it would be helpful to know whether or not Rowley actually performed the role of Sancho. Sancho certainly has the guileless overenthusiasm of Rowley's other clown roles, and as I have noted, the comic partnership between him and Soto is reminiscent of Chough and Trimtram in *A Fair Quarrel*. However, *The Spanish Gypsy* was performed by Lady Elizabeth's Men, and Rowley is not known to have acted for this company at this time. As far as is known, he was still a member of Prince Charles's Men in 1622 when he wrote *The Changeling* for Lady Elizabeth's, and from 1623 to 1625 he was acting with the King's Men but apparently writing as a freelancer.[76] However, Rowley's earliest documented association with the King's Men is the licence for his and Fletcher's *The Maid in the Mill* on 29 August 1623, while *The Spanish Gypsy* was licensed on 9 July, just under two months previously. Nels Anchor Christensen, who believes Sancho to be 'undeniably Rowleyan,' thus proposes that Rowley could have played Sancho if there was cooperation between Prince Charles's and Lady Elizabeth's companies in 1623, or if he was hired for a special performance.[77]

However, despite the superficial similarities between Sancho and Rowley's other clowns, there is one important difference. Sancho is very musical: he and Soto sing six times in *The Spanish Gypsy* and perform a dance at the end of the play. This contrasts with all of Rowley's other known roles, in which the clown rarely sings or dances more than once, and it suggests that the role may have been written for a clown with different specialities.[78] The fact that Taylor (cautiously) considers Thomas Dekker to have written the bulk of the Sancho and Soto scenes may also suggest that these clown roles were not as closely associated with Rowley as those in other plays. The evidence, then, seems to lean against Rowley's performing Sancho.

There are various explanations for the insertion of the cluster of Rowleyan in-jokes into the play. The simplest, of course, is that Rowley lacked inspiration and recycled his old jokes in the absence of new ones. If an audience member experienced them this way, the encounter with Rowley's presence would result in a groan of weary recognition and the desire *not* to be reminded of the agents who created the text. However, it may be unfair to call these jokes recycled; they are more like catchphrases or running gags, because the humour of each of them requires recollection of an earlier play (even the Bucephalus gag is so truncated that it may require a memory of the other examples in order to make it amusing). If Rowley did perform the role, such moments might well be pleasurable in the same way that the character of Pretiosa seems intended to be: the audience is encouraged to take pleasure in a specific actor's presence on the stage, and in this case, to laugh as his former career is paraded before them.

But if, as seems more likely, Rowley did not perform Sancho, the conjuring of his presence in the text might seem rather more discordant. If our understanding of his movements is correct, Rowley and Prince

Charles's Men probably left the Phoenix in 1622, almost certainly having had an unpleasant experience with the theatre's manager, Christopher Beeston, who was known for withholding the property of companies who left his theatre.[79] Hearing these references to Rowley's clowning in *The Spanish Gypsy* might thus produce, in addition to a sense of his presence in the text, a sense of his absence from the stage, perhaps even inviting a contrast between the new clown and the departed Rowley. As such, a very strong sense of discoherence would be created here, as the awareness of one writer's presence – and of an actor's absence – would break the unity of the play's world, right at the centre of a scene already packed with metatheatrical jokes. It could be a sad moment: the traces of the author would be like the ghostly presence of a figure that is no longer there.

It is ghostly presences such as this that I have tried to reveal, however fleetingly, in this book. The previous chapters have, I hope, indicated some of the many kinds of collaboration that went into the creation of Middleton and Rowley's drama. Not only did the playwrights themselves collaborate in different ways and with other dramatists, but numerous other personalities and institutions were also involved; I have focused in particular on actors, playing companies, playhouse reputations, and powerful patrons. It is often said that theatre is the most collaborative of art forms, and the approach of this book in no way seeks to deny that.

However, this study has contended that some critical studies of English Renaissance drama have defended collaboration by celebrating the unity of the authors to such a degree that, in a curious paradox, they have risked denying the multiplicity of voices within the text. I have argued that privileging the internal harmonies of collaborative plays risks obscuring the ways in which elements associated with distinct personalities or institutions may be identified within the texts. I have tried to avoid the extreme of rejecting any possibility of recognizing authorial presences as well as the extreme of demanding that only a perfectly unified work can be admired. Both approaches result in a textual idealism that prevents engagement with the grubby realities of collaboration – that is, the fact of definable, recognizable personalities and institutions imperfectly working together. The collaborative nature of theatre is too often celebrated without scepticism about the extent to which absolute unity and harmony is either possible or desirable.

I have thus approached the Middleton-Rowley plays by trying to identify individual authorial voices within them. This approach is not possible with all of the plays, as the presences of Middleton and Rowley are not always distinguishable. But just because they are sometimes indistinguishable does not mean they are always so, and even when we can admire the dramatists' attempts at seamlessly blending their work, there often remain ways in which their distinct presences can be discerned. In *The Changeling*, the different religious perspectives of the authors can be seen to clash within the text and produce some of the complexities that make the characters so fascinating. In *Wit at Several Weapons* and *A Fair Quarrel*, the authors' backgrounds in different kinds of comedy result in plays in which genres clash in theatrically exciting ways, especially in those moments at which one author writes scenes or parts of scenes that complicate the generic nature of other scenes.

Many other kinds of presence can be felt in a dramatic text. The popular actor is the most obvious example, and the need to incorporate William Rowley's distinct persona had important effects on the nature of *Wit at Several Weapons* and *A Game at Chess*. Similarly, the popularity of an individual boy actor seems to have inspired the nature of two characters in *The Changeling* and *The Spanish Gypsy*. Other personalities detectable in the plays include Prince Charles and King James, as knowledge of their personal attitudes may strongly affect the way we read *A Fair Quarrel*, *The World Tossed at Tennis*, and *The Old Law*. Finally, playing companies and playhouses can also be seen as 'personalities' when they specialize in performing specific kinds of plays, creating expectations in their regular audience members; this seems to have generated the shifts by Prince Charles's Men into generic experiments such as *Wit at Several Weapons*, *A Fair Quarrel*, and *The Old Law*.

The gallants who demanded at the stage door to know 'whose play it is,' the balladeer who sang of the 'fat foole of the Curtin,' the publishers who made the effort, if not always accurately, to identify collaborative authors, and the playwrights whose works drew attention to individual actors and to their well-known patrons all understood that recognizing an individual presence can sometimes be an important part of the experience of theatre. I have tried to show that awareness of the multiple agents that contribute to works of collaborative fiction need not result simply in a celebration of voices singing in unison. The recognition of distinct voices within the choir can be useful in helping us to understand how a text was written and can be interpreted. And as with the ghostly trace of Rowley that lingers in the self-reflexive humour of *The Spanish Gypsy*, the encounter with distinct voices within the multivocal text may have been pleasurable and even moving for the collaborators' original audience, just as it can be for us.

Appendix: A Middleton-Rowley Chronology

This is a chronological list of Middleton's and Rowley's plays and of the incidents in their careers discussed in this book. Plays on which Middleton collaborated with Rowley (as writer or as actor) are highlighted in bold. Masques, pageants, lost plays, and non-dramatic works are excluded unless relevant to the arguments in this book.

The dates, authorship, and company attributions for plays written in whole or in part by Middleton are based on those suggested in Gary Taylor and John Lavagnino, *Thomas Middleton and Early Modern Textual Culture*.[1] Those for Rowley's (aside from the Middleton collaborations) are based on each play's entry in G.E. Bentley, *The Jacobean and Caroline Stage*, unless otherwise indicated. The dates of significant events in the authors' careers are derived from Andrew Gurr, *The Shakespearian Playing Companies*, unless otherwise indicated.[2]

I assume that Rowley did not write *A Match at Midnight*, attributed to him in 1656, as neither the external nor the internal evidence is strong.[3] Rowley's play *The Thracian Wonder* does not appear on this list because it is difficult to date it or attribute it to a company; its date range is 1609–26, although such evidence as there is suggests the latter end of the spectrum.[4]

1603–4	*The Phoenix*, by Thomas Middleton (for the Children of Paul's)
1604	*The Honest Whore, Part 1*, by Middleton and Thomas Dekker (for Prince Henry's Men)
1604–6	*Michaelmas Term*, by Middleton (for the Children of Paul's)
1604–7	*A Trick to Catch the Old One*, by Middleton (for the Children of Paul's)

1605	*A Yorkshire Tragedy*, by Middleton (for the King's Men)
1605–6	*A Mad World, My Masters*, by Middleton (for the Children of Paul's); *Timon of Athens*, by Middleton and William Shakespeare (for the King's Men)
1606	*The Puritan*, by Middleton (for the Children of Paul's); *The Revenger's Tragedy*, by Middleton (for the King's Men)
1607	*The Travels of the Three English Brothers*, by William Rowley, John Day, and George Wilkins (for Queen Anne's Men);[5] *Your Five Gallants*, by Middleton (for the Blackfriars Boys)
1607–9	*Fortune by Land and Sea*, by Rowley and Thomas Heywood (for Queen Anne's Men)[6]
1608	The Duke of York's Men (later Prince Charles's Men) is founded; Rowley is among its members by at least 1609
1608–9	*The Bloody Banquet*, by Middleton and Dekker (company uncertain)
1611	*The Roaring Girl*, by Middleton and Dekker, and *No Wit, No Help Like a Woman's*, by Middleton (both for Prince Henry's Men); *The Second Maiden's Tragedy*, by Middleton (for the King's Men)
1611–15	*A New Wonder: A Woman Never Vexed*, by Rowley (for Prince Charles's Men)[7]
1613	*A Chaste Maid in Cheapside*, by Middleton (for Lady Elizabeth's Men); by this year, Prince Charles's Men are likely performing at the Curtain playhouse
1613–15	***Wit at Several Weapons***, by Middleton and Rowley (for Prince Charles's Men)[8]
1614	Prince Charles's Men merges with Lady Elizabeth's Men, and the merged company continues under Charles's name, performing at the Hope playhouse; *More Dissemblers Besides Women*, by Middleton (for the King's Men)
1615–16	*The Widow*, by Middleton (for the King's Men)
1616	Prince Charles becomes Prince of Wales; *The Witch*, by Middleton, and Middleton's revision of *Macbeth* (for the King's Men); ***A Fair Quarrel***, by Middleton and Rowley (for Prince Charles's Men, likely performed before the king on 28 December)[9]
1617	By this year, Prince Charles's Men are performing at the Red Bull playhouse
1618	*The Peacemaker*, pamphlet by Middleton.

ca. 1618–20	Very approximate date of *A Shoemaker a Gentleman*, by Rowley (probably for Prince Charles's Men)[10]
1618–19	***The Old Law***, by Middleton, Rowley, and Heywood (for Prince Charles's Men)
1618–20	*All's Lost by Lust*, by Rowley (for Prince Charles's Men)
1619	***The Inner Temple Masque, or, Masque of Heroes***, by Middleton (for Prince Charles's Men); Prince Charles's Men move to the Phoenix (or Cockpit) playhouse
1619–20	An unnamed play performed at court by Prince Charles's Men causes offence to the king; ***The World Tossed at Tennis***, by Middleton and Rowley (for Prince Charles's Men)
1620	*Hengist, King of Kent*, by Middleton (for the King's Men)
1621	*Women Beware Women*, by Middleton (company unknown); *Anything for a Quiet Life*, by Middleton and John Webster, and Middleton's revision of *Measure for Measure* (both for the King's Men); *The Witch of Edmonton* by Rowley, Dekker, and John Ford (for Prince Charles's Men)
1622	Prince Charles's Men leave the Phoenix playhouse, to be replaced by a re-formed Lady Elizabeth's Men; ***The Changeling***, by Middleton and Rowley (for Lady Elizabeth's Men); *The Nice Valour*, by Middleton (company unknown); *The Birth of Merlin*, by Rowley (for Prince Charles's Men)[11]
1623	The Prince's Men are performing at the Red Bull by at least July;[12] Rowley leaves Prince Charles's Men for the King's Men, by at least August;[13] ***The Spanish Gypsy***, by Middleton, Rowley, Dekker, and Ford (for Lady Elizabeth's Men); *The Maid in the Mill*, by John Fletcher and Rowley (for the King's Men)
1624	***A Game at Chess***, by Middleton (for the King's Men); *A Cure for a Cuckold*, by Rowley, Heywood, and Webster (for Prince Charles's Men); *The Late Murder in Whitechapel, or Keep the Widow Waking*, by Rowley, Dekker, Ford, and Webster (lost; for Prince Charles's Men); Rowley likely performs in Fletcher, *Rule a Wife and Have a Wife*, and *A Wife for a Month* (for the King's Men)[14]
1624–5	Rowley likely performs in Philip Massinger, *The Unnatural Combat* (for the King's Men)[15]
1625	Death of Middleton
1626	Death of Rowley

Notes

1. Middleton *and* Rowley

1 Hoy, 'Critical and Aesthetic Problems,' 6.
2 Vickers, *Shakespeare, Co-Author*, 439; Masten, *Textual Intercourse*, 18.
3 Aside from Hoy's article, the major interlocutors in this debate are Masten, *Textual Intercourse*; McMullan, '"Our Whole Life Is Like a Play,"' 454; Hirschfield, *Joint Enterprises*; and Vickers, *Shakespeare, Co-Author*. Several important essays by John Jowett are cited at appropriate points below.
4 Taylor, 'Thomas Middleton: Lives and Afterlives,' 44.
5 Bromham and Hutchings, *Middleton and His Collaborators*, 73–87.
6 The following overview of Middleton's and Rowley's careers is derived from Taylor, 'Thomas Middleton: Lives and Afterlives'; and Gunby, 'Rowley, William.' Except where noted, information on the authorship and dates of the plays derives from the relevant entries in Taylor and others, 'Works Included.'
7 For a discussion of the date and playing company of this play, see chapter 3.
8 Daalder, *The Changeling*, xii–xiii, xvii–xix; Dutton, 'Women Beware Women,' xxvii–xxviii.
9 Dutton, 'Women Beware Women,' xxvii–xxviii. Similarly, Daalder writes, 'I do not think that, from a critical point of view, we need to know, or to try and establish who was the most important author. On the contrary, I think we should approach the play as a fully integrated artefact' (*The Changeling*, xviii).
10 See, for example, Heinemann, *Puritanism and Theatre*; Stachniewski, 'Calvinist Psychology in Middleton's Tragedies'; Chakravorty, *Society and Politics*; and Heller, *Penitent Brothellers*. The conclusions of these writers are

varied, but all see Middleton as a writer with discernible political and religious attitudes that can be traced throughout his work.
11 Hoy, 'Shares of Fletcher and His Collaborators (V)'; Lake, *The Canon of Thomas Middleton's Plays*; and Jackson, *Studies in Attribution*. Other important attribution work appears throughout Taylor and others, 'Works Included.'
12 Hoy, 'Critical and Aesthetic Problems,' 4; see also Vickers, *Shakespeare, Co-Author*, 439. The major exception is Mooney, '"Framing" as Collaborative Technique'; I discuss Mooney's essay below.
13 Hoy, 'Critical and Aesthetic Problems,' 6.
14 Ibid., 4.
15 Masten, *Textual Intercourse*, 19.
16 Vickers, *Shakespeare, Co-Author*, 433–500.
17 Munro, *Children of the Queen's Revels*, 12.
18 Ibid., 4.
19 I am quoting Little, '"Trans-Shaped" Women,' 25, but formulations such as this are common.
20 Chambers, 'The Disintegration of Shakespeare.'
21 Honigmann, 'Shakespeare as a Reviser,' 3; Hugh Grady, 'Disintegration and Its Reverberations.'
22 Gosse, *The Jacobean Poets*, 131; Swinburne, introduction to *Thomas Middleton*, 1:xxii.
23 Ellis-Fermor, *Jacobean Drama*, 144; Barker, *Thomas Middleton*, 129. Barker's late expression of 'disintegrationist' attitudes was published in 1958 but written in the early 1940s (see p. vii).
24 Eliot, 'Thomas Middleton,' 92. Ironically, Eliot demonstrates Middleton's genius by citing Beatrice's death speech, which is now generally agreed to have been written by Rowley.
25 Empson, 'Double Plots,' 52. See also Bradbrook, *Themes and Conventions*, 214, 217, 222–4. Bradbrook's study was inspired by a pre-publication version of Empson's (see *Themes and Conventions*, vii, 221).
26 Empson, 'Double Plots,' 50–1, 52; Bradbrook, *Themes and Conventions*, 221, 223.
27 Empson, 'Double Plots,' 48.
28 Daalder, *The Changeling*, xviii.
29 For examples of the same approach applied to other early modern collaborative plays, see Gossett, 'Editing Collaborative Drama,' 214.
30 Classic studies include Ricks, 'The Moral and Poetic Structure'; Levin, *Multiple Plot*, 34–48; and Mooney, '"Framing" as Collaborative Technique,' 132–7. As Mooney notes (p. 136), some of these studies describe image chains that are in fact restricted to the scenes of one playwright: those of

Middleton in Ricks, and of Rowley in Mooney's own study. The evidence thus implies some degree of separate composition rather than fully collaborative organization.

31 Bradbrook, *Themes and Conventions*, 213.
32 These include some important studies of the play; for example, Baines, *The Lust Motif*, 97–126; Morrison, 'Cangoun in Zombieland'; and Stachniewski, 'Calvinist Psychology in Middleton's Tragedies.'
33 McLuskie, 'The Plays and Playwrights,' 173n1.
34 Ribner, *Jacobean Tragedy*, 124.
35 Holmes, *Art of Thomas Middleton*, 217, 219. Holmes argues that Rowley did not in fact write the scenes attributed to him, and that his contribution to the play was minimal. He justifies this claim with an attack on the methodology of Wiggin's *Inquiry* and a defence of Dunkel's article, 'Did Not Rowley Merely Revise Middleton?' Dunkel's evidence is that events in scenes supposedly by Rowley can be paralleled in other plays by Middleton; Schoenbaum argues that such evidence does not outweigh the more objective data provided by stylistic attribution; see *Middleton's Tragedies*, 214. The stylistic evidence of Hoy, Lake, and Jackson has validated Wiggin's theories.
36 Tomlinson, *A Study of Elizabethan and Jacobean Tragedy*, 185.
37 Little, '"Trans-Shaped" Women,' 25; Neill, *Issues of Death*, 171.
38 Wiggin ponders this question, but concludes that 'we notice nothing incoherent' (*Inquiry into the Authorship*, 54). I take issue with this conclusion in chapter 2.
39 McAlindon, *English Renaissance Tragedy*, 195. Other studies that use similar formulations include White, *Middleton and Tourneur*, 94; Daalder, *The Changeling*, xviii–xix; Dutton, 'Women Beware Women,' xxvii–xxviii.
40 Brooks, *From Playhouse to Printing House*, 1.
41 McMullan, '"Our Whole Life Is Like a Play,"' 454.
42 Bromham and Bruzzi, '*The Changeling*' and the Years of Crisis.
43 Heinemann, *Puritanism and Theatre*, 177n9. See also Chakravorty, *Society and Politics*, 146, who notes that Rowley wrote the opening scene but does not comment on the significance of this fact; and Malcolmson, '"As Tame as the Ladies": Politics and Gender,' 320, who calls the author 'Middleton and Rowley' but discusses the play's politics only in relation to Middleton's 'opposition drama.'
44 Simmons, 'Diabolical Realism in *The Changeling*.'
45 Mooney, '"Framing" as Collaborative Technique,' 139.
46 Rabkin, 'Problems in the Study of Collaboration,' 11.
47 Foucault, 'What Is an Author?,' 101.

48 Masten, *Textual Intercourse*, 15; Brooks, *From Playhouse to Printing House*, 1.
49 Masten, *Textual Intercourse*, 20.
50 Greenblatt, 'Towards a Poetics of Culture,' 12. See also McGann, *A Critique of Modern Textual Criticism*, 100: 'Literary production is not an autonomous and self-reflexive activity; it is a social and an institutional event'; de Grazia and Stallybrass, 'The Materiality of the Shakespearean Text,' 276: 'the authorial name ties the work not to a sole agent or "onlie begetter" but to a productive and reproductive network.'
51 Orgel, 'What Is a Text?,' 83.
52 McMullan, '"Our Whole Life Is Like a Play,"' 438; see also Masten, 'Beaumont and/or Fletcher,' 345, who writes that 'collaboration is more the condition of discourse than its exception.'
53 Masten, *'More* or Less,' 117–19.
54 Ibid., 119–20.
55 Hirschfeld, *Joint Enterprises*, 4, 104–17, 117.
56 Taylor, 'Thomas Middleton, Thomas Dekker and *The Bloody Banquet*,' 197.
57 Masten, *Textual Intercourse*, 19. See also McMullan, '"Our Whole Life Is Like a Play,"' 454.
58 Foucault, 'What Is an Author?,' 119.
59 Masten, *Textual Intercourse*, 26; Orgel, 'What Is an Editor?,' 29.
60 McMullan, '"Our Whole Life Is Like a Play,"' 455n39. See also Jowett, 'Varieties of Collaboration,' 111.
61 Burke, 'Introduction: Reconstructing the Author,' xxviii.
62 Jowett, 'Middleton and Debt,' 233n34.
63 McMullan, '"Our Whole Life Is Like a Play,"' 454.
64 On collaboration and the relationship between playwrights and playing companies, see Bentley, *Profession of Dramatist*, 62–87, 198–234. On the mediation of texts, see, for example, Orgel, 'What Is a Text?'; De Grazia and Stallybrass, 'Materiality of the Shakespearean Text'; and Brooks, *From Playhouse to Printing House*.
65 Masten, *Textual Intercourse*, 21.
66 Ibid., 13.
67 Masten, 'Playwriting: Authorship and Collaboration,' 371, 370.
68 Masten, *Textual Intercourse*, 16.
69 Ibid., 121. Hirschfeld, *Joint Ventures*, explicitly follows Masten's suggestion that scholars 'trace different kinds of collaborative endeavors' (p. 5). See also Jowett, 'Varieties of Collaboration.'
70 Knapp, *Shakespeare Only*, 14.
71 Dekker, *The Guls Horn-booke*, 29.

72 Vickers, *Shakespeare, Co-Author*, 17.
73 Hirschfield, *Joint Enterprises*, 23–8.
74 Knapp, *Shakespeare Only*, 128–9, 191n26.
75 It does, however, appear in non-dramatic works: Knapp notes the example of John Dod and Robert Cleaver's *Ten Sermons* (1609), which carefully identifies the author of each sermon. See *Shakespeare Only*, 128.
76 Brooks, *From Playhouse to Printing House*, 24–43.
77 Masten, *Textual Intercourse*, 16.
78 Ben Jonson, 'To the Readers,' lines 43–8, in Herford and Simpson, *Ben Jonson*, 4:350–1.
79 Knapp, 'What Is a Co-Author,' 8.
80 Langbaine, *An Account of the English Dramatick Poets*, 370; Kewes, *Authorship and Appropriation*, 146–7.
81 Hirschfield, *Joint Enterprises*, 100.
82 Ibid., 102–3.
83 Bentley, *Profession of Dramatist*, 30.
84 Nicol, 'The Repertory of Prince Charles's (I) Company,' 62–3.
85 Bentley, *Profession of Dramatist*, 36.
86 Hirschfield, *Joint Enterprises*, 102. The plays are *More Dissemblers Besides Women* (1614), *The Widow* (ca. 1615), *The Witch* (ca. 1616), *Hengist, King of Kent* (1620), and *A Game at Chess* (1624).
87 Hirschfield, *Joint Enterprises*, 102, 101.
88 Among the collaborations with Rowley, *Wit at Several Weapons* (ca. 1613–15), *A Fair Quarrel* (1616), *The Old Law* (1618–19), and *The World Tossed at Tennis* (1619–20) were written for Prince Charles's Men, and *The Changeling* (1622) and *The Spanish Gypsy* (1623) for Lady Elizabeth's.
89 Hirschfield, *Joint Enterprises*, 102.
90 Bentley, *Jacobean and Caroline Stage*, 5:1016.
91 Nicol, 'The Repertory of Prince Charles's (I) Company,' 62–3.
92 Bentley, *Jacobean and Caroline Stage*, 2:556.
93 The rather defensive prologue to Rowley's *All's Lost by Lust* may not have been written by him, since it also appears before a play by Dekker; see Bentley, *Jacobean and Caroline Stage*, 5:1020–1.
94 Streitberger, 'Personnel and Professionalization,' 347–9.
95 Masten, 'Beaumont and/or Fletcher,' 339.
96 Gurr, *Shakespearian Playing Companies*, 396.
97 His name appears in the company patent of 1610; see Chambers and Greg, 'Dramatic Records from the Patent Rolls,' 3:272–4. The company had been formed only a year previously, so it is likely that Rowley was involved from the start.

158 Notes to pages 20–3

98 Cook and Wilson, eds., 'Dramatic Records in the Declared Accounts,' 51–2, 54, 60, 67.
99 Bentley, *Jacobean and Caroline Stage*, 1:199–200.
100 Cook and Wilson, 'Dramatic Records in the Declared Accounts,' 148; Bentley, *Jacobean and Caroline Stage*, 6:134.
101 See the lists of plays in Bentley, *Jacobean and Caroline Stage*, 1:214–15; and Gurr, *Shakespearian Playing Companies*, 409.
102 On the presence of actor-playwrights during rehearsal, see Stern, *Rehearsal from Shakespeare to Sheridan*, 86–8.
103 See, for example, Symons, 'Middleton and Rowley,' 85; Ribner, *Jacobean Tragedy*, 135; Sālgādo, *Three Jacobean Tragedies*, 34; Holmes, *Art of Thomas Middleton*, 218.
104 Barker, *Thomas Middleton*, 100; my italics.
105 Schoenbaum, *Middleton's Tragedies*, 216–17; my italics. These formulations are criticised by Daalder, *The Changeling*, xvii–xviii, although he does not go on to describe Rowley's position in the theatre company.
106 Wiggin, *An Inquiry into the Authorship*, 28.
107 Stork, *William Rowley*, 39–50; Robb, 'The Canon of William Rowley's Plays'; Barker, *Thomas Middleton*, 177–93.
108 Masten, *Textual Intercourse*, 16–20; see also Masten, 'Playwriting: Authorship and Collaboration,' 371–4; Nochimson, '"Sharing" *The Changeling*.' Masten's critique is also echoed in McMullan, *King Henry VIII*, 188–96.
109 Hoy, 'Shares of Fletcher and His Collaborators (I),' 130.
110 Masten, *Textual Intercourse*, 16–20.
111 Nochimson, '"Sharing" *The Changeling*,' 38–42.
112 Hirschfield, *Joint Enterprises*, 15; Bromham and Hutchings, *Middleton and His Collaborators*, 75.
113 Nochimson makes valid points about discrepancies in Jackson's comments on the occurrence of parentheses and the words *I'd* and *ye* in Rowley ('"Sharing" *The Changeling*,' 40). But elsewhere his assumption that authorship attributers believe in absolute authorial divisions leads him to see discrepancies where the attributer is in fact being sensitive to complexities. He claims that Jackson, finding the Middletonian *on't* becoming more frequent at the very end of the supposedly Rowleyan last scene of *A Fair Quarrel*, is 'forced to conclude' that 'Middleton had a hand in the closing pages' of the play, a notion already proposed by Robb (Nochimson, '"Sharing" *The Changeling*,' 40; Jackson, *Studies in Attribution*, 123–4). But Jackson is not being 'forced' here; rather, his linguistic evidence reveals a possible subtlety of the authorial division; indeed, as I discuss in chapter 4, it may echo the curiously detachable quality of this section of the play.

When he turns to Hoy's discovery that the spelling *'um* for *'em* is associated with Rowley, Nochimson claims that Hoy assumes 'compositorial accuracy or inaccuracy according to his convenience' ('"Sharing" *The Changeling*,' 41–2). He notes Hoy's claim that Rowley wrote the first few lines of *The Changeling* 4.2, a scene otherwise by Middleton, and protests that Hoy does not suggest Middleton's presence in Rowley's 1.1 when it begins with an *'em* (pp. 41–2; referring to Hoy, 'Shares of Fletcher and His Collaborators (V),' 87–8). Yet Hoy's logic is implicit: since *'um* is un un- usual spelling likely to be occasionally corrected by compositors, its absence cannot be evidence of Rowley's absence, but its surviving presence is a sign of Rowley's hand (and although Hoy doesn't say it, the obvious reason for believing that these lines might be written by a different author than that of the rest of the scene is that they are disconnected from the subject matter of the rest of the scene and also represent a rare moment in which the play's two plotlines meet).
114 Hoy, 'Shares of Fletcher and His Collaborators (I),' 134; my italics. See also Hoy's later comment, 'With all linguistic evidence, it is all, finally, a matter of more or less,' in 'Shares of Fletcher and His Collaborators (VII),' 87.
115 Jackson, 'Early Modern Authorship,' 87.
116 Jowett, 'Pattern of Collaboration,' 183.
117 Hoy, 'Critical and Aesthetic Problems,' 4. Bentley was generally suspicious of Hoy's studies for not taking sufficient account of the possibility of revision, but admitted that Hoy's analysis of Fletcher and Massinger was 'highly suggestive' (*Profession of Dramatist*, 232n29).
118 Hoy, 'Shares of Fletcher and His Collaborators (V),' 97.
119 Ibid., 91.
120 Jackson, 'Early Modern Authorship,' 88.
121 Rabkin, 'Problems in the Study of Collaboration,' 12.
122 Hirschfield, *Joint Enterprises*, 43–7.
123 Masten, *Textual Intercourse*, 17–18. McMullan, '"Our Whole Life Is Like a Play,"' 451–2.
124 Masten, *Textual Intercourse*, 16–18, citing Hoy, 'Shares of Fletcher and His Collaborators (I),' 130.
125 Jackson, 'Early Modern Authorship,' 87.
126 Craig, 'Style, Statistics, and New Models of Authorship,' par. 31.
127 Jowett, 'Pattern of Collaboration,' 183.
128 Nochimson, '"Sharing" *The Changeling*,' 51.
129 Ibid., 52.
130 I borrow this image from Burns, *King Henry VI, Part I*, 79.

131 Vickers, *Shakespeare, Co-Author*, 43.
132 Jackson, *Defining Shakespeare*, 7; Jackson, 'Early Modern Authorship,' 88.
133 Lake, *Canon of Thomas Middleton's Plays*, 3.
134 Bentley, *Profession of Dramatist*, 227–34, concludes that division by act was 'quite common,' claiming that Hoy's study of Beaumont and Fletcher reveals that 'joint composition was basically by acts' (p. 232). However, Bentley misrepresents the diversity of Hoy's findings. Nochimson, '"Sharing" *The Changeling*,' 42–8, sets out the evidence against Bentley's argument.
135 Vickers, *Shakespeare, Co-Author*, 21–3; for an example of one of these 'plots,' see Adams, 'The Author Plot.'
136 Chillington, 'Playwrights at Work,' 461.
137 Sisson, '*Keep the Widow Waking*,' 257.
138 Burns, *King Henry VI*, 80.
139 Ibid., 80–2. Sisson, who discovered the document, interpreted Dekker's statement to mean that the other playwrights also took on an entire act each ('*Keep the Widow Waking*,' 246–7), but there is no evidence for this.
140 McMullan, '"Our Whole Life Is Like a Play,"' 448.
141 Lake, *Canon of Thomas Middleton's Plays*, 202; Hoy, 'Shares of Fletcher and His Collaborators (V),' 88; Taylor, '*The Spanish Gypsy*, July 1623.'
142 Jackson, *Defining Shakespeare*, 7–8.
143 Lake, *Canon of Thomas Middleton's Plays*, 204–5. See also Hoy, 'Shares of Fletcher and His Collaborators (V),' 87–8, and Jackson, *Studies in Attribution*, 124–5.
144 These two short scenes comprise a continuous flow of action, and so I group them as one.
145 Mooney, '"Framing" as Collaborative Technique,' 139.
146 Ibid., 132, 138.
147 Ibid., 136.
148 Hoy, 'Shares of Fletcher and His Collaborators (V),' 96–7.
149 Lake, *Canon of Thomas Middleton's Plays*, 211–14; see also Hoy, 'Shares of Fletcher and His Collaborators (V),' 89–92; Jackson, *Studies in Attribution*, 125–7.
150 Lake, *Canon of Thomas Middleton's Plays*, 212, and Jackson, *Studies in Attribution*, 126–7, both acknowledge the sparse authorial evidence of 2.3. Lake (p. 213) follows Hoy in suspecting traces of an original Fletcherian play in 5.1; Jackson (p, 127) thinks that 'Middleton may have written patches' of act 5.
151 Lake, *Canon of Thomas Middleton's Plays*, 200–2; Jackson, *Studies in Attribution*, 120–4. Jackson (p. 122) considers 4.3 to be 'of mixed authorship with

Middleton's hand dominant.' Lake (pp. 201–2) suspects, but finds no evidence for, Middleton's authorship of the final section of act 5; Jackson (pp. 123–4) identifies some minor stylistic evidence for this possibility.
152 Lake, *Canon of Thomas Middleton's Plays*, 201–2, offers stylistic evidence for Middleton's presence in act 1 but is purely impressionistic on act 5; Jackson, *Studies in Attribution*, 123–4, adds some minor evidence for Middleton 'in the closing pages of the play.'
153 Mooney, '"Framing" as Collaborative Technique,' 140n5.
154 Lake, *Canon of Thomas Middleton's Plays*, 208; Jackson, *Studies in Attribution*, 127–8.
155 For a summary of scholarship on the play's authorship, see Taylor, '*An/The Old Law*,' 405–7.
156 Lake, *Canon of Thomas Middleton's Plays*, 209–10. Jackson, *Studies in Attribution*, 130, sees no third collaborator and attributes the whole of act 5 to Rowley.
157 See Lake, *Canon of Thomas Middleton's Plays*, 210; he believes Rowley's hand to be the dominant one, since most of the features point to him. Jackson, *Studies in Attribution*, 129, thinks Rowley wrote it, apart, perhaps, from 'a few sentences' contributed by Middleton.
158 For a similar conclusion about other dramatists, see Cathcart, 'Plural Authorship, Attribution, and the Children of the King's Revels,' par. 36.
159 Jowett, 'Varieties of Collaboration,' 115.
160 Vickers, *Shakespeare, Co-Author*, 433–500.
161 Jowett, *Timon of Athens*, 144.
162 McMullan, 'A Rose for Emilia,' 131, 145.
163 Jowett, *Timon of Athens*, 145.
164 Ibid., 151, 152. See also Jowett, 'Middleton and Debt,' in which he argues that the play's dual authorship creates a situation in which 'the play incorporates two concepts of how money means' (pp. 230–1).
165 Pentzell, '*The Changeling*: Notes on Mannerism,' 276.
166 Ibid.,' 278–9. Similarly, Morrison calls the play 'a freak half-finished with an arm too many and a leg too few,' but curiously ignores the dual authorship, implying that the disunities in the play are deliberate decisions by Middleton ('Cangoun in Zombieland,' 236).
167 Munro, *Children of the Queen's Revels*, 4.
168 McMillin and MacLean, *The Queen's Men and Their Plays*, xi.
169 Knutson, *Repertory of Shakespeare's Company*; McMillin and MacLean, *Queen's Men and Their Plays*; Bly, *Queer Virgins and Virgin Queans*; Gurr, *Shakespeare Company*; Munro, *Children of the Queen's Revels*.

170 Wiles, *Shakespeare's Clown*.
171 Leggatt, *Jacobean Public Theatre*.
172 Foucault, 'What Is an Author?,' 119.
173 Bly, *Queer Virgins and Virgin Queans*, 32–3, 121.

2. Collaborators and Individual Style

1 Symons, 'Middleton and Rowley,' 86. Symons claims to see slight 'traces of Middleton' in the first scene, but does not elaborate.
2 Ibid., 87.
3 Ibid., 83–4, 86–7.
4 Ibid., 86–7. In the latter phrase, Symons is quoting Leigh Hunt.
5 Bentley, *Jacobean and Caroline Stage*, 5:1020.
6 Arthur Golding's 1567 translation reads, 'The best I see and like: the worst I follow headlong still'; see Golding, *Ovid's Metamorphoses*, 7.25. On Renaissance responses to this concept, see Waswo, 'Damnation, Protestant Style,' 68–9.
7 See, for example, Sanders, *The Dramatist and the Received Idea*, 312–13; Waswo, 'Damnation, Protestant Style'; Sinfield, *Literature in Protestant England*, 99–100; Rozett, *Doctrine of Election*, 291–300; White, *Natural Law*, 41–2.
8 Sinfield, *Literature in Protestant England*, 99.
9 Aristotle, *Nichomachean Ethics*, 7.2–3.
10 Bamford, *Sexual Violence on the Jacobean Stage*, 107.
11 Dent, *Plaine Mans Path-Way*, 288.
12 Milton, *Catholic and Reformed*, 413.
13 Lake, *Moderate Puritans and the Elizabethan Church*, 151–3.
14 Tyacke, 'Puritanism, Arminianism and Counter-Revolution,' 119. Tyacke states this description as fact, but it is better considered an influential mischaracterization of the movement by its enemies, who sought to associate it with Pelagianism; see White, *Predestination, Policy and Polemic*, 32–3; Milton, *Catholic and Reformed*, 417–18.
15 Tyacke, *Anti-Calvinists: The Rise of English Arminianism*, 102–6. White, *Predestination, Policy and Polemic*, 203–14 is more sceptical about the existence of defined groups of English 'Arminianists' at this time but acknowledges that an oversimplified understanding of the term was current among laymen (p. 214).
16 Reay, *Popular Cultures in England*, 96–8.
17 Watt, 'Piety in the Pedlar's Pack,' 242, 247–8.
18 Capp, *The World of John Taylor the Water-Poet*, 133–4.

19 Bouwsma, 'Hooker in the Context of European Cultural History,' 148. On the second theory's connections with Calvinism, see pp. 149 and 151.
20 Bouwsma, 'Hooker in the Context of European Cultural History,' 149.
21 Wright, *Passions of the Mind in Generall*, 8–9.
22 Wilks, *Idea of Conscience*, 11–14.
23 White, *Natural Law*, 2–3, 31–2.
24 Calvin, *Institution of Christian Religion*, 2.2.12. On Calvin's pessimism about natural law and reason, see Hoopes, *Right Reason in the English Renaissance*, 110–12; Wilks, *Idea of Conscience*, 29–31; White, *Natural Law*, 38–40.
25 Bouwsma, 'Hooker in the Context of European Cultural History,' 151.
26 Perkins, 'A Golden Chaine,' in *The Workes*, 1:372; Dyke, *Mystery of Selfe-Deceiving*, 140.
27 Dyke, *Mystery of Selfe-Deceiving*, 139. Dyke is paraphrasing Calvin, *Institution of Christian Religion*, 2.2.27.
28 Perkins, 'A Golden Chaine,' in *The Workes*, 1:372. Rozett, *Doctrine of Election*, 295, discusses this passage, although her quotation of Perkins is inaccurate, an error originating with her source, George and George, *The Protestant Mind*, 49.
29 Rozett, *Doctrine of Election*, 68–9.
30 Dent, *Plaine Mans Path-Way*, 30, 31; the phrases appear in a list of 'infallible notes and tokens of a regenerate mind' and a list of 'manifest signes of damnation,' respectively; see Rozett, *Doctrine of Election*, 69–70.
31 Calvin, *Institution of Christian Religion*, 4.10.3.
32 White, *Natural Law*, 39.
33 Dyke, *Mystery of Selfe-Deceiving*, 140.
34 Waswo, 'Damnation, Protestant Style,' 65–71; Stachniewski, 'Calvinist Psychology in *Macbeth*,' 173–5.
35 Rozett, *Doctrine of Election*, 295.
36 Ibid.
37 On the Moor in *All's Lost* as a symbol of the devil, see Barthelemy, *Black Face, Maligned Race*, 117–20.
38 White, *Natural Law*, 41. White is critiquing George C. Herndl, who found Calvinist pessimism in most Jacobean tragedies because their characters are 'helpless before the power of lust' and because they depict 'the helplessness of conscience or of reason, before contrary nature'; see Herndl, *High Design*, 153.
39 White, *Natural Law*, 42.
40 Ferrell, introduction to *The Two Gates of Salvation*, 680–1. See also Mulholland, '*The Two Gates of Salvation*: Typology, and Thomas Middleton's Bibles'; Heller, *Penitent Brothellers*, 1–34.

41 Stachniewski, 'Calvinist Psychology in Middleton's Tragedies'; Heller, *Penitent Brothellers*.
42 Heinemann's thesis is set out in *Puritanism and Theatre*; for rebuttals, see Chakravorty, *Society and Politics*, 9–13; and Bawcutt, 'Was Thomas Middleton a Puritan Dramatist?'
43 Heller, *Penitent Brothellers*, 32.
44 Engleberg, 'Tragic Blindness,' 21; for a similar description of Middleton's tragedies, see Ribner, *Jacobean Tragedy*, 125–6.
45 Stachniewski, 'Calvinist Psychology in Middleton's Tragedies,' 240–1.
46 Classic articulations of this view include Sanders, '*The Revenger's Tragedy*'; and Dollimore, *Radical Tragedy*, 139–50.
47 See Stachniewski, 'Calvinist Psychology in *Macbeth*,' 180.
48 Herndl, *High Design*, 221.
49 From a predestinarian catechism bound into editions of the English Geneva Bible, 1579–1615, cited by Tyacke, *Anti-Calvinists: The Rise of English Arminianism*, 2.
50 Heller, *Penitent Brothellers*, 74–5.
51 Frost, *Selected Plays of Thomas Middleton*, 411. Frost demonstrates the play's Calvinist influence via a different approach to mine: he observes that several characters are represented as subconsciously aware that their lives are running to a predestined pattern (pp. 411–12).
52 The traditional interpretation is that the scene dramatizes a seduction, but I am following those critics who argue that the Duke forces himself on Bianca; see Anthony Dawson, '*Women Beware Women* and the Economy of Rape,' 303–5; Carroll, *Women Beware Women*, xxiv; Daileader, *Eroticism on the Renaissance Stage*, 25–31.
53 There are several other scenes that feature self-deceiving characters. Isabella is reluctant to commit incest with her uncle, but once tricked into believing that they are not related, she is happy to countenance adultery (1.2.185–232). Elsewhere, the Cardinal warns the Duke and Bianca before their marriage that 'Religious Honors done to sin, / Disparage Vertues reverence, and will pull / Heavens thunder upon *Florence*' (4.3.1–3), but Bianca blithely puts a positive gloss on the event: 'Heaven and Angels / Take great delight in a converted sinner' (55–6). In one instance, the warning comes too late: the violated Bianca tells Guardiano, 'Beware of offring the first-fruits to sin' (2.2.433), but since he has already done so, the warning becomes irrelevant. But in most of these events, the warnings are received but the recipient fails to understand it. There is a similar instance in the only moment of mental conflict in Middleton's one-act *Yorkshire Tragedy*: the Husband suffers anguish when he learns that his gambling habit is

causing his brother to starve at university (4.55–93), but like the Duke, his reaction is to commit a worse crime: the murders of his children.
54 Dyke, *Mystery of Selfe-Deceiving*, 39.
55 Dent, *Plaine Mans Path-Way*, 10–11.
56 Quotations are from the Portland manuscript, one of the two early texts. The 1661 quarto, which presents a shortened version of the play, omits the assassins' pity: '*he kneels and spreads his arms, they kill him, hurry him off.*'
57 Line references are to the left-hand column of the parallel-text edition in Taylor and Lavagnino, *Thomas Middleton: The Collected Works*.
58 Schoenbaum, *Middleton's Tragedies*, 57–8; Farley-Hills, *Jacobean Drama*, 124.
59 The meanings of the title are discussed by Holzknecht, 'The Dramatic Structure of *The Changeling*'; Levin, *Multiple Plot*, 44–6; Frost, *Selected Plays of Thomas Middleton*, 413; and Morrison, 'Cangoun in Zombieland.'
60 For variations on this idea, see Daalder, 'Folly and Madness in *The Changeling*,' 11–18, and Daalder, *The Changeling*, xxxvii–xl, who describes the characters' desires as 'unconscious' and the madmen behind the tiring-house facade as an emblem of the shrouding of secrets; Garber, 'The Insincerity of Women,' who discusses the masculine anxiety caused by the impossibility of knowing whether women are genuinely sexually aroused; Stachniewski, 'Calvinist Psychology in Middleton's Tragedies,' 228, 244–5, who describes the play as illustrating a pre-Freudian concept of unconscious motivation inspired by Calvinist theology; Neill, *Issues of Death*, 168–97, who describes the play's cathartic representation of the discovery and expulsion of evil; and Boehrer, 'Alsemero's Closet,' who sees Alsemero's closet as a symbol of inward secrets.
61 Stachniewski, 'Calvinist Psychology in Middleton's Tragedies,' 228; see also Ribner, *Jacobean Tragedy*, 129, 131, who describes the same process but does not link it to Calvinism.
62 On the moral blindness of Beatrice, see Ellis-Fermor, *Jacobean Drama*, 146–9; Engleberg, 'Tragic Blindness,' passim; Levin, *Multiple Plot*, 38–9; Baines, *The Lust Motif*, 116–17; Wymer, *Suicide and Despair in the Jacobean Drama*, 50–1; Stachniewski, 'Calvinist Psychology in Middleton's Tragedies,' 231–7.
63 The quarto reads 'or' for 'of.'
64 See Reynolds, *The Triumphs of Gods Revenege* [sic], Book 1, R1^v; the source of Alsemero's speech is noted by Holmes, *Art of Thomas Middleton*, 174n37; and Randall, 'Some Perspectives on the Spanish Setting,' 204.
65 Hillman, *Self-Speaking in Medieval and Early Modern English Drama*, 185.
66 Daalder, 'Folly and Madness in *The Changeling*,' 8. See also Hillman, *Self-Speaking in Medieval and Early Modern English Drama*, 184–5. Holmes goes

to the opposite extreme, calling Alsemero's speech hypocrisy (*Art of Thomas Middleton*, 172n32); but since Alsemero is speaking in soliloquy we should probably assume that the speech represents a sincere expression of his thought processes, even though his attempts at justifying himself are unconvincing.

67 Neill, *Issues of Death*, 175, 181–2.
68 Daalder, 'Folly and Madness in *The Changeling*,' 9.
69 In the following description I am referring to the relationship between Beatrice and Alsemero as sinful, and thus according with DeFlores's patriarchal assumption that her rejection of her father's choice, Alonzo, is 'A kind / Of whoredome in [her] heart' (3.4.146–7). While individual audience members might sympathize with Beatrice's reluctance to marry Alonzo, both Middleton and Rowley seem to be directing the audience's sympathy away from such sentiments by making her a murderess and by not making Alonzo obviously unpleasant. See Belsey, *The Subject of Tragedy*, 202; Malcolmson, '"As Tame as the Ladies,"' 329, who argues that the play's solution to gender conflicts is not equality but a wiser and stronger patriarchy; and Burks, '"I'll Want My Will Else,"' 776, for whom Beatrice's wilfulness is represented as a dangerously exaggerated version of that discouraged in all women.
70 Reynolds, *The Triumphs of Gods Revenege* [sic], Q3^r, R2^r, R3^v, S1^v.
71 Ibid., Q3^r.
72 White, *Middleton and Tourneur*, 94, notes this alteration of the source material but does not make the connection with Calvinist theology.
73 Proponents of this view include Ellis-Fermor, *Jacobean Drama*, 146–8; Engleberg, 'Tragic Blindness'; Levin, *Multiple Plot*, 38–9; Baines, *Lust Motif*, 116–17; Wymer, *Suicide and Despair*, 50–1; Stachniewski, 'Calvinist Psychology in Middleton's Tragedies,' 231–7.
74 Wright, *Passions of the Mind in Generall*, 9.
75 Sara Eaton, 'Beatrice-Joanna and the Rhetoric of Love,' 279.
76 The scene's didactic representation of the purging of evil is noted in Whigham, 'Reading Social Conflict in the Alimentary Tract,' 340; Stachniewski, 'Calvinist Psychology in Middleton's Tragedies,' 239; Burks, '"I'll Want My Will Else,"' 781–2; Neill, *Issues of Death*, 195–6.
77 For this reading of Isabella, see Daalder, 'The Role of Isabella in *The Changeling*.'
78 Neill, *Issues of Death*, 170; Morrison, 'Cangoun in Zombieland,' 233. For others examples, see Holmes, *Art of Thomas Middleton*, 184, who calls Alsemero a 'grotesque moraliser'; Burks, '"I'll Want My Will Else,"' 782, who notes the 'barrenness' of the play's attempts at closure; and Hillman, *Self-Speaking in Medieval and Early Modern English Drama*, 187–8, who says that

Alsemero takes on the role of moral spokesman 'so as to reclaim his status as innocent outsider.'
79 Pentzell, 'The Changeling: Notes on Mannerism,' 279–80.
80 Rozett, Doctrine of Election, 291.
81 Schoenbaum, Middleton's Tragedies, 130.
82 Randall, 'Some Observations on the Theme of Chastity'; and Burks, '"I'll Want My Will Else,"' 776–9.
83 'Parks' can refer to women's bodies (see A Mad World, My Masters, 1.1.144–50), while 'rangers' can mean 'rakes'; see Partridge, Shakespeare's Bawdry, 158, 172; and Oxford English Dictionary, 'ranger,' 2.a.
84 Although the Oxford English Dictionary's definition of 'changeling' states that the human child is replaced by an obviously 'stupid or ugly' fairy-child (A.sb.3), there are versions of the myth in which the child's appearance is unchanged, and only its behaviour indicates its malevolent nature; see Spence, The Fairy Tradition in Britain, 231. In this sense, Beatrice and Alsemero can be compared to folkloric changelings.
85 Wiggin, An Inquiry into the Authorship, 56.
86 Daalder, The Changeling, xviii.

3. The Actor as Collaborator

1 On the performance of World Tossed, see Bentley, Jacobean and Caroline Stage, 4:908–11; on Rowley's clown roles, see 2:556–7.
2 The preface is clearly by Rowley because it is signed 'Simplicitie' and is also similar to the preface he wrote for A Fair Quarrel: its dedication ('To the well-wishing, well-reading Understander') uses similar words to that of Fair Quarrel ('his poor well-Willer wisheth his best wishes'), and both prefaces refer to the play as a child going out into the world (World Tossed, Epistle, 10–26; A Fair Quarrel, Epistle, 19–26). The phrase 'well-willer' also appears twice in the dedicatory epistle to The Travels of the Three English Brothers by Rowley, Day, and Wilkins (1607).
3 Johnson, Actor as Playwright, 23.
4 Bentley, Jacobean and Caroline Stage, 2:556.
5 On the probability that Middleton adapted the play to include Rowley, see Howard-Hill, Game at Chess, 30–2. Further evidence that Rowley played the Fat Bishop can be found in Ben Jonson's The Staple of News (1626): Rowley died shortly before Jonson wrote this play, which alludes to the death of the actor who had played the Fat Bishop in A Game at Chess, and to the fact that the King's Men currently lacked a clown actor; see Parr, The Staple of News, 171n, 109n.
6 Bentley, Profession of Player, 206–7, 223–8.

7 Palfrey and Stern, *Shakespeare in Parts*, 41.
8 Wiles, *Shakespeare's Clown*, xi.
9 Ibid., 99–103, 158–63, 178.
10 The signifying power of well-known actors has been articulated more effectively by theorists of film than by theorists of theatre. In *Heavenly Bodies*, 1–8, Richard Dyer describes the actor's 'star image' as a combination of the character he or she is playing, his or her previous performances, and the viewer's knowledge of his or her real life. Similarly, both Stephen Heath and James Naremore draw a distinction between characters, actors, and star images; see Heath, *Questions of Cinema*, 178–93, and Naremore, *Acting in the Cinema*, 158. 'Star studies' is not perfectly applicable to Elizabethan actors (there is little evidence that early modern audiences were interested in the actors' personal lives, nor is there evidence of a marketing machine for actors), but what is useful is the concept of the persona as a fictional character that is a recognizable continuation of the actor's previous roles and which affects the audience's perception of the character created by the writer.
11 Leishman, *The Three Parnassus Plays*, 129. The play's author is alluding to Sir Philip Sidney, who criticized plays that 'thrust in the clown by head and shoulders'; see Sidney, 'A Defence of Poetry,' 114, lines 32–3.
12 On the printing and thematic relevance of the 'new additions,' see Gossett, textual introduction to *A Fair Quarrel*, 633.
13 See the responses collected in Howard-Hill, *Game at Chess*, 193, 199, 200, 202, 211, in which the character is usually referred to as the 'Bishop of Spalato.'
14 Sargent, 'Theme and Structure in Middleton's *A Game at Chess*,' 721, 727.
15 Taylor, introduction to *A Game at Chess*, 1827.
16 Patterson, 'Dominis, Marco Antonio de.'
17 Howard-Hill, 'Political Interpretations,' 285; see also Howard-Hill, *Game at Chess*, 31.
18 Howard-Hill, 'Political Interpretations,' 285; Howard-Hill, *Game at Chess*, 31.
19 Johnson, *Actor as Playwright*, 20. See, for example, Bristol, *Carnival and Theater*, 140–55; Wiles, *Shakespeare's Clown*; Weimann, *Author's Pen and Actor's Voice*, 99–102.
20 Johnson, *Actor as Playwright*, 27.
21 Nicol, 'The Title Page of *The World Tossed at Tennis*.' Other clown actors who were depicted on title pages of plays include Robert Armin on *The Two Maids of Moreclacke*, Thomas Greene on *Greene's Tu Quoque*, and pos-

sibly Richard Tarlton on *Friar Bacon and Friar Bungay*; see Levin, 'Tarlton in *The Famous History of Friar Bacon and Friar Bungay.*'
22 Johnson, *Actor as Playwright*, 20, 27.
23 Armin wrote one, possibly two plays (see ibid., 44). The only other playwright-clown of the period was Robert Wilson, who wrote at least three plays for the Queen's Men in the 1580s.
24 See the divisions of authorship suggested by the three major stylistic analyses: Hoy, 'Shares of Fletcher and His Collaborators (V)'; Lake, *The Canon of Thomas Middleton's Plays*, 200–13; and Jackson, *Studies in Attribution*, 119–31.
25 Bentley, *Jacobean and Caroline Stage*, 2:556.
26 The 1633 quarto of *All's Lost* states in the *dramatis personae* that Jaques was 'personated by the Poet.' Rowley is listed as Plumporridge in the *dramatis personae* of *The Inner Temple Masque*. The evidence for *World Tossed* and *Chess* has been noted earlier.
27 For a list of this company's plays, see Nicol, 'The Repertory of Prince Charles's (I) Company.' On the dating of *A Shoemaker*, see Nicol, '*A Shoemaker a Gentleman.*'
28 Bentley, *Jacobean and Caroline Stage*, 2:556, lists most of Rowley's King's Men roles. He does not include *The Unnatural Combat*, presumably because of uncertainty over its date, but Philip Edwards and Colin Gibson date the play to 1624–5 (*The Plays and Poems of Philip Massinger*, 2:181–2), and Belgarde is a suitable role for a fat actor (see, for example, 3.1.25–8). Bentley lists the Cook in *Rollo, Duke of Normandy* and the Clown in *The Fair Maid of the Inn* as Rowley roles, but later studies give *Rollo* dates incompatible with Rowley (see Williams, textual introduction to *Rollo, Duke of Normandy*, 155–7), and *Fair Maid* may have been written after Rowley's death, at the same time as *The Staple of News* (see Bowers, textual introduction to *Fair Maid of the Inn*, 555).
29 Bentley, *Jacobean and Caroline Stage*, 2:556. In a recent article, Brandon Centerwall suggests that Rowley began his career with the Children of Paul's and that further roles may thus be detectable within that repertory. However, the evidence (apparent puns on Rowley's name in the playtexts of that company), while intriguing, is too speculative to be reliable. See Centerwall, 'A Greatly Exaggerated Demise.'
30 Bakhtin, *Rabelais and His World*, 308–9.
31 Breton, *The Good and the Badde*, D4^r.
32 Bakhtin, *Rabelais and His World*, 292; Laroque, *Shakespeare's Festive World*, 49.
33 Bakhtin, *Rabelais and His World*, 292.

34 Knowles, *King Henry VI, Part II*, 102–3.
35 Those who see a radical function for the clown include Bristol, *Carnival and Theater*, 140–50; and Patterson, *Shakespeare and the Popular Voice*, 67–70. Those who describe a more conservative function include Levin, *Multiple Plot*, 111–16, 139–47, for whom clowns are a 'foil to set off an elevated main action,' not to parody it (146–7); Weimann, *Shakespeare and the Popular Tradition*, 186–8, for whom the clown unifies rather than divides the audience; and Helgerson, *Forms of Nationhood*, 216–18, 221–2, for whom popular rebellion is critiqued through its association with the clown.
36 Knowles, *King Henry VI, Part II*, 103.
37 Burton, *The Anatomy of Melancholy*, 2:207.
38 Shakespeare's roles for Kemp contain this type of humour, but since it is also used by Kemp's clown in *A Knack to Know a Knave* (see Felver, *Robert Armin, Shakespeare's Fool*, 9–10), it was clearly a skill associated with the actor rather than a distinctive quality of Shakespeare's writing.
39 Welsford, *The Fool*, 322.
40 Cohen, *Drama of a Nation*, 360.
41 Stylistic analyses indicate that the section of the masque that includes Simplicity was essentially divided in half between the writers; see Hoy, 'Shares of Fletcher and His Collaborators (V),' 86–7; Lake, *Canon of Thomas Middleton's Plays*, 203–4; and Jackson, *Studies in Attribution*, 125.
42 The stage directions and speech prefixes usually refer to him as *Jaques*, but at several points, the stage direction reads '*Enter Clowne*' (3.2.27, 3.3.20, and 5.3.9), and at 3.2.28, the speech-prefix reads '*Clo., Ja.*' In addition, the *dramatis personae* calls him 'a simple Clownish gentleman.' All of this indicates that Jaques is a role written for the company's clown.
43 Bakhtin, *Rabelais and His World*, 20; see also Laroque, *Shakespeare's Festive World*, 45.
44 This is implied when Margaretta says, shortly before Jaques's first appearance after the marriage, 'A coat of tissue / If a foole weares it, is but a fooles coat' (3.2.7–8).
45 Bakhtin, *Rabelais and His World*, 20.
46 Lothario refers to 'this burthen of flesh that I beare about me' which 'Hath made me so heavy,' and later says, 'heavy as I am' (3.1.66–7, 155); Jacinta calls him a 'fleshly fiend' (3.1.4); Roderick tells him, 'pocks of your heavy flesh!' and calls him a 'hatefull lumpe' (3.1.132, 145). There is some evidence that Rowley sometimes worked in a double act with another fat actor: in *A Fair Quarrel*, the clown Chough is teamed with a servant whose name, Trimtram, alludes to the proverb 'trim, tram, like master like man,' and may thus refer to a similar physical appearance between the two actors.

47 Karen Bamford points out, for example, that Jacinta's furious anger at the rapist King Roderick is directed only at his servant Lothario, not at the king himself; see *Sexual Violence on the Jacobean Stage*, 197n70.
48 For an expanded version of this argument, see Nicol, 'Interrogating the Devil.'
49 On Rogation ceremonies, see Thomas, *Religion and the Decline of Magic*, 71–4.
50 Mooney, '"Common Sight,"' 315–17.
51 Udall, *A Critical, Old-Spelling Edition of 'The Birth of Merlin,'* 8, 69–70.
52 On Compass's function as a moral guideline for the main plot characters, see Gunby, 'Critical Introduction,' 277–9; on the role's Rowleyan nature, see Carnegie, 'Theatrical Introduction,' 287–8, 290–1. Carnegie theorizes that Rowley may have written the role for himself but that the play was rejected by his then company, the King's Men.
53 Wiles, *Shakespeare's Clown*, 63–4.
54 Ibid.
55 See also McElroy, *Parody and Burlesque*, 246.
56 Although the other characters call him 'Gnothos,' he is labelled *Clown* in all the quarto's speech prefixes and stage directions. I use 'Gnothos' in this chapter for the sake of clarity.
57 Printed as irregular verse in the quarto, but clearly intended to be prose.
58 Masten, 'Family Values,' 450–4.
59 Hoy, 'Shares of Fletcher and His Collaborators (V),' 92; Lake, *Canon of Thomas Middleton's Plays*, 213–14; Jackson, *Studies in Attribution*, 125–7; Michael Dobson, '*Wit at Several Weapons*, Late 1613.'
60 Nicol, 'Repertory of Prince Charles's (I) Company,' 64–7, 71n30.
61 McMullan, *Politics of Unease*, 13.
62 The date of the text as we have it is derived from its references to the New River, which was completed in September 1613. Lake (*Canon of Thomas Middleton's Plays*, 198) and Dobson ('*Wit at Several Weapons*, Late 1613,' 376) both claim that the play must have been written in 1613, when the New River was still topical. However, its novelty value could surely have lasted longer than a few months, and Jackson rightly prefers a less specific date of 1613–15 (*Studies in Attribution*, 127).
63 He is labelled *Clown* in the stage directions and speech-headings in the folio text, but I refer to him as 'Pompey' for the sake of clarity.
64 Lake, *Canon of Thomas Middleton's Plays*, 213. The stylistic evidence in question is the contractions *I've* and *we're*.
65 The lines are 28–78, 120, 140–3, 143–6, 175, 223–31, and 249–62.
66 Dobson, introduction to *Wit at Several Weapons*, 982.

67 The spelling of 'rolling' is conceivably a pun on the actor's name.
68 On master/servant inversion in Carnival festivities, see Burnett, *Masters and Servants*, 97–111.
69 In these and subsequent quotations I follow the lineation of Michael Dobson's edition in Taylor and Lavagnino, *Thomas Middleton: The Collected Works*, which corrects the often confused lineation of the original text.
70 In *The Witch of Edmonton*, Cuddy does not mourn when he learns that Kate Carter is not really in love with him (5.1.109–14). In *A New Wonder*, the rejected Roger prepares to throw himself onto his sword, but puts his cap on the point first so as not to injure himself (2.1.320–39).
71 McKeithan, *The Debt to Shakespeare*, 192–9; Frost, *The School of Shakespeare*, 243.
72 Cohen, *Drama of a Nation*, 282.
73 See Bristol, *Carnival and Theater*, 202–4. Bristol points out that Sir Toby also receives a 'bloody coxcomb' and Malvolio threatens to be revenged, so that in Shakespeare's play, the battle of Carnival and Lent is not concluded, reflecting the circularity of the seasons. Rowley's play is less conventional in that Carnival is thoroughly quashed and Lent triumphs.

4. Collaborators and Playing Companies

1 Turner, *Turners Dish of Lentten Stuffe*.
2 On the presence of Prince Charles's Men (then called the Duke of York's Men) at the Curtain, see Gurr, *Shakespearian Playing Companies*, 396–7.
3 For exceptionally detailed studies of the thematic and linguistic parallels connecting the play's plotlines, see Levin, *Multiple Plot*, 66–75; Baines, *The Lust Motif*, 65–77; Holdsworth, *A Fair Quarrel*, xxii–xxxix; Mooney, '"Common Sight"'; and Pacheco, '"A Mere Cupboard of Glasses."'
4 Gossett, 'Major/Minor,' 34–5.
5 Bly, *Queer Virgins and Virgin Queans*, 28. Related studies include Knutson, *The Repertory of Shakespeare's Company*; McMillin and MacLean, *The Queen's Men and Their Plays*; Gurr, *Shakespeare Company*; Munro, *Children of the Queen's Revels*.
6 Theodore B. Leinwand, for example, attributes 'the flowering of city comedy' to the unprecedented social mobility between 1540 and 1640 and the debates about social roles that it sparked; see Leinwand, *City Staged*, 39.
7 Bliss, 'Pastiche, Burlesque, Tragicomedy,' 258–60. See also Brittin, *Thomas Middleton*, 95–6; Mooney, '"Common Sight,"' 321–2; and Asp, *Study of Middleton's Tragicomedies*, 98–100.
8 McElroy, *Parody and Burlesque*, 1–34; Parker, 'Fair Quarrel,' 54–5.

9 See Cohen, *Drama of a Nation*, 282–92; and Manley, *Literature and Culture*, 431–77. Both studies take their inspiration from Fredric Jameson's analysis of the politics of romance narratives in *The Political Unconscious*, 103–50.
10 Manley, *Literature and Culture*, 434; and *A Most Pleasant Comedie of Mucedorus*, A3^v, F3^r.
11 Manley, *Literature and Culture*, 441–3; see also Leinwand, *City Staged*, 8, 200n4; Hunter, 'Bourgeois Comedy,' 10–11.
12 Manley, *Literature and Culture*, 441–2.
13 Howard, 'Sex and Social Conflict,' 178.
14 Heinemann, *Puritanism and Theatre*, 101.
15 Manley, *Literature and Culture*, 444.
16 Ibid., 445; on *Chaste Maid*, see pp. 449–51.
17 Cohen, *Drama of a Nation*, 283.
18 Ibid., 289–90.
19 Wright, *Middle-Class Culture in Elizabethan England*, 652–3.
20 Heinemann, *Puritanism and Theatre*, 95; Barber, *A Trick to Catch the Old One*, 2–4.
21 See, for example, Rowe, *Thomas Middleton and the New Comedy*, 75; Chakravorty, *Society and Politics*, 58; Wayne, *A Trick to Catch the Old One*, note to 5.3.188–200.
22 Chakravorty, *Society and Politics*, 63.
23 Leinwand, *City Staged*, 120–1.
24 Chakravorty, *Society and Politics*, 62. Chakravorty corrects Heinemann, who claims that 'the satire is principally at the expense of aristocratic and court vices like lechery, dandyism, duelling and gambling' (*Puritanism and Theatre*, 94), pointing out that the sinners in question are citizens trying to be gentlemen and are defeated by a *true* gentleman (*Society and Politics*, 62n58).
25 Harbage, *Shakespeare and the Rival Traditions*, 274.
26 On the parody of romance in *Chaste Maid*, see Gibbons, *Jacobean City Comedy*, 128–9; Manley, *Literature and Culture*, 449–50.
27 Leggatt, *Citizen Comedy*, 70n8, finds the central character to alternate too clumsily between sentimentality and 'witty knavery'; Michael Taylor, '*A Mad World, My Masters*' and Other Plays, xvi, calls it 'a transitional piece between satire and romance.' Some see the awkwardness as a deliberate choice: Rowe, *Thomas Middleton and the New Comedy*, 129, considers it a commentary on the 'unnatural fiction' of the romance resolution, as does Chakravorty, *Society and Politics*, 108; but Jowett, introduction to *No Wit/Help Like a Woman's*, 779, finds that the emphasis nonetheless remains on tolerance rather than discord.

28 Taylor calls Rowley a gentleman (see 'Thomas Middleton: Lives and Afterlives,' 44), but Rowley's biographers do not: see Howard-Hill, 'William Rowley'; and Gunby, 'Rowley, William.' Certainly, the title pages of *A Fair Quarrel* and *The World Tossed at Tennis* describe both Middleton and Rowley as '*Gent*.' Furthermore, in 1614 Rowley is referred to as 'William Rowley of St. Leonard, Shoreditch, gent.' in one of his appearances in the records of the Middlesex magistrates court. However, other records from before and after this date do not give him this label; see Eccles, 'Brief Lives,' 117. Laura Caroline Stevenson points out that the word 'gentleman' was often used loosely as a 'respectful form of address' rather than as an accurate description of a person's social status; see Stevenson, *Praise and Paradox*, 84–6.
29 Rowley, 'To the Publique Reader,' C2^r.
30 Harbage, *Shakespeare and the Rival Traditions*, 277.
31 It was known as the Duke of York's company or the Duke of Albany's company until 1612, using the then titles of its patron, the young Prince Charles. When Prince Henry died in 1612, the company became known as Prince Charles's.
32 Gurr, *Shakespearian Playing Companies*, 396–7.
33 Orrell, 'The London Stage in the Florentine Correspondence,' 171.
34 On the dating of this play, see Cheatham, '*A New Wonder*,' 19–23. For some time, the date of composition was thought to be 1624 (see Shapiro, '*Tityretu* and the Date of William Rowley's *Woman Never Vext*'), but Cheatham disproves this claim and makes a case for the earlier dates based on topical allusions. That the play was written for Prince Charles's Men can be confirmed by the fact that the quarto's printer, Francis Constable, bought most of his copy from the theatre impresario Christopher Beeston (Cheatham, '*A New Wonder*,' 2); Beeston would have acquired the playtext when he retained the repertory of Prince Charles's Men after they left his Phoenix playhouse in 1622; see Nicol, 'The Repertory of Prince Charles's (I) Company,' 58, 67.
35 On *The Shoemaker's Holiday*, see Leggatt, *Citizen Comedy*, 18–19, and McLuskie, *Dekker and Heywood*, 68–9. On *If You Know Not Me*, see Stevenson, *Praise and Paradox*, 146.
36 Leinwand, *City Staged*, 8. By 'mature city comedies,' Leinwand refers to those plays that depict social rivalry (typically, the private theatre satires). See also McLuskie, *Dekker and Heywood*, 61–6.
37 Leggatt, *Citizen Comedy*, 16–17.
38 In this and all subsequent quotations from *A New Wonder*, lineation follows

Darby, *A Critical Old-Spelling Edition of William Rowley's 'A New Wonder: A Woman Never Vexed,'* which corrects the often-confused lineation of the original text.
39 Harbage, *Shakespeare and the Rival Traditions*, 277.
40 The play most likely belongs to the late 1610s; see Nicol, '*A Shoemaker a Gentleman.*' This means that it was probably written for Prince Charles's Men, since Rowley was an attached playwright for the company at that time.
41 In quotations from *A Shoemaker*, lineation follows of Stork, *William Rowley: His 'All's Lost by Lust' and 'A Shoemaker a Gentleman,'* which corrects the often confused lineation of the original text.
42 Rowley's source for this section was Pedro Mexia, *The Foreste*, a grab bag of information on all manner of subjects, which includes a list of low-born men who successfully climbed the social ladder. Mexia's purpose in providing this list is 'That men borne of base condition should not leave by all meanes possible to attempt to reach and aspire unto honour'; see Mexia, *The Foreste, or Collection of Historyes*, 80^v; and Nicol, '*A Shoemaker a Gentleman,*' 442.
43 Butler, *Theatre and Crisis*, 234.
44 Ibid., 205.
45 Stevenson, *Praise and Paradox*, 193–4.
46 Ibid., 186–9.
47 Manley, *Literature and Culture*, 470.
48 Cohen puts it differently, saying that the plays have a foot in both sides of the theatrical divide; see *Drama of a Nation*, 292.
49 Nicol, 'Repertory of Prince Charles's (I) Company,' 64–7.
50 Bolton, *The Cities Advocate*, passim, especially sig. K1^v.
51 According to the 1679 *dramatis personae*.
52 Jameson, *Political Unconscious*, 138.
53 Levin, *Multiple Plot*, 8–9, 72–3.
54 On the sibling theme, see Gossett, 'Sibling Power,' 437–57. Although Gossett does not refer to Lady Ager and Russell's relationship in this article, she notes it in the same context in 'Major/Minor,' 33, as well as in her introduction to *A Fair Quarrel*, 1210, 1211–12.
55 Levin, *Multiple Plot*, 6–7.
56 Gossett, 'Major/Minor,' 33, and introduction to *A Fair Quarrel*, 1211–12.
57 *The Peace-Maker: or, Great Brittaine's Blessing* (London: Thomas Purfoot, 1618); line references are to Paul Mulholland's edition in Taylor and Lavagnino, *Thomas Middleton: The Collected Works*.
58 Barber, *The Idea of Honour*, 332 and 268; see also Parker, '*Fair Quarrel*,' 57–8.

On *The Peacemaker*'s aim of reforming gentry morality, see Amussen, introduction to *The Peacemaker*, 1305–6.

59 Swetnam, *The Schoole of the Noble and Worthy Science*, 32. For other examples, see Peltonen, *Duel in Early Modern England*, 42–4 (on the need to repulse attacks to maintain honour), and 44–58 (on duelling manuals).
60 Bacon, *The Charge of Sir Francis Bacon*, 43; italics added. For further examples of this notion, see Bowers, 'Middleton's Fair Quarrel,' 40–1, 54.
61 Critics who see Ager as an heroic observer of the duelling code include Lamb, *Specimens of English Dramatic Poets*, 1:334; Swinburne, *Age of Shakespeare*, 162–3; Bowers, 'Middleton's *Fair Quarrel*'; Barker, *Thomas Middleton*, 106–9; Schoenbaum, 'Middleton's Tragicomedies,' 16–18; Levin, *Multiple Plot*, 66–75; Holmes, *Art of Thomas Middleton*, 113–21; Brittin, *Thomas Middleton*, 90–6; Asp, *Study of Thomas Middleton's Tragicomedies*, 103–47; and Price, *A Fair Quarrel*, xxi–xxvi.
62 For a detailed account, see Peltonen, *Duel in Early Modern England*, 80–145; for a summary, see Parker, '*Fair Quarrel*,' 60–2.
63 Dunlap, 'James I, Bacon, Middleton, and the Making of *The Peacemaker*'; see also Mulholland, '*Peacemaker*, July 1618.'
64 Peltonen, *Duel in Early Modern England*, 142–5.
65 Maxwell, 'The Attitude toward the Duello.'
66 Parker, '*Fair Quarrel*,' 63–4; Mulholland, '*Peacemaker*, July 1618,' 404.
67 On the parallels with *The Peacemaker*, see Holdsworth, *Fair Quarrel*, note to 3.1.86–7.
68 Critics who argue that Ager must be viewed with scepticism because of this scene include McElroy, *Parody and Burlesque*, 302–9; Baines, *Lust Motif*, 72–3; Holdsworth, *Fair Quarrel*, xxvii; Kistner and Kistner, 'Themes and Structures,' 36–8; Parker, '*Fair Quarrel*,' 71; White, *Middleton and Tourneur*, 90–1; Pacheco, '"A Mere Cupboard of Glasses,"' 445–7; Gossett, introduction to *A Fair Quarrel*, 1209–10. Peltonen notes that even proponents of the duelling code were uncomfortably aware that it was opposed to Christian forgiveness and tended to brush the problem aside (*Duel in Early Modern England*, 78–9).
69 Bowers, 'Middleton's *Fair Quarrel*,' 63.
70 Pacheco, '"A Mere Cupboard,"' 454. This 'battle' is also noted by Kistner and Kistner, 'Themes and Structures,' 40–1, although they differ in considering the Colonel's generosity to be the play's moral exemplar.
71 On Chough's roaring as a parody of the duelling code, see Mooney, '"Common Sight"'; see also Holdsworth, *Fair Quarrel*, xxxii–xxxv.
72 Levin, *Multiple Plot*, 70–1, 74–5; McElroy, *Parody and Burlesque*, 272–4; and Holdsworth, *Fair Quarrel*, xxx–xxxi.

73 Parker, 'Fair Quarrel,' 69; Kirsch, *Jacobean Dramatic Perspectives*, 81–2; McElroy, *Parody and Burlesque*, 273 n19.
74 Levin, *Multiple Plot*, 71.
75 Leggatt, *Citizen Comedy*, 107–8; Gossett, 'Major/Minor,' 34.
76 Pacheco, '"A Mere Cupboard,"' 460.
77 Chakravorty, *Society and Politics*, 115.
78 Pacheco, '"A Mere Cupboard,"' passim; Gossett, introduction to *Fair Quarrel*, 1210–11.
79 Bliss, 'Pastiche, Burlesque, Tragicomedy,' 258.
80 Pacheco, '"A Mere Cupboard,"' 462.
81 For influential studies of Lady Ager's 'tragedy,' see Barker, *Thomas Middleton*, 106–10, and Schoenbaum, 'Middleton's Tragicomedies,' 16–18.
82 Pacheco, '"A Mere Cupboard,"' 451.
83 Jackson, *Studies in Attribution*, 123–4, offers some minor stylistic evidence for the presence of Middleton 'in the closing pages of the play.' For a summary of scholarly opinions about the authorship of this section, see Gossett, '*A Fair Quarrel*, Late 1616,' 399. The presence of the word *h'um* at line 431 might seem to indicate Rowley's hand in this sequence, if it is interpreted as an unusual variant of his common spelling of *'um* for *'em*. However, some editors consider it instead a misreading of the word *him*; see Gossett's defence of this reading, textual note to *A Fair Quarrel*, 5.1.431, in Taylor and Lavagnino, *Thomas Middleton and Early Modern Textual Culture*, 637. The authorship of the section thus remains uncertain.
84 Baines, *Lust Motif*, 73; Holdsworth, *Fair Quarrel*, xxvii–xxix; White, *Middleton and Tourneur*, 90–2; Gossett, 'Sibling Power,' 453; Chakravorty, *Society and Politics*, 115–16.
85 Elder brothers took on the authority of deceased fathers over their sisters; see Gossett, 'Sibling Power,' 439–44.
86 Holdsworth, *Fair Quarrel*, xxviii; Gossett, 'Sibling Power,' 453.
87 Levin, *Multiple Plot*, 75.
88 For the former, see Schoenbaum, 'Middleton's Tragicomedies,' 18; Holdsworth, *Fair Quarrel*, xxxix. For the latter, see McElroy, *Parody and Burlesque*, 320.
89 Kistner and Kistner, 'Themes and Structures,' 38.
90 Mooney, '"Common Sight,"' 321–2.
91 Between 1615 and 1617 Prince Charles's Men were performing first at the Hope on Bankside and later at the Red Bull; see Gurr, *Shakespearian Playing Companies*, 401–2. While the Red Bull acquired a reputation for lower-class audiences, there is evidence that gentlemen frequented it too; see Straznicky, 'Red Bull Repertory,' 150–1.

5. A Presence in the Crowd

1. In this and other quotations from *The Spanish Gypsy*, lineation follows Gary Taylor's edition in Taylor and Lavagnino, *Thomas Middleton: The Collected Works*, which corrects the often confused lineation of the original text.
2. Hoy, *Introductions, Notes and Commentaries*, 3:234; Taylor, 'Thomas Middleton, *The Spanish Gypsy*, and Collaborative Authorship,' 269; Taylor, '*Spanish Gypsy*, July 1623,' 433.
3. Lake, *Canon of Thomas Middleton's Plays*, 209–10; Jackson, *Studies in Attribution*, 128–9; see also Gary Taylor's critique of their work in Taylor, '*An/The Old Law*,' 405.
4. Taylor, 'Middleton and Rowley – and Heywood'; Taylor, '*An/The Old Law*,' 405–6.
5. Taylor, 'Thomas Middleton, *The Spanish Gypsy*, and Collaborative Authorship,' 241; Taylor '*Spanish Gypsy*, July 1623,' 433.
6. The case for Ford was first proposed by Sykes, *Sidelights on Elizabethan Drama*, 183–99. Oliphant, *Shakespeare and His Fellow Dramatists*, 2:18, was the first to propose Dekker as co-author in 1929, writing that *The Spanish Gypsy* 'seems in the main to be from the workshop of Ford and Dekker; but there are also a few uncertain signs of Middleton.' The first systematic attempt to prove this assertion was Lake, *Canon of Thomas Middleton's Plays*, 215–30.
7. Taylor, '*Spanish Gypsy*, July 1623,' 433.
8. Ibid., 434.
9. Taylor, 'Thomas Middleton, *The Spanish Gypsy*, and Collaborative Authorship,' 264.
10. Taylor, '*Spanish Gypsy*, July 1623,' 434.
11. Taylor, 'Thomas Middleton, *The Spanish Gypsy*, and Collaborative Authorship' 264–5.
12. Bruster, textual introduction to *The Changeling*, 1094. *The Spanish Gypsy* is actually set in Madrid.
13. Ibid.
14. The addition of an extra 'Thyself' to make sense of this line is Taylor's emendation, following the anonymous annotator of the copy of the quarto in the Dyce collection, who seems to have had access to 'another authoritative source' for the playtext; see Taylor, textual introduction to *The Spanish Gypsy*, 1108.
15. Bullen, *Thomas Middleton*, 6:139n.
16. Bentley, *Jacobean and Caroline Stage*, 4:894.

17 On the variety of characters who could be called 'changelings' in the play, see Holzknecht, 'The Dramatic Structure of *The Changeling.*'
18 Bruster, textual introduction to *The Changeling*, 1094.
19 There are two potential objections to taking the word 'little' to refer to the actor's size. Lake notes that Dekker had a tendency toward 'running to death' the word 'little'; his characters often call others 'my little ...' or 'you little ... ,' with the addition of a choice epithet (Lake, *Canon of Thomas Middleton's Plays*, 84). Although Lake does not apply this observation to *The Spanish Gypsy*, it is worth testing the applicability of this claim. A search conducted with the *Literature Online* database shows that only Dekker's *Satiromastix* and *Blurt, Master Constable* contain a notable preponderance of these phrases, and they are used differently than in *The Spanish Gypsy*. In *Satiromastix*, the phrases are used almost entirely by Tucca, who applies them indiscriminately to many characters; in *Blurt*, they are employed by several characters, again indiscriminately. This is a very different situation to that of *The Spanish Gypsy*, in which the word 'little,' when applied to a person, is only ever applied to Pretiosa, indicating that it is particularly suited to this character. A different argument is offered by Taylor ('*Spanish Gypsy*, July 1623,' 437), who considers the repeated use of the word 'little' to be evidence that the play was inspired directly by the original Spanish source's title, 'Novela de la Gitanilla' (The Story of the Little Gypsy) rather than the French version, which is called instead 'La Belle Égyptienne' (The Beautiful Gypsy). Whether or not this is true, there would still be no point repeating the word 'little' if the actor were tall.
20 However, the anonymous annotator of the quarto in the Dyce collection adjusted this adjective to 'lovely.'
21 In these and subsequent quotations from *The Changeling*, I follow the lineation of Douglas Bruster's edition in Taylor and Lavagnino, *Thomas Middleton: The Collected Works*, which corrects the often-confused lineation of the original text.
22 I am grateful to Jennette White for these insights.
23 The date of composition of *Match Me in London* is uncertain, but it could plausibly have been written for Lady Elizabeth's Men (rather than being revived by them). Cyrus Hoy notes that although Sir Henry Herbert called it an 'Old Play,' this simply means that he was re-licensing a play licensed by his predecessor, Sir George Buc, who retired in May 1622 because of insanity (the same year in which the re-formed Lady Elizabeth's Men began performing in London; see Bentley, *Jacobean and Caroline Stage*, 1:182–3). Hoy dates *Match Me* to 1620–1, but his reason for saying 1621 rather than 1622 is unclear (see Hoy, *Introductions, Notes and Commentaries*, 3:143–8);

the play could have been written by Dekker for Lady Elizabeth's Men in 1622, licensed by Buc, and then re-licensed by Herbert in 1623, and thus originally conceived for the same team of actors as *The Changeling* and *The Spanish Gypsy*.

24 For the satire on tobacco-smoking, see 4.1.213–47.
25 Mulholland, 'The Peacemaker, July 1618,' 404.
26 Nicol, 'Middleton and Rowley's *A Fair Quarrel*.'
27 Cook and Wilson, 'Dramatic Records in the Declared Accounts,' xxvi.
28 See the list of recorded court performances, which for the period concerned is primarily based on the Chamber Accounts, in Astington, *English Court Theatre*, 242–51.
29 Cook and Wilson, 'Dramatic Records in the Declared Accounts,' 67.
30 Quoted in Bentley, *Jacobean and Caroline Stage*, 1:204.
31 Weldon, *The Court and Character of King James*, 77–8.
32 Cust, *Charles I*, 3; on the combative relationship between James and Henry, see Carlton, *Charles I*, 10.
33 Butler, *The Stuart Court Masque and Political Culture*, 423n35.
34 Quoted in Gardiner, *Letters and Other Documents*, 2:148.
35 Kernan, 'What the King Saw, What the Poet Wrote,' 160–1. Finkelpearl also compares the incident to Hamlet; see '"The Comedians' Liberty,"' 127.
36 Quoted in Bentley, *Jacobean and Caroline Stage*, 1:204.
37 Andrew Gurr incorrectly states that the offensive play caused 'infrequency' in the company's court appearances, and even states that it 'did not appear at court at all in the following season'; see Gurr, *Shakespearian Playing Companies*, 405. In fact, they appeared twice a year before the king for two years afterward (Cook and Wilson, 'Dramatic Records in the Declared Accounts,' 74, 76), and the records for the years 1618–22 show that Prince Charles's Men was the second most frequent playing company at the King's court every year (after the King's Men); see ibid., 69–76.
38 Cust, *Charles I*, 3–4.
39 Patterson, *King James VI and I and the Reunion of Christendom*, 303–4.
40 Quoted in Gardiner, *Letters and Other Documents*, 1:140. See also Carlton, *Charles I*, 28.
41 Cust, *Charles I*, 6.
42 Gardiner, *Letters and Other Documents*, 2:148, 149. See also Carlton, *Charles I*, 28.
43 Cust, *Charles I*, 6, 5.
44 Greg, *A Bibliography of the English Printed Drama*, 2:517.
45 The 'Princes Armes' mentioned in the Stationers' Register has been identified either as an inn in Leadenhall (Lawrence, 'Early Substantive Theatre

Masques') or as a rare alternative name for the Swan theatre on Bankside. The latter is more likely, since Rowley's epistle to the reader describes the masque as 'born on the Bankside of Helicon' (11; see Bentley, *Jacobean and Caroline Stage*, 4:910). The masque was probably also performed at the Phoenix, the regular theatre of Prince Charles's Men at the time, since it seems to appear in the repertories of later companies at that theatre (ibid., 4:910–11). Given the interpretation put forward in this chapter, the use of the name 'Prince's Arms' for the Swan is intriguingly appropriate.
46 Martin Butler is the exception among scholars of the play in assuming that the masque *did* receive its court performance; he speculates that the performance took place on 4 March 1620 (Butler, *Stuart Court Masque*, 251 and 423n36).
47 Lawrence, 'Early Substantive Theatre Masques.'
48 Bentley, *Jacobean and Caroline Stage*, 4:909.
49 McGee, introduction to *The World Tossed at Tennis*, 1407 and note to line 867.
50 Butler, 'To Warm the Cold Night,' 14.
51 McGee, *World Tossed Tossed at Tennis*, note to Induction, lines 78–9.
52 Cook and Wilson, 'Dramatic Records in the Declared Accounts,' 148.
53 McGee, *World Tossed at Tennis*, 1406.
54 Ibid., 1406.
55 Yachnin, 'The Populuxe Theatre,' in Yachnin and Dawson, *The Culture of Playgoing in Shakespeare's England: A Collaborative Debate*, 40–3.
56 McGee, *World Tossed at Tennis*, note to line 820.
57 *The Old Law* has traditionally been dated 1618, but Gary Taylor has observed that the topical allusions supporting this date could have had a longer shelf life than has been presumed by earlier scholars; in addition, a 1619 date fits better with his evidence for Heywood's presence; see Taylor, 'Middleton and Rowley – and Heywood,' 167–70, 210–13.
58 Chambers, review of *The King's Office of the Revels*, 482, 484.
59 Carlton, *Charles I*, 25–6; Cust, *Charles I*, 5.
60 Taylor, '*An/The Old Law*,' 406.
61 Cooper, 'Butler, William.'
62 Rowe, *Thomas Middleton and the New Comedy*, 198.
63 Quoted in Carlton, *Charles I*, 29.
64 Bromham, 'Contemporary Significance of *The Old Law*.'
65 Ibid., 331. See also Chakravorty, *Society and Politics*, 119; and Masten, introduction to *An/The Old Law*, 1333.
66 Schoenbaum, 'Middleton's Tragicomedies,' 13.
67 The quarto reads 'nature' for 'mature.'

68 Carlton, *Charles I*, 20–1, 29–30; Bergeron, *Royal Family, Royal Lovers*, 157–60; Cust, *Charles I*, 6.
69 Quoted in Gardiner, *Letters and Other Documents*, 1:140; noted by Carlton, *Charles I*, 29; Cust, *Charles I*, 6. Italics added.
70 Taylor, '*Spanish Gypsy*, July 1623,' 433, 436–7.
71 Carnegie, 'Theatrical Introduction,' 2:290–1.
72 Tilley, *A Dictionary of the Proverbs in England*, T525. The allusion is noted by Christensen, 'Playwrights, Actors and Acting Companies,' 174, but he does not observe the scene's other references to Rowley's roles.
73 For examples in *A Fair Quarrel*, see 2.2.205–40; 4.1.172–82, 215–36; 4.4.148–55, 167–210; 5.1.125–42, 172–84, 310–35. For *The Spanish Gypsy*, see 2.1.173–94; 2.2.166–79; 3.1.31–9, 60–70; 4.1.126–34.
74 Nicol, 'The Date of *The Thracian Wonder*.'
75 Nolan, '*The Thracian Wonder* by William Rowley and Thomas Heywood, 177, notes to 4.2.165 and 171.
76 Bentley, *Jacobean and Caroline Stage*, 2:556; Nicol, 'Repertory of Prince Charles's (I) Company,' 62–3.
77 Christensen, 'Playwrights, Actors and Acting Companies,' 136, 116–23, 150–1.
78 In *The Spanish Gypsy*, Sancho and Soto sing in 2.1, 3.1, twice in 3.2, and twice in 4.1, in addition to dancing at the end of the play. Rowley's clown does not sing or dance in *A New Wonder*, *The Old Law*, *The Birth of Merlin*, *A Wife for a Month*, *Rule a Wife and Have a Wife*, *The Unnatural Combat*, or *A Game at Chess*. Barnaby sings a dirge in *A Shoemaker a Gentleman* (4.3), Chough and Trimtram sing once in *A Fair Quarrel* (5.1), and the Clown sings once in *The Thracian Wonder* (1.2) and dances twice (2.2). In *Wit at Several Weapons*, the clown merely 'Hums "Loath to Depart,"' a popular song (2.2.248). In *All's Lost by Lust*, Jaques may dance at 1.3.119 and sings in 3.3; in *The Witch of Edmonton*, Cuddy dances the Morris once (3.4).
79 Bentley, *Jacobean and Caroline Stage*, 1:205–9; Nicol, 'Repertory of Prince Charles's (I) Company,' 58.

Appendix

1 Taylor and others, 'Works Included,' 335–443.
2 Gurr, *Shakespearian Playing Companies*, 394–415.
3 Young, *A Critical Old-Spelling Edition of 'A Match at Midnight*,' 22–37.
4 Nicol, 'The Date of *The Thracian Wonder*.'
5 Parr, *Three Renaissance Travel Plays*, 8–9, 55n.
6 Doh, *A Critical Edition of 'Fortune by Land and Sea*,' 37.

7 Cheatham, 'A New Wonder,' 19–23. Given the date, it was likely written for Prince Charles's Men; see Nicol, 'The Repertory of Prince Charles's (I) Company,' 63.
8 See chapter 3 for a discussion of the date and company of this play.
9 Nicol, 'Middleton and Rowley's *A Fair Quarrel*.'
10 *A Shoemaker* most likely dates from the late 1610s, before 1620; see Nicol, '*A Shoemaker a Gentleman*.' As such, it was likely written for Prince Charles's Men, given Rowley's status as an attached playwright for the company at that time.
11 On *The Birth of Merlin*, see Bawcutt, *Control and Censorship of Caroline Drama*, 136.
12 Bentley, *Jacobean and Caroline Stage*, 1:205–9.
13 Ibid., 5:1016.
14 See chapter 3 for discussion of Rowley's acting roles.
15 See chapter 3 for discussion of Rowley's acting roles.

Bibliography

Adams, Joseph Quincy. 'The Author Plot of an Early Seventeenth Century Play.' *The Library*, 4th ser., 26 (1945): 17–27.
Aggeler, Geoffrey. *Nobler in the Mind: The Stoic-Sceptic Dialectic in English Renaissance Tragedy*. Newark: University of Delaware Press, 1998.
Amussen, Susan Dwyer. Introduction to *The Peacemaker; or, Great Britain's Blessing*. In Taylor and Lavagnino, *Thomas Middleton: The Collected Works*, 1303–6.
Anderson, Donald K., Jr. *John Ford*. New York: Twayne, 1972.
Aristotle. *Nichomachean Ethics*. In *The Works of Aristotle*, vol. 9. Translated by W.D. Ross. Oxford: Oxford University Press, 1915.
Asp, Carolyn. *A Study of Thomas Middleton's Tragicomedies*. Salzburg: Universität Salzburg, 1974.
Astington, John. *English Court Theatre, 1558–1642*. Cambridge: Cambridge University Press, 1999.
Bacon, Francis. *The Charge of Sir Francis Bacon Knight his Majesties Attourney Generall, Touching Duells*. London: Robert Wilson, 1614. STC 1125.
Baines, Barbara J. *The Lust Motif in the Plays of Thomas Middleton*. Salzburg: Universität Salzburg, 1973.
Bakhtin, Mikhail M. *Rabelais and His World*. 1965. Translated by Hélène Iswolsky. Cambridge, MA: Massachusetts Institute of Technology, 1968.
Baldwin, Thomas Whitfield. *The Organization and Personnel of the Shakespearean Company*. Princeton, NJ: Princeton University Press, 1927.
Bamford, Karen. *Sexual Violence on the Jacobean Stage*. Basingstoke: Macmillan, 2000.
Barber, Charles L. *The Idea of Honour in the English Drama, 1591–1700*. Göteborg: Elanders Boktryckeri Aktiebolog, 1957.
– ed. *A Trick to Catch the Old One*. Berkeley: University of California Press, 1968.

186 Bibliography

Barker, Richard Hindry. *Thomas Middleton*. New York: Columbia University Press, 1958.
Barthelemy, Anthony Gerard. *Black Face, Maligned Race: The Representation of Blacks in English Drama from Shakespeare to Southerne*. Baton Rouge: Louisiana State University Press, 1987.
Bawcutt, N.W., ed. *The Changeling*. London: Methuen, 1958.
– *The Control and Censorship of Caroline Drama: The Records of Sir Henry Herbert, Master of the Revels, 1623–73*. Oxford: Clarendon Press, 1996.
– 'Was Thomas Middleton a Puritan Dramatist?' *Modern Language Review* 94 (1999): 925–39.
Belsey, Catherine. *The Subject of Tragedy: Identity and Difference in Renaissance Tragedy*. London: Methuen, 1985.
Bentley, G.E. *The Jacobean and Caroline Stage*. 7 vols. Oxford: Oxford University Press, 1941–68.
– *The Profession of Dramatist in Shakespeare's Time, 1590–1642*. Princeton, NJ: Princeton University Press, 1971.
– *The Profession of Player in Shakespeare's Time, 1590–1642*. Princeton, NJ: Princeton University Press, 1984.
Bergeron, David M. *Royal Family, Royal Lovers: King James of England and Scotland*. Columbia: University of Missouri Press, 1991.
Berry, Edward. *Shakespeare's Comic Rites*. Cambridge: Cambridge University Press, 1984.
Billington, Sandra. *A Social History of the Fool*. Brighton: Harvester, 1984.
Bliss, Lee. 'Pastiche, Burlesque, Tragicomedy.' In *The Cambridge Companion to Renaissance Drama*, edited by A.R. Braunmuller and Michael Hattaway, 237–61. Cambridge: Cambridge University Press, 1984.
Bly, Mary. *Queer Virgins and Virgin Queans on the Early Modern Stage*. Oxford: Oxford University Press, 2000.
Boehrer, Bruce. 'Alsemero's Closet: Privacy and Interiority in *The Changeling*.' *Journal of English and Germanic Philology* 96, no. 3 (1997): 349–68.
Bolton, Edmund. *The Cities Advocate, in this Case or Question of Honor and Armes; Whether Apprentiship Extinguisheth Gentry?* London: W. Lee, 1629. STC 3219.
Bonahue, Edward T., Jr. 'Citizen History: Stow's *Survey of London*.' *Studies in English Literature* 38 (1998): 61–85.
Bouwsma, William J. 'Hooker in the Context of European Cultural History.' In *Religion and Culture in Renaissance England*, edited by Claire McEachern and Debora Kuller Shuger, 142–58. Cambridge: Cambridge University Press, 1997.
Bowers, Fredson, ed. *The Dramatic Works in the Beaumont and Fletcher Canon*. Cambridge: Cambridge University Press, 1966–96.

- ed. *The Dramatic Works of Thomas Dekker*. Cambridge: Cambridge University Press, 1953–61.
- 'Middleton's *Fair Quarrel* and the Duelling Code.' *Journal of English and Germanic Philology* 36 (1937): 40–65.
- Textual introduction to *The Fair Maid of the Inn*. In Bowers, *The Dramatic Works in the Beaumont and Fletcher Canon*, 10: 555–7.

Bradbrook, M.C. *Themes and Conventions of Elizabethan Tragedy*. 1935. Reprint, Cambridge: Cambridge University Press, 1960.

Breton, Nicholas. *The Good and the Badde, or Descriptions of the Worthies, and Unworthies of this Age*. London: George Purslowe for John Budge, 1616. STC 3656.

Bristol, Michael D. *Carnival and Theater: Plebeian Culture and the Structure of Authority in Renaissance England*. New York: Routledge, 1985.

Brittin, Norman. *Thomas Middleton*. New York: Twayne, 1972.

Bromham, A.A. 'The Contemporary Significance of *The Old Law*.' *Studies in English Literature* 24 (1984): 327–39.

Bromham, A.A., and Zara Bruzzi. *'The Changeling' and the Years of Crisis, 1619–1624: A Hieroglyph of Britain*. London: Pinter, 1990.

Bromham, A.A., and Mark Hutchings. *Middleton and His Collaborators*. Horndon: Northcote House, 2008.

Brooks, Douglas A. *From Playhouse to Printing House: Drama and Authorship in Early Modern England*. Cambridge: Cambridge University Press, 2000.

Bruster, Douglas. Textual introduction to *The Changeling*. In Taylor and Lavagnino, *Thomas Middleton and Early Modern Textual Culture*, 1094–6.

Bullen, A.H., ed. *Thomas Middleton*. 8 vols. London: John C. Nimmo, 1885.

Burke, Peter. *Popular Culture in Early Modern Europe*. London: Temple Smith, 1978.

Burke, Seán. 'Introduction: Reconstructing the Author.' In *Authorship: From Plato to the Postmodern: A Reader*, xv–xxx. Edinburgh: Edinburgh University Press, 1995.

Burks, Deborah G. '"I'll Want My Will Else": *The Changeling* and Women's Complicity with Their Rapists.' *English Literary History* 62 (1995): 759–90.

Burnett, Mark Thornton. *Masters and Servants in English Renaissance Drama and Culture: Authority and Obedience*. Basingstoke: Macmillan, 1997.

Burns, Edward, ed. *King Henry VI, Part 1*. London: Arden Shakespeare, 2000.

Burton, Robert. *The Anatomy of Melancholy*. 1628. Edited by Thomas C. Faulkner and others. 6 vols. Oxford: Clarendon Press, 1989–2000.

Butler, Martin. *The Stuart Court Masque and Political Culture*. Cambridge: Cambridge University Press, 2008.

- *Theatre and Crisis, 1632–1642*. Cambridge: Cambridge University Press, 1984.

- 'To Warm the Cold Night.' *Times Literary Supplement*, 7 December 2007, 13–14.
Calvin, John. *The Institution of Christian Religion*. Translated by Thomas Norton. London: Reinolde Wolfe and Richarde Harrison, 1561. STC 4415.
Capp, Bernard. *The World of John Taylor the Water-Poet, 1578–1653*. Oxford: Oxford University Press, 1994.
Carlton, Charles. *Charles I: The Personal Monarch*. London: Routledge and Kegan Paul, 1983.
Carnegie, David. 'Theatrical Introduction.' In Hammond, Gunby, Carnegie, and Jackson, *The Works of John Webster*, 2:282–93.
Carroll, William C., ed. *Women Beware Women*. London: A & C Black, 1994.
Cathcart, Charles. 'Plural Authorship, Attribution, and the Children of the King's Revels.' In *Renaissance Forum* 4, no. 2 (2000). http://www.hull.ac.uk/renforum/v40no2/cathcart.htm.
Centerwall, Brandon. 'A Greatly Exaggerated Demise: The Remaking of the Children of Paul's as the Duke of York's Men (1608).' *Early Theatre* 9 (2006): 85–107.
Cerasano, S.P. 'Competition for the King's Men? Alleyn's Blackfriars Venture.' *Medieval and Renaissance Drama in England* 4 (1989): 173–86.
Chakravorty, Swapan. *Society and Politics in the Plays of Thomas Middleton*. Oxford: Clarendon Press, 1996.
Chambers, E.K. 'The Disintegration of Shakespeare.' 1924. Reprinted in *Aspects of Shakespeare*, edited by J.W. Mackail, 23–48. Oxford: Oxford University Press, 1933.
- *The Elizabethan Stage*. 4 vols. Oxford: Clarendon Press, 1923.
- Review of *The King's Office of the Revels, 1610–1622*, by Frank Marcham. *Review of English Studies* 1 (1925): 479–84.
Chambers, E.K., and W.W. Greg. 'Dramatic Records from the Patent Rolls: Company Licenses.' In *Malone Society Collections 1*, 3:260–84. Oxford: Oxford University Press, 1909.
Cheatham, George, ed. *'A New Wonder, a Woman Never Vext': An Old-Spelling Critical Edition*. New York: Peter Lang, 1993.
Cherry, Caroline Lockett. *The Most Unvaluedst Purchase: Women in the Plays of Thomas Middleton*. Salzburg: Universität Salzburg, 1973.
Chillington, Carol A. 'Playwrights at Work: Henslowe's, Not Shakespeare's *Book of Sir Thomas More*.' *English Literary Renaissance* 10 (1980): 439–79.
Christensen, Nels Anchor. 'Playwrights, Actors and Acting Companies: Domains of Collaboration in Middleton-Rowley's *A Fair Quarrel*, *The Changeling* and *The Spanish Gypsy* (1615–23).' PhD diss., Michigan State University, 2005.

Cohen, Walter. *Drama of a Nation: Public Theater in Renaissance England and Spain*. Ithaca, NY: Cornell University Press, 1985.
Cook, David, and F.P. Wilson, eds. 'Dramatic Records in the Declared Accounts of the Treasurer of the Chamber, 1558–1642.' *Malone Society Collections 6*, 1–175. Oxford: Oxford University Press, 1962.
Cooper, Thompson. 'Butler, William (1535–1618).' Revised by Sarah Bakewell. In *Oxford Dictionary of National Biography*, edited by H.C.G. Matthew and Brian Harrison. Oxford: Oxford University Press, 2004. Online ed., edited by Lawrence Goldman, 2008. http://www.oxforddnb.com/view/article/4217.
Corbin, Peter, and Douglas Sedge, eds. *The Witch of Edmonton*. Manchester: Manchester University Press, 1999.
Craig, Hugh. 'Style, Statistics, and New Models of Authorship.' *Early Modern Literary Studies* 15, no. 1 (2009–10). http://purl.oclc.org/emls/15-1/craistyl.htm.
Cust, Richard. *Charles I: A Political Life*. Harlow: Pearson, 2007.
Daalder, Joost, ed. *The Changeling*. 5th impr. London: A & C Black, 1995.
– 'Folly and Madness in *The Changeling*.' *Essays in Criticism* 38 (1988): 1–21.
– 'The Role of Isabella in *The Changeling*.' *English Studies* 73 (1992): 22–9.
Daileader, Celia R. *Eroticism on the Renaissance Stage: Transcendence, Desire and the Limits of the Visible*. Cambridge: Cambridge University Press, 1998.
Darby, Trudi L., ed. *A Critical, Old-Spelling Edition of William Rowley's 'A New Wonder, A Woman Never Vexed.'* New York: Garland, 1988.
Dawson, Anthony B. '*Women Beware Women* and the Economy of Rape.' *Studies in English Literature* 27 (1987): 303–20.
De Grazia, Margreta, and Peter Stallybrass. 'Love among the Ruins: Response to Pechter.' *Textual Practice* 11 (1997): 69–79.
– 'The Materiality of the Shakespearean Text.' *Shakespeare Quarterly* 44 (1993): 255–83.
Dekker, Thomas. *The Guls Horn-booke*. London: R.S., 1609. STC 6500.
– *The Magnificent Entertainment Given to King James, Queene Anne his Wife, and Henry Frederick the Prince*. Edinburgh: Thomas Finlason, 1604. STC 6512.
– *A Tragi-Comedy: Called, Match Mee in London*. London: H. Seile, 1631. STC 6529.
Dekker, Thomas, John Ford, and William Rowley. *The Witch of Edmonton: A Known True Story. Composed into a Tragi-Comedy*. London: Edward Blackmore, 1658. Wing R2097.
Dent, Arthur. *The Plaine Mans Path-Way to Heaven*. 1601. 6th impr., London: R. Dexter, 1603. STC 6627.
Dobson, Michael. Introduction to *Wit at Several Weapons*. In Taylor and Lavagnino, *Thomas Middleton: The Collected Works*, 980–2.

- 'Wit at Several Weapons, Late 1613.' In Taylor and Lavagnino, *Thomas Middleton and Early Modern Textual Culture*, 375–7.
Doh, Herman, ed. *A Critical Edition of 'Fortune by Land and Sea,' by Thomas Heywood and William Rowley*. New York: Garland, 1980.
Dollimore, Jonathan. *Radical Tragedy: Religion, Ideology and Power in the Drama of Shakespeare and His Contemporaries*. 2nd ed. Brighton: Harvester, 1989.
Dunkel, W.F. 'Did Not Rowley Merely Revise Middleton?' *Papers of the Modern Language Association* 48 (1933): 799–805.
Dunlap, Rhodes. 'James I, Bacon, Middleton and the Making of *The Peace-Maker*.' In *Studies in the English Renaissance Drama*, edited by Josephine Bennett, Oscar Cargill, and Vernon Hall, Jr., 82–94. New York: New York University Press, 1959.
Dutton, Richard, ed. *'Women Beware Women' and Other Plays*. Oxford: Oxford University Press, 1999.
Dyer, Richard. *Heavenly Bodies: Film Stars and Society*. Basingstoke: Macmillan, 1987.
Dyke, Daniel. *The Mystery of Selfe-Deceiving, or a Discourse and Discovery of the Deceitfulnesse of Mans Heart*. London: Ralph Mab, 1614. STC 7398.
Early English Books Online. http://eebo.chadwyck.com/home.
Eaton, Sara. 'Beatrice-Joanna and the Rhetoric of Love.' 1984. Reprinted in *Staging the Renaissance: Reinterpretations of Elizabethan and Jacobean Drama*, edited by David Scott Kastan and Peter Stallybrass, 275–89. London: Routledge, 1991.
Eccles, Mark. 'Brief Lives: Tudor and Stuart Authors.' *Studies in Philology* 79, no. 4 (1982): 1–135.
Edwards, Philip, and Colin Gibson, eds. *The Plays and Poems of Philip Massinger*. 5 vols. Oxford: Oxford University Press, 1976.
Eliot, T.S. 'Thomas Middleton.' 1927. Reprinted in *Elizabethan Dramatists*, 83–93. London: Faber, 1962.
Ellis-Fermor, Una. *The Jacobean Drama: An Interpretation*. 2nd ed. London: Methuen, 1947.
Empson, William. 'Double Plots: Heroic and Pastoral in the Main Plot and Sub-Plot'. In *Some Versions of Pastoral*, 27–86. 1935. 3rd impr. London: Chatto & Windus, 1968.
Engleberg, Edward. 'A Middleton-Rowley Dispute.' *Notes and Queries* 198 (1953): 330–2.
- 'Tragic Blindness in *The Changeling* and *Women Beware Women*.' *Modern Language Quarterly* 23 (1962): 20–8.
Evans, G. Blakemore, ed. *The Riverside Shakespeare*. Boston: Houghton Mifflin, 1974.

Farley-Hills, David. *Jacobean Drama: A Critical Study of the Professional Drama, 1600–25*. Basingstoke: Macmillan, 1988.

Farr, Dorothy M. *Thomas Middleton and the Drama of Realism*. Edinburgh: Oliver and Boyd, 1973.

Felver, Charles S. *Robert Armin, Shakespeare's Fool: A Biographical Essay*. Kent, OH: Kent State University, 1961.

Ferrell, Lori Anne. Introduction to *The Two Gates of Salvation*. In Taylor and Lavagnino, *Thomas Middleton: The Collected Works*, 679–82.

Finkelpearl, Philip. '"The Comedians' Liberty": Censorship of the Jacobean Stage Reconsidered.' *English Literary Renaissance* 16 (1986): 123–38.

Fletcher, John. *Rule a Wife and Have a Wife. A Comedy*. Oxford: Leonard Lichfield, 1640. STC 11073.

– 'A Wife for a Moneth.' In *Comedies and Tragedies Written by Francis Beaumont and John Fletcher*. London: Humphrey Robinson and Humphrey Moseley, 1647. Wing B1581.

Foucault, Michel. 'What Is an Author?' 1979. Translated by Josué V. Harari. Reprinted in *The Foucault Reader*, edited by Paul Rabinow, 101–20. Harmondsworth: Penguin, 1984.

Frost, David L. *The School of Shakespeare: The Influence of Shakespeare on English Drama, 1600–42*. Cambridge: Cambridge University Press, 1968.

– ed. *The Selected Plays of Thomas Middleton*. Cambridge: Cambridge University Press, 1978.

Garber, Marjorie. 'The Insincerity of Women.' In *Desire in the Renaissance: Psychoanalysis and Literature*, edited by Valeria Finucci and Regina Schwartz, 19–38. Princeton, NJ: Princeton University Press, 1994.

Gardiner, S.R., ed. *Letters and Other Documents Illustrating the Relations Between England and Germany at the Commencement of the Thirty Years' War*. 2 vols. London: Camden Society, 1885–9.

George, Charles H., and Katherine George. *The Protestant Mind of the English Reformation, 1570–1640*. Princeton, NJ: Princeton University Press, 1961.

Gibbons, Brian. *Jacobean City Comedy: A Study of Satiric Plays by Jonson, Marston and Middleton*. 2nd ed. London: Methuen, 1980.

Golding, Arthur, trans. *Ovid's Metamorphoses: The Arthur Golding Translation, 1567*. Edited by John Frederick Nims. New York: Macmillan, 1965.

Gosse, Edmund. *The Jacobean Poets*. London: John Murray, 1894.

Gossett, Suzanne. 'Editing Collaborative Drama.' *Shakespeare Survey* 59 (2006): 213–24.

– '*A Fair Quarrel*, Late 1616.' In Taylor and Lavagnino, *Thomas Middleton and Early Modern Textual Culture*, 398–400.

– Introduction to *A Fair Quarrel*. In Taylor and Lavagnino, *Thomas Middleton: The Collected Works*, 1209–12.

- 'Major/Minor, Main Plot/Subplot, Middleton/and.' *The Elizabethan Theatre* 15 (2002): 21–38.
- 'Sibling Power: Middleton and Rowley's *A Fair Quarrel*.' *Philological Quarterly* 71 (1992): 437–57.
- Textual introduction to *A Fair Quarrel*. In Taylor and Lavagnino, *Thomas Middleton and Early Modern Textual Culture*, 633–5.
- Textual notes to *A Fair Quarrel*. In Taylor and Lavagnino, *Thomas Middleton and Early Modern Textual Culture*, 636–7.

Grady, Hugh. 'Disintegration and Its Reverberations.' In *The Appropriation of Shakespeare: Post-Renaissance Reconstructions of the Works and the Myth*, edited by Jean I. Marsden, 111–27. Hemel Hempstead: Harvester, 1991.

Greenblatt, Stephen. 'Towards a Poetics of Culture.' In *The New Historicism*, edited by H. Aram Veeser, 1–12. New York: Routledge, 1989.

Greg, W.W. *A Bibliography of the English Printed Drama to the Restoration*. 4 vols. London: Oxford University Press, 1939–59.

Gunby, David, 'Critical Introduction.' In Hammond, Gunby, Carnegie, and Jackson, *The Works of John Webster*, 2:264–81.

- 'Rowley, William (1585?–1626).' In *Oxford Dictionary of National Biography*, edited by H.C.G. Matthew and Brian Harrison. Oxford: Oxford University Press, 2004. Online ed., edited by Lawrence Goldman, 2008. http://www.oxforddnb.com/view/article/24227.

Gurr, Andrew. *The Shakespeare Company, 1594–1642*. Cambridge: Cambridge University Press, 2004.

- *The Shakespearian Playing Companies*. Oxford: Clarendon Press, 1996.

Hallett, Charles A., and Elaine S. Hallett. *The Revenger's Madness: A Study of Revenge Tragedy Motifs*. Lincoln: University of Nebraska Press, 1980.

Hammond, Anthony, David Gunby, David Carnegie, and MacDonald P. Jackson, eds. *The Works of John Webster*. Cambridge: Cambridge University Press, 1995–2008.

Harbage, Alfred. *Shakespeare and the Rival Traditions*. New York: Macmillan, 1952.

Heath, Stephen. *Questions of Cinema*. Bloomington: Indiana University Press, 1981.

Heinemann, Margot. *Puritanism and Theatre: Thomas Middleton and Opposition Politics under the Early Stuarts*. Cambridge: Cambridge University Press, 1980.

Helgerson, Richard. *Forms of Nationhood: The Elizabethan Writing of England*. Chicago: University of Chicago Press, 1992.

Heller, Herbert Jack. *Penitent Brothellers: Grace, Sexuality and Genre in Thomas Middleton's City Comedies*. Newark: University of Delaware Press, 2000.

Herford, C.H., and Percy Simpson, eds. *Ben Jonson*. Vol. 4. Oxford: Clarendon Press, 1932.
Herndl, George C. *The High Design: English Renaissance Tragedy and the Natural Law*. Lexington: University of Kentucky, 1970.
Heywood, Thomas, and William Rowley. *Fortune by Land and Sea. A Tragicomedy*. London: John Sweeting and Robert Pollard, 1655. Wing H1783.
Hillman, Richard. *Self-Speaking in Medieval and Early Modern English Drama: Subjectivity, Discourse and the Stage*. Basingstoke: Macmillan, 1997.
Hirschfield, Heather Anne. *Joint Enterprises: Collaborative Drama and the Institutionalization of the English Renaissance Theater*. Amherst: University of Massachusetts Press, 2004.
Holdsworth, R.V., ed. *A Fair Quarrel*. London: Ernest Benn, 1974.
Holmes, David M. *The Art of Thomas Middleton: A Critical Study*. Oxford: Clarendon Press, 1970.
Holzknecht, Karl L. 'The Dramatic Structure of *The Changeling*.' 1954. Reprinted in *Shakespeare's Contemporaries*, edited by Max Bluestone and Norman Rabkin, 263–72. Englewood Cliffs, NJ: Pentice-Hall, 1961.
Honigmann, E.A.J. 'Shakespeare as a Reviser.' In *Textual Criticism and Literary Interpretation*, edited by Jerome J. McGann, 1–22. Chicago: University of Chicago Press, 1985.
Hoopes, Robert. *Right Reason in the English Renaissance*. Cambridge, MA: Harvard University Press, 1962.
Howard, Jean. 'Sex and Social Conflict: The Erotics of *The Roaring Girl*.' In *Erotic Politics on the Renaissance Stage*, edited by Susan Zimmerman, 170–90. London: Routledge, 1992.
Howard-Hill, T.H., ed. *A Game at Chess*. Manchester: Manchester University Press, 1993.
– *Middleton's 'Vulgar Pasquin': Essays on 'A Game at Chess.'* London: Associated University Presses, 1995.
– 'Political Interpretations of Middleton's *A Game at Chess* (1624).' *Yearbook of English Studies* 21 (1991): 274–85.
– 'William Rowley.' In *Dictionary of Literary Biography*. Vol. 58, *Jacobean and Caroline Dramatists*, edited by Fredson Bowers, 241–8. Detroit: Bruccoli Clark Layman, 1987.
Hoy, Cyrus. 'Critical and Aesthetic Problems of Collaboration in Renaissance Drama.' *Research Opportunities in Renaissance Drama* 19 (1976): 3–6.
– *Introductions, Notes and Commentaries to Texts in 'The Dramatic Works of Thomas Dekker.'* 4 vols. Cambridge: Cambridge University Press, 1980.
– 'Massinger as Collaborator: The Plays with Fletcher and Others.' In *Philip Massinger: A Critical Reassessment*, edited by Douglas Howard, 51–82. Cambridge: Cambridge University Press, 1985.

- 'The Shares of Fletcher and His Collaborators in the Beaumont and Fletcher Canon (I).' *Studies in Bibliography* 8 (1956): 129–46.
- 'The Shares of Fletcher and His Collaborators in the Beaumont and Fletcher Canon (V).' *Studies in Bibliography* 13 (1960): 77–108.
- 'The Shares of Fletcher and His Collaborators in the Beaumont and Fletcher Canon (VII).' *Studies in Bibliography* 15 (1962): 71–90.

Hunter, George K. 'Bourgeois Comedy: Shakespeare and Dekker.' In *Shakespeare and His Contemporaries: Essays in Comparison*, edited by E.A.J. Honigmann, 1–15. Manchester University Press, 1986.
- *The Oxford History of English Literature*. Vol. 6, *English Drama, 1586–1642: The Age of Shakespeare*. Oxford: Oxford University Press, 1997.

Jackson, MacDonald P. *Defining Shakespeare: 'Pericles' as Test Case*. Oxford: Oxford University Press, 2003.
- 'Early Modern Authorship: Canons and Chronologies.' In Taylor and Lavagnino, *Thomas Middleton and Early Modern Textual Culture*, 80–97.
- *Studies in Attribution: Middleton and Shakespeare*. Salzburg: Universität Salzburg, 1979.

Jameson, Fredric. *The Political Unconscious: Narrative as a Socially Symbolic Act*. London: Methuen, 1981.

Johnson, Nora. *The Actor as Playwright in Early Modern Drama*. Cambridge: Cambridge University Press, 2003.

Jowett, John. Introduction to *No Wit/Help Like a Woman's*. In Taylor and Lavagnino, *Thomas Middleton: The Collected Works*, 779–83.
- 'Middleton and Debt in *Timon of Athens*.' In *Money and the Age of Shakespeare*, edited by Linda Woodbridge, 219–36. Basingstoke: Palgrave, 2003.
- 'The Pattern of Collaboration in *Timon of Athens*.' In *Words That Count: Essays on Early Modern Authorship in Honor of MacDonald P. Jackson*, edited by Brian Boyd, 181–208. Cranbury: Associated University Presses, 2004.
- ed. *Timon of Athens*. Oxford: Oxford University Press, 2004.
- 'Varieties of Collaboration in Shakespeare's Problem Plays and Late Plays.' In *A Companion to Shakespeare's Works*, edited by Richard Dutton and Jean E. Howard, 4:106–28. Oxford: Blackwell, 2003.

Kernan, Alvin. 'What the King Saw, What the Poet Wrote.' In *Time, Memory, and the Verbal Arts: Essays on the Thought of Walter Ong*, edited by Dennis L. Weeks and Jane Hoogestraat, 155–68. Selinsgrove, PA: Susquehanna University Press, 1998.

Kewes, Paulina. *Authorship and Appropriation: Writing for the Stage in England, 1660–1710*. Oxford: Oxford University Press, 1998.

Kirsch, Arthur. *Jacobean Dramatic Perspectives*. Charlottesville: University Press of Virginia, 1972.

Kistner, A.L., and M.K. Kistner. 'The Themes and Structures of *A Fair Quarrel.*' *Tennessee Studies in Literature* 23 (1978): 31–46.
Knapp, Jeffrey. *Shakespeare Only*. Chicago: University of Chicago Press, 2009.
– 'What Is a Co-Author?' *Representations* 89 (2005): 1–29.
Knights, L.C. *Drama and Society in the Age of Jonson*. 1937. Reprint, London: Chatto & Windus, 1962.
Knowles, Ronald, ed. *King Henry VI, Part II*. London: Thomson Learning, 1999.
Knutson, Roslyn Lander. *The Repertory of Shakespeare's Company, 1594–1613*. Fayetteville: University of Arkansas Press, 1991.
Lake, David J. *The Canon of Thomas Middleton's Plays*. Cambridge: Cambridge University Press, 1975.
Lake, Peter. *Moderate Puritans and the Elizabethan Church*. Cambridge: Cambridge University Press, 1982.
Lamb, Charles. *Specimens of English Dramatic Poets*. 2 vols. Edited by William MacDonald. London: J.M. Dent, 1903.
Langbaine, Gerard. *An Account of the English Dramatick Poets*. Oxford: L.L. for George West and Henry Clements, 1691. Wing L373.
Laroque, François. *Shakespeare's Festive World: Elizabethan Seasonal Entertainment and the Professional Stage*. Translated by Janet Lloyd. Cambridge: Cambridge University Press, 1991.
Lawrence, W.J. 'Early Substantive Theatre Masques.' *Times Literary Supplement*, 8 December 1921, 814.
Leggatt, Alexander. *Citizen Comedy in the Age of Shakespeare*. Toronto: University of Toronto Press, 1976.
– *Jacobean Public Theatre*. London: Routledge, 1992.
Leinwand, Theodore B. *The City Staged: Jacobean Comedy, 1603–13*. Madison: University of Wisconsin Press, 1986.
Leishman, J.B., ed. *The Three Parnassus Plays (1598–1601)*. London: Nicholson and Watson, 1949.
Levin, Richard. *The Multiple Plot in English Renaissance Drama*. Chicago: University of Chicago Press, 1971.
– 'Tarlton in *The Famous History of Friar Bacon and Friar Bungay.*' *Medieval and Renaissance Drama in England* 12 (1999): 84–98.
Literature Online. http://lion.chadwyck.com/marketing/index.jsp.
Little, Arthur L., Jr. '"Trans-Shaped" Women: Virginity and Hysteria in *The Changeling.*' *Themes in Drama* 15 (1993): 19–42.
Malcolmson, Christina. '"As Tame as the Ladies": Politics and Gender in *The Changeling.*' *English Literary Renaissance* 20 (1990): 320–39.

Manley, Lawrence. *Literature and Culture in Early Modern London*. Cambridge: Cambridge University Press, 1995.

Marcham, Frank. *The King's Office of the Revels 1610–1622: Fragments of Documents in the Department of Manuscripts, British Museum*. London: Frank Marcham, 1925.

Masten, Jeffrey. 'Beaumont and/or Fletcher: Collaboration and the Interpretation of Renaissance Drama.' *English Literary History* 59 (1992): 337–56.

– 'Family Values: Euthanasia, Editing and *The Old Law*.' *Textual Practice* 9 (1995): 445–58.

– Introduction to *An/The Old Law*. In Taylor and Lavagnino, *Thomas Middleton: The Collected Works*, 1331–4.

– '*More* or Less: Editing the Collaborative.' *Shakespeare Studies* 29 (2001): 109–31.

– ed. *An/The Old Law*. In Taylor and Lavagnino, *Thomas Middleton: The Collected Works*, 1335–96.

– 'Playwriting: Authorship and Collaboration.' In *A New History of Early English Drama*, edited by John D. Cox and David Scott Kastan, 357–82. New York: Columbia University Press, 1997.

– *Textual Intercourse: Collaboration, Authorship and Sexualities in Renaissance Drama*. Cambridge: Cambridge University Press, 1997.

Maxwell, Baldwin. 'The Attitude toward the Duello in the Beaumont and Fletcher Plays.' In *Studies in Beaumont, Fletcher and Massinger*, 84–106. 1939. Reprint, New York: Octagon, 1966.

McAlindon, T. *English Renaissance Tragedy*. Basingstoke: Macmillan, 1986.

McCabe, Richard. *Incest, Drama and Nature's Law, 1550–1700*. Cambridge: Cambridge University Press, 1993.

McElroy, John F. *Parody and Burlesque in the Tragicomedies of Thomas Middleton*. Salzburg: Universität Salzburg, 1972.

McGann, Jerome. *A Critique of Modern Textual Criticism*. Chicago: Chicago University Press, 1983.

McGee, C.E. Introduction to *The World Tossed at Tennis*. In Taylor and Lavagnino, *Thomas Middleton: The Collected Works*, 1405–8.

– ed. *The World Tossed at Tennis*. In Taylor and Lavagnino, *Thomas Middleton: The Collected Works*, 1408–30.

McKeithan, D.M. *The Debt to Shakespeare in the Beaumont and Fletcher Plays*. 1938. Reprint, New York: AMS, 1970.

McLuskie, Kathleen. *Dekker and Heywood*. Basingstoke: Macmillan, 1994.

– 'The Plays and Playwrights, 1613–42.' In *The Revels History of Drama in English*. Vol. 4, *1613–1642*, edited by G.E. Bentley and others, 127–252. London: Methuen, 1981.

McMillin, Scott, and Sally-Beth MacLean. *The Queen's Men and Their Plays*. Cambridge: Cambridge University Press, 1998.
McMullan, Gordon, ed. *King Henry VIII*. London: Thomson Learning, 2000.
– '"Our Whole Life Is Like a Play": Collaboration and the Problem of Editing.' *Textus: English Studies in Italy* 9 (1996): 437–60.
– *The Politics of Unease in the Plays of John Fletcher*. Amherst: University of Massachusetts Press, 1994.
– 'A Rose for Emilia: Collaborative Relations in *The Two Noble Kinsmen*.' In *Renaissance Configurations: Voices/Bodies/Spaces, 1580–1690*, 129–47. London: Macmillan, 1998.
Mexia, Pedro. *The Foreste, or Collection of Historyes, Dooen out of Frenche*. Translated by T. Fortescue (from the translation from Spanish of C. Gruget). 2nd ed. London: J. Day, 1576. STC 17850.
Middleton, Thomas. *A Game at Chess*. Edited by T.H. Howard-Hill. Oxford: Oxford University Press, 1990.
– *Hengist, King of Kent*. Edited by Grace Ioppolo. Oxford: Oxford University Press, 2003.
– *Michaelmas Terme*. London: A.I., 1607. STC 17890.
– *The Peace-Maker: or, Great Brittaines Blessing*. London: Thomas Purfoot, 1618. STC 14387.
– *The Revengers Tragaedie*. London: G. Eld, 1607. STC 24149.
– *The Second Maiden's Tragedy*. Edited by W.W. Greg. Oxford: Oxford University Press, 1910.
– 'Women Beware Women'. In *Two New Playes*. London: Humphrey Moseley. 1657. Wing M1989.
Middleton, Thomas, and Thomas Dekker. *The Roaring Girle. Or Moll Cut-Purse*. London: Thomas Archer, 1611. STC 17908.
Middleton, Thomas, and William Rowley. *The Changeling*. London: Humphrey Moseley, 1653. Wing M1980.
– *A Courtly Masque: The Device Called The World Tost at Tennis*. STC 17909.
– *The Excellent Comedy Called, The Old Law, or, A New Way to Please You*. London: Edward Archer, 1656. Wing M1048.
– *A Faire Quarrell with New Additions of Mr. Chaughs and Trimtrams Roaring, and the Bauds Song, Never Before Printed*. London: I.T., 1617. STC 17911a.
– *The Spanish Gipsie*. London: Richard Marriot, 1653. Wing M1986.
– 'Wit at Severall Weapons.' In *Comedies and Tragedies Written by Francis Beaumont and John Fletcher*. London: Humphrey Robinson and Humphrey Moseley, 1647. Wing B1581.
Milton, Anthony. *Catholic and Reformed: The Roman and Protestant Churches in*

English Protestant Thought, 1600–1640. Cambridge: Cambridge University Press, 1995.
Mooney, Michael E. '"The Common Sight": Rowley's Embedded Jig in *A Fair Quarrel*.' *Studies in English Literature* 20 (1980): 305–23.
– '"Framing" as Collaborative Technique: Two Middleton-Rowley Plays.' *Comparative Drama* 13 (1979): 127–41.
Morrison, Peter. 'A Cangoun in Zombieland: Middleton's Teratological Changeling.' In *'Accompaninge the Players': Essays Celebrating Thomas Middleton, 1580–1980*, edited by Kenneth Friedenreich, 219–41. New York: AMS, 1983.
A Most Pleasant Comedie of Mucedorus. London: William Jones, 1610. STC 18232.
Mulholland, Paul, '*The Peacemaker*, July 1618.' In Taylor and Lavagnino, *Thomas Middleton and Early Modern Textual Culture*, 402–4.
– ed. *The Peacemaker*. In Taylor and Lavagnino, *Thomas Middleton: The Collected Works*, 1306–19.
– '*The Two Gates of Salvation*: Typology, and Thomas Middleton's Bibles.' *English Language Notes* 23, no. 2 (1985): 27–36.
Munro, Lucy. *Children of the Queen's Revels: A Jacobean Theatre Repertory*. Cambridge: Cambridge University Press, 2005.
Naremore, James. *Acting in the Cinema*. Berkeley: University of California Press, 1988.
Neill, Michael. *Issues of Death: Mortality and Identity in English Renaissance Tragedy*. Oxford: Oxford University Press, 1997.
Nicol, David. 'The Date of *The Thracian Wonder*.' *Notes and Queries* 253 (2008): 223–5.
– 'Interrogating the Devil: Social and Demonic Pressure in *The Witch of Edmonton*.' *Comparative Drama* 38 (2004): 425–45.
– 'Middleton and Rowley's *A Fair Quarrel* at the Court of King James.' *Notes and Queries* 254 (2009): 201–3.
– 'The Repertory of Prince Charles's (I) Company, 1608–1625.' *Early Theatre* 9, no. 2 (2006): 57–72.
– '*A Shoemaker a Gentleman*: Dates, Sources and Influence.' *Notes and Queries* 248 (2003): 441–3.
– 'The Title Page of *The World Tossed at Tennis*: A Portrait of a Jacobean Playing Company?' *Notes and Queries* 251 (2006): 158–9.
Nochimson, Richard L. '"Sharing" *The Changeling* by Playwrights and Professors: The Certainty of Uncertain Knowledge about Collaboration.' *Early Theatre* 5 (2002): 37–57.
Nolan, Michael, ed. *'The Thracian Wonder' by William Rowley and Thomas Heywood: A Critical Edition*. Salzburg: Universität Salzburg, 1997.

Oliphant, E.H.C. *Shakespeare and His Fellow Dramatists*. New York: Prentice-Hall, 1929.
Oliver, H.J. *The Problem of John Ford*. Melbourne: Melbourne University Press, 1955.
Orgel, Stephen. 'What Is a Text?' 1981. Reprinted in *Staging the Renaissance: Reinterpretations of Elizabethan and Jacobean Drama*, edited by David Scott Kastan and Peter Stallybrass, 83–7. London: Routledge, 1991.
– 'What Is an Editor?' *Shakespeare Studies* 24 (1996): 23–9.
Orlin, Lena Cowen. *Private Matters and Public Culture in Post-Reformation England*. Ithaca, NY: Cornell University Press, 1994.
Orrell, John. 'The London Stage in the Florentine Correspondence, 1604–1618.' *Theatre Research International* 3 (1978): 157–76.
Ovid. *Metamorphoses*. Translated by Frank Justur Miller. London: Heinemann, 1946.
Pacheco, Anita. '"A Mere Cupboard of Glasses": Female Sexuality and Male Honor in *A Fair Quarrel*.' *English Literary Renaissance* 28 (1998): 441–63.
Palfrey, Simon, and Tiffany Stern. *Shakespeare in Parts*. Oxford: Oxford University Press, 2007.
Parker, Brian. '*A Fair Quarrel* (1617), the Duelling Code and Jacobean Law.' In *Rough Justice: Essays on Crime in Literature*, edited by M.L. Friedland, 52–75. Toronto: University of Toronto Press, 1991.
Parr, Anthony, ed. *The Staple of News*. Manchester: Manchester University Press, 1988.
– ed. *Three Renaissance Travel Plays*. Manchester: Manchester University Press, 1995.
Partridge, Eric. *Shakespeare's Bawdy*. Rev. ed. London: Routledge and Kegan Paul, 1968.
Patterson, Annabel. *Shakespeare and the Popular Voice*. Oxford: Basil Blackwell, 1989.
Patterson, W.B. 'Dominis, Marco Antonio de (1560–1624).' In *Oxford Dictionary of National Biography*, edited by H.C.G. Matthew and Brian Harrison. Oxford: Oxford University Press, 2004. Online ed., edited by Lawrence Goldman, January 2008. http://www.oxforddnb.com/view/article/7788.
– *King James VI and I and the Reunion of Christendom*. Cambridge: Cambridge University Press, 1997.
Peltonen, Markku. *The Duel in Early Modern England: Civility, Politeness and Honour*. Cambridge: Cambridge University Press, 2003.
Pentzell, Raymond J. '*The Changeling*: Notes on Mannerism in Dramatic Form.' 1975. Reprinted in *Drama in the Renaissance: Comparative and Critical Essays,*

edited by Clifford Davidson, C.J. Gianakaris, and John H. Stroupe, 274–99. New York: AMS, 1986.

Perkins, William. *The Workes*. 3 vols. London: John Legatt, 1612–13. STC 19650.

Price, George R., ed. *A Fair Quarrel*. Lincoln: University of Nebraska Press, 1976.

Rabkin, Norman. 'Problems in the Study of Collaboration.' *Research Opportunities in Renaissance Drama* 19 (1976): 7–13.

Randall, Dale B. 'Some Observations on the Theme of Chastity in *The Changeling*.' *English Literary Renaissance* 14 (1984): 347–66.

– 'Some Perspectives on the Spanish Setting of *The Changeling* and Its Sources.' *Medieval and Renaissance Drama in England* 3 (1986): 189–216.

Reay, Barry. *Popular Cultures in England, 1550–1750*. London: Longman, 1998.

Reynolds, John. *The Triumphs of Gods Revenege* [sic], *against the Crying, and Execrable Sinne of Murther*. London: William Lee, 1621. STC 20942.

Ribner, Irving. *Jacobean Tragedy: The Quest for Moral Order*. London: Methuen, 1962.

Ricks, Christopher. 'The Moral and Poetic Structure of *The Changeling*.' *Essays in Criticism* 10 (1960): 290–306.

Robb, Dewar M. 'The Canon of William Rowley's Plays.' *Modern Language Review* 45 (1950): 129–41.

Rowe, George E., Jr. *Thomas Middleton and the New Comedy Tradition*. Lincoln: Nebraska University Press, 1979.

Rowley, William. *A Merrie and Pleasant Comedy: Never Before Printed, Called A Shoo-Maker a Gentleman*. London: John Cowper, 1638. STC 21422.

– *A New Wonder, a Woman Never Vext. A Pleasant Conceited Comedy*. London: Francis Constable, 1632. STC 21423.

– 'To the Publique Reader.' In *Greate Britaine All in Blacke*, edited by John Taylor, 2nd ed, C2^r. London: J. Wright, 1612. STC 23760.5.

– *A Tragedy Called All's Lost by Lust*. London: Thomas Harper, 1633. STC 21425.

Rowley, William, and John Webster. *A Cure for a Cuckold. A Pleasant Comedy*. London: Francis Kirkman, 1661. Wing W1220.

– *The Thracian Wonder. A Comical History*. London: Francis Kirkman, 1661. Wing T1078A.

Rozett, Martha Tuck. *The Doctrine of Election and the Emergence of Elizabethan Tragedy*. Princeton, NJ: Princeton University Press, 1984.

Sālgādo, Gamini, ed. *Three Jacobean Tragedies*. Harmondsworth: Penguin, 1965.

Salkeld, Duncan. *Madness and Drama in the Age of Shakespeare*. Manchester: Manchester University Press, 1993.

Sanders, Leslie, '*The Revenger's Tragedy*: A Play on the Revenge Play.' *Renaissance and Reformation* 10 (1974): 25–36.

Sanders, Wilbur. *The Dramatist and the Received Idea: Studies in the Plays of Marlowe and Shakespeare*. Cambridge: Cambridge University Press, 1968.
Sargent, Roussel. 'Theme and Structure in Middleton's *A Game at Chess.*' *Modern Language Review* 66 (1971): 721–30.
Schoenbaum, S. *Internal Evidence and Elizabethan Dramatic Authorship: An Essay in Literary History and Method*. London: Edward Arnold, 1966.
– *Middleton's Tragedies: A Critical Study*. New York: Columbia University Press, 1955.
– 'Middleton's Tragicomedies.' *Modern Philology* 54 (1956): 7–19.
Shakespeare, William. *Mr. William Shakespeares Comedies, Histories & Tragedies*. London: Isaac Jaggard and Edward Blount, 1623. STC 22273.
Shapiro, I.A. '*Tityre-tu* and the Date of William Rowley's *Woman Never Vext.*' *Review of English Studies*, n.s., 2 (1960): 55–6.
Shenk, Robert. *The Sinner's Progress: A Study of Madness in English Renaissance Drama*. Salzburg: Universität Salzburg, 1978.
Sidney, Philip. 'A Defence of Poetry.' In *Miscellaneous Prose of Sir Philip Sidney*, edited by Katherine Duncan-Jones and Jan van Dorsten, 59–121. Oxford: Clarendon Press, 1973.
Simmons, J.L. 'Diabolical Realism in *The Changeling.*' *Renaissance Drama* 11 (1980): 135–70.
Sinfield, Alan. *Literature in Protestant England, 1560–1660*. London: Croom Helm, 1983.
Sisson, C.J. '*Keep the Widow Waking*: A Lost Play by Dekker.' *The Library*, 4th ser., 8 (1927): 39–57, 233–59.
– *Lost Plays of Shakespeare's Age*. Cambridge: Cambridge University Press, 1936.
Slater, A.P. 'Hypallage, Barley-Break and *The Changeling.*' *Review of English Studies* 136 (1983): 429–40.
Spence, Lewis. *The Fairy Tradition in Britain*. London: Rider, 1948.
Stachniewski, John. 'Calvinist Psychology in *Macbeth.*' *Shakespeare Studies* 20 (1988): 169–89.
– 'Calvinist Psychology in Middleton's Tragedies.' In *New Casebooks: Three Jacobean Revenge Tragedies*, edited by R.V. Holdsworth, 226–46. Basingstoke: Macmillan, 1990.
– *The Persecutory Imagination: English Puritanism and the Literature of Religious Despair*. Oxford: Oxford University Press, 1991.
Stern, Tiffany. *Rehearsal from Shakespeare to Sheridan*. Oxford: Oxford University Press, 2000.
Stevenson, Laura Caroline. *Praise and Paradox: Merchants and Craftsmen in Elizabethan Popular Literature*. Cambridge: Cambridge University Press, 1984.

Stork, Charles Wharton, ed. *William Rowley: His 'All's Lost by Lust' and 'A Shoemaker a Gentleman,' with an Introduction on Rowley's Place in the Drama.* Philadelphia: University of Pennsylvania Press, 1910.

Straznicky, Marta. 'The Red Bull Repertory in Print, 1605–60.' *Early Theatre* 9, no. 2 (2006): 144–56.

Streitberger, W.R. 'Personnel and Professionalization.' In *A New History of Early English Drama*, edited by John D. Cox and David Scott Kastan, 337–56. New York: Columbia University Press, 1997.

Swetnam, Joseph. *The Schoole of the Noble and Worthy Science of Defence.* London: Nicholas Okes, 1617. STC 23543.

Swinburne, A.C. *The Age of Shakespeare.* 1908. Reprint, New York: AMS Press, 1965.

– Introduction to *Thomas Middleton*, 1:vii–xxxviii. London: T. Fisher Unwin, [1894?].

Sykes, H. Dugdale. *Sidelights on Elizabethan Drama.* Oxford: Oxford University Press, 1924.

Symons, Arthur. 'Middleton and Rowley.' In *The Cambridge History of English Literature*, vol. 6, *The Drama to 1642, Part Two*, edited by A.W. Ward and A.R. Waller, 66–91. Cambridge: Cambridge University Press, 1910.

Taylor, Gary. Introduction to *A Game at Chess: A Later Form.* In Taylor and Lavagnino, *Thomas Middleton: The Collected Works*, 1825–9.

– 'Middleton and Rowley – and Heywood: *The Old Law* and New Technologies of Attribution.' *Papers of the Bibliographical Society of America* 96 (2002): 165–217.

– '*An/The Old Law*, 1618–19.' In Taylor and Lavagnino, *Thomas Middleton and Early Modern Textual Culture*, 405–8.

– 'The Order of Persons.' In Taylor and Lavagnino, *Thomas Middleton and Early Modern Textual Culture*, 31–79.

– '*The Spanish Gypsy*, July 1623.' In Taylor and Lavagnino, *Thomas Middleton and Early Modern Textual Culture*, 433–8.

– Textual introduction to *The Spanish Gypsy*. In Taylor and Lavagnino, *Thomas Middleton and Early Modern Textual Culture*, 1105–9.

– 'Thomas Middleton: Lives and Afterlives.' In Taylor and Lavagnino, *Thomas Middleton: The Collected Works*, 25–58.

– 'Thomas Middleton, *The Spanish Gypsy*, and Collaborative Authorship.' In *Words That Count: Essays on Early Modern Authorship in Honour of MacDonald P. Jackson*, edited by Brian Boyd, 241–73. Cranbury: Associated University Presses, 2004.

– 'Thomas Middleton, Thomas Dekker and *The Bloody Banquet*.' *Papers of the Bibliographical Society of America* 94 (2000): 197–233.

Taylor, Gary, and John Lavagnino, eds. *Thomas Middleton: The Collected Works*. Oxford: Clarendon Press, 2007.
– eds. *Thomas Middleton and Early Modern Textual Culture: A Companion to the Collected Works*. Oxford: Clarendon Press, 2007.
Taylor, Gary, and others. 'Works Included in This Edition: Canon and Chronology.' In Taylor and Lavagnino, *Thomas Middleton and Early Modern Textual Culture*, 335–443.
Taylor, Michael, ed. *'A Mad World, My Masters' and Other Plays*. World's Classics. Oxford: Oxford University Press, 1995.
Thomas, Keith. *Religion and the Decline of Magic: Studies in Popular Beliefs in Sixteenth and Seventeenth-Century in England*. Harmondsworth: Penguin, 1971.
Thornton Burnett, Mark. *Masters and Servants in English Renaissance Drama and Culture: Authority and Obedience*. Basingstoke: Macmillan, 1997.
Tilley, Morris P. *A Dictionary of the Proverbs in England in the Sixteenth and Seventeenth Centuries*. Ann Arbor: University of Michigan Press, 1950.
Tomlinson, T.B. *A Study of Elizabethan and Jacobean Tragedy*. Cambridge: Cambridge University Press, 1964.
Turner, W. *Turners Dish of Lentten Stuffe, or, A Galymaufery to the Tune of Watton Townes End*. London: J.W., 1612. STC 24350.
Tyacke, Nicholas. *Anti-Calvinists: The Rise of English Arminianism c. 1590–1640*. Oxford: Oxford University Press, 1987.
– 'Puritanism, Arminianism and Counter-Revolution.' In *The Origins of the English Civil War*, edited by Conrad Russell, 119–43. London: Methuen, 1987.
Udall, Joanna, ed. *A Critical, Old-Spelling Edition of 'The Birth of Merlin' (Q 1662)*. London: MHRA, 1991.
Vickers, Brian. *Shakespeare, Co-Author: A Historical Study of Five Collaborative Plays*. Oxford: Clarendon Press, 2002.
Waswo, Richard. 'Damnation, Protestant Style: *Macbeth, Faustus* and Christian Tragedy.' *Journal of Medieval and Renaissance Studies* 4 (1974): 63–99.
Watt, Tessa. 'Piety in the Pedlar's Pack: Continuity and Change, 1578–1630.' In *The World of Rural Dissenters, 1520–1725*, edited by Margaret Spufford, 255–72. Cambridge: Cambridge University Press, 1995.
Wayne, Valerie, ed. *A Trick to Catch the Old One*. In Taylor and Lavagnino, *Thomas Middleton: The Collected Works*, 373–413.
Webster, John. *The Tragedy of the Dutchesse of Malfy*. London: John Waterson, 1623. STC 25176.
Weimann, Robert. *Author's Pen and Actor's Voice: Playing and Writing in Shakespeare's Theatre*. Cambridge: Cambridge University Press, 2000.

- *Shakespeare and the Popular Tradition in the Theater: Studies in the Social Dimension of Dramatic Form and Function*. Edited and translated by Robert Schwartz. Baltimore: Johns Hopkins University Press, 1978.
Weldon, Anthony. *The Court and Character of King James*. London: R.I., 1651. Wing W1274.
Welsford, Enid. *The Fool: His Social and Literary History*. 1935. Reprint, Gloucester, MA: Peter Smith, 1966.
Whigham, Frank. 'Reading Social Conflict in the Alimentary Tract: More on the Body in Renaissance Drama.' *English Literary History* 55 (1988): 333–50.
White, Martin. *Middleton and Tourneur*. Basingstoke: Macmillan, 1992.
White, Peter. *Predestination, Policy and Polemic: Conflict and Consensus in the English Church from the Reformation to the Civil War*. Cambridge: Cambridge University Press, 1992.
White, R.S. *Natural Law in English Renaissance Literature*. Cambridge: Cambridge University Press, 1996.
Wiggin, Pauline G. *An Inquiry into the Authorship of the Middleton-Rowley Plays*. Boston: Ginn, 1897.
Wiles, David. *Shakespeare's Clown: Actor and Text in the Elizabethan Playhouse*. Cambridge: Cambridge University Press, 1987.
Wilks, John S. *The Idea of Conscience in Renaissance Tragedy*. London: Routledge, 1990.
Williams, George Walton. Textual introduction to *Rollo, Duke of Normandy*. In Bowers, *The Dramatic Works in the Beaumont and Fletcher Canon*, 10:147–65.
Wright, Louis B. *Middle-Class Culture in Elizabethan England*. Chapel Hill: University of North Carolina Press, 1935.
Wright, Thomas. *The Passions of the Mind in Generall*. Edited by Thomas O. Sloan. Urbana: University of Illinois Press, 1971.
Wrightson, Keith. *English Society, 1580–1680*. 1982. Reprint, London: Routledge, 1993.
Wymer, Rowland. *Suicide and Despair in the Jacobean Drama*. Brighton: Harvester, 1986.
Yachnin, Paul, and Anthony B. Dawson. *The Culture of Playgoing in Shakespeare's England: A Collaborative Debate*. Cambridge: Cambridge University Press, 2001.
Young, Stephen Blase, ed. *A Critical, Old-Spelling Edition of 'A Match at Midnight.'* New York: Garland, 1980.

Index

actors:
- clown actors: as author-like figures (*see* authorship in the theatre: and actors); and celebrity, 66, 70–1; dramatic functions of, 72–5, 170n35; and festivity, 73, 75, 81, 88, 89–90, 172n73; as holy fools, 72, 73, 75; and love, 87–90; and nature, 72–3, 78, 80; as obligatory presences in plays, 67–8; personae of, 67–8, 124; and plain-speaking, 72, 74–80, 82, 87–8, 90–1; as playwrights, 71–2, 73; and plebeianness, 73, 77, 170n35; and reversals of hierarchical roles, 73, 75, 76, 77–80, 82–3, 88, 170n35; and satire, 84, 87, 89–90; and selfishness, 72–3, 75, 77. *See also names of individual clown actors*
- distinctive boy actor in Lady Elizabeth's Men, 128–30, 179–80n23
- general: as author-like figures (*see* authorship in the theatre: and actors); personae of, 66–8, 124, 148, 168n10. *See also names of individual actors*

All's Lost by Lust: auspices and date of, 151; and change, 64; and choice, 37–41, 42, 45–52, 54, 56–9, 61; clown role in, 71–2, 73, 75–80, 84, 90, 170nn42, 46, 182n78; critical neglect of, 5; prologue to, 157n93; and satire, 90; solo authorship of, 20, 37; stylistic analysis of, 24

Anything for a Quiet Life, 19, 151

Aristotle, 39

Armin, Robert, 67, 71, 74, 168–9n21, 169n23

Arminianism, 42, 162nn14–15

Augustine, Saint, 44

authorship attribution: and criticism, 6, 32; debates over validity of, 15, 22–4, 25–6; methodologies for, 22, 25–6, 123–4, 155n35; value of, 21–2, 24–32, 161n158. *See also under titles of individual plays*

authorship in the theatre: and actors, 7, 34–5, 67–8, 70–1, 119, 124–5, 148; early modern attitudes toward, 3, 6, 15–18, 19–20; and individuality, 3, 6–7, 12–18, 19–20, 32–5; and patrons, 7, 34–5, 124, 138, 142–3, 148; and playing companies, 7, 34–5, 118–19, 124, 148; and playhouses, 35, 148; and presence, 122–3, 124–

5, 128, 130–1, 138, 143, 146–8. *See also* collaborative drama

Bakhtin, Mikhail, 72–3, 76, 78
Bankside, 92, 103, 180–1n45
Barber, C.L., 96, 107–8
Barker, R.H., 9, 21, 22
Bartholomew Fair, 97
Beaumont, Francis, 22, 23, 94–5
Beeston, Christopher, 147, 174n34
Belsey, Catherine, 166n69
Bentley, G.E.: on actors in *The Spanish Gypsy*, 126; on auspices and dates of plays, 134; on authorship attribution, 159n117; on playwriting and collaboration, 18–19, 25, 160n134
Birth of Merlin, The, 72, 73, 82, 151, 182n78
Blackfriars Boys, 97, 150
Bliss, Lee, 113
Bloody Banquet, The, 150
Blurt, Master Constable, 179n19
Bly, Mary, 34, 35, 94
body, the: and clowns, 73, 79; and the soul (*see* mind, structure of the)
Boehrer, Bruce, 165n60
Bolton, Edmund, 104
Bouwsma, William, 43–4
Bowers, Fredson, 110
Bradbrook, M.C., 9–10, 154n25
Breton, Nicholas, 72–3
Bristol, Michael D., 172n73
Bromham, A.A., 4, 11, 141
Brooks, Douglas A., 11, 12, 156n64
Bruster, Douglas, 126
Bruzzi, Zara, 11
Buc, Sir George, 133, 179–80n23
Bullen, A.H., 126
Burke, Séan, 14–15

Burks, Deborah G., 62, 166n69, 166–7n78
Burns, Edward, 25–6
Burton, Robert, 74
Butler, Martin, 102, 132, 181n46
Butler, William, 140

Calvin, John. *See* Calvinism
Calvinism: and change, 42, 52–3; and choice, 42–5, 46–7, 48, 50; and conscience, 45, 163n38; and natural law, 43–4; opposition to, 42; and predestination, 42–3, 44, 45–6, 48, 53, 56, 60, 63–4, 164n51; and reason, 43, 45, 163n38; and security, 48; and self-deceit, 50; structure of the mind in, 43–4, 46, 47, 63–4; and *synderesis*, 45; and tragedy, 37, 45–54, 56, 62, 63–4, 163n38; and the unconscious, 53
Carlton, Charles, 142
Carnegie, David, 171n52
Cathcart, Charles, 161n158
Catholicism, 42
Centerwall, Brandon, 169n29
Chakravorty, Swapan, 155n43, 173nn24, 27
Chambers, E.K., 8
change. *See under All's Lost by Lust; Calvinism; Changeling, The*
Changeling, The: allusions to, 145; attribution of authorship of, 22, 26, 154n24, 158–9n113, 162n1; auspices and date of, 5, 19, 125, 151; and change, 52–3, 57–8, 64, 126, 165nn59–60, 166–7n78, 167n84; and choice, 42, 52–65, 165n60, 165–6n66; clown role in, 83; critical approaches to collaborative nature of, 4, 5, 7–15, 36–7; and distinctive

boy actor, 124, 126–7, 128–31, 148; disunities within, 14, 34, 37, 57–65, 90–1, 122, 148, 161n166; method of collaborative composition of, 8–9, 21, 24–5, 26–32, 36–7, 54, 160n134; multiple authorial visions within, 3, 5, 36–7, 64–5; and patriarchy, 166n69; relationship between main plot and subplot of, 9–10, 24–5; and *The Spanish Gypsy*, 125–7

Charles, Prince of Wales: as author-like figure, 142–3, 148; influence on drama of, 131–43, 148; investiture of, 131–2; and James I, 131–43; as patron of Prince Charles's Men, 20, 35, 125, 131–2, 135–6, 140, 142

Chaste Maid in Cheapside, A, 18, 96, 97, 103, 150

Cheatham, George, 174n34

Children of Paul's, 96, 97, 149–50, 169n29

Children of the Queen's Revels, 34, 85–6, 103

choice: in theology, 39, 41–7, 48, 50; in tragedy, 46–7, 61. *See also under* Middleton and Rowley (playwriting team): differences between; *titles of individual plays*

Christensen, Nels Anchor, 146

class relations in drama. *See under* romance (genre of London comedy); satire (genre of London comedy)

Cleaver, Robert, 157n75

clowns. *See under* actors

Cockpit playhouse. *See* Phoenix playhouse

Cohen, Walter, 89, 95, 96, 99, 106, 114, 173n9, 175n48

collaborative drama: actors and (*see under* authorship in the theatre);
critical approaches to, 3–4, 8–15, 32, 33, 36–7, 118, 147–8; disunity within, 4, 7, 12, 32–4, 37, 64–5, 90–1, 118, 124, 143, 147–8, 161n164; early modern attitudes toward, 17, 19–20, 157n75; friendship between writers of, 18–19; methods of composition of, 6, 15, 24–32, 123–4, 160nn135, 139; patrons and (*see under* authorship in the theatre); playhouses and (*see under* authorship in the theatre); playing companies and (*see under* authorship in the theatre); and presence (*see under* authorship in the theatre); unity within, 26, 27, 148. *See also* authorship in the theatre; *names of individual plays and playwrights*

commedia dell'arte, 120–1

conscience, 43, 45, 46, 163n38

Constable, Francis, 174n34

Craig, Hugh, 24

Cure for a Cuckold, A, 83, 101, 115, 144, 151, 171n52

Curtain playhouse, 92, 98, 118, 150

Cust, Richard, 134

Daalder, Joost, 55, 65, 153n9, 158n105, 165n60

Day, John, 150

de Dominis, Marco Antonio, 67, 68, 69

de Grazia, Margareta, 156nn50, 64

Dekker, Thomas: on authorship in the theatre, 16; on collaboration, 17, 25, 160n139; as collaborator with both Middleton and Rowley, 5, 122–4, 125, 128, 143, 146, 151, 178n6; as collaborator with Middleton, 9, 19–20, 95–6, 149–50; as

208 Index

collaborator with Rowley, 25, 151; and distinctive boy actor in Lady Elizabeth's Men, 128, 130, 179n19; and romance, 95, 99. *See also titles of individual works*
Dent, Arthur, 44, 50, 163n30
Devil's Lawcase, The, 17
disintegration, 8–9, 32
disunity. *See under* collaborative drama
Dobson, Michael, 171n62
Dod, John, 157n75
double predestination. *See* Calvinism: and predestination
Duchess of Malfi, The, 17, 19, 46
Duke of Albany's Men. *See* Prince Charles's Men
Duke of York's Men. *See* Prince Charles's Men
Dunkel, W.F., 155n35
Dutch Courtesan, The, 103
Dyer, Richard, 168n10
Dyke, Daniel, 44, 50, 163n27

Eastward Ho, 24, 96
elect, the. *See* Calvinism: and predestination
Elector Palatine. *See* Frederick, Elector Palatine
Eliot, T.S., 9, 154n24
Elizabeth, Queen of Bohemia, 133, 135
Ellis-Fermor, Una, 9
Empson, William, 9–10, 154n25
Engleberg, Edward, 47

Fair Quarrel, A: allusions to, 144, 145; attribution of authorship of, 22, 26, 29–30, 158–9n113, 160–1n151, 161n152, 167n2, 177n83; auspices and date of, 4, 92, 131–2, 150; and class relations, 106–19, 171n47; clown role in, 68, 72, 73, 82, 91, 170n46, 182n78; disunity within, 34, 68, 118, 123, 148; and duelling, 107–10, 176n68; method of collaborative composition of, 29–30, 32, 115; and Prince Charles's Men, 35, 93, 118; and romance, 91, 92–5, 114, 115–19, 148; Rowley's attitude toward authorship of, 20, 167n2; and the royal family, 109, 118, 131–2, 148, 150; and satire, 91, 92–5, 114, 115–19, 148; unity within, 68, 118
Fair Maid of the Inn, The, 169n28
Fletcher, John: as collaborator (general), 4, 18; as collaborator with Beaumont, 22, 23; as collaborator with Massinger, 23, 159n117; as collaborator with Rowley, 23, 28, 31, 146, 151; as collaborator with Shakespeare, 24; revised by Middleton and Rowley, 85–6, 103, 160n150; and tragicomedy, 94–5, 97, 142; as writer of clown role for Rowley, 71–2, 74, 75. *See also titles of individual works*
Ford, John, 5, 25, 122–4, 125, 151, 178n6. *See also titles of individual works*
Fortune by Land and Sea, 98, 101, 102, 150
Fortune playhouse, 95
Foucault, Michel, 6, 12, 13, 14, 35
framing (method of collaboration). *See under* Middleton and Rowley (playwriting team): methods of composition used by
Frederick, Elector Palatine, 132–3, 135, 142

Index 209

free will. *See* choice
Freud, Sigmund, 53, 165n60
Friar Bacon and Friar Bungay, 168–9n21
Frost, David L., 49, 164n51

Game at Chess, A: auspices and date of, 151; actors as collaborators in, 5, 67–70; clown role in, 67–70, 71, 73–4, 86, 90–1, 148, 167n5, 182n78; political allegory in, 68–70
Garber, Marjorie, 165n60
Gascoigne, George, 17
Globe playhouse, 92
Golding, Arthur, 162n6
Gondomar, Count of (ambassador of Spain), 68, 70
Gorboduc, 17
Gosse, Edmund, 9
Gossett, Suzanne, 93–4, 107, 154n29, 177n83
grace. *See* Calvinism: and predestination
Greene, Thomas, 168–9n21
Greene's Tu Quoque, 168–9n21
Gurr, Andrew, 34, 180n37

Hamlet, 46, 83, 133, 139
Harbage, Alfred, 98, 100
Heath, Stephen, 168n10
Heinemann, Margot, 11, 47, 96, 173n24
Helgerson, Richard, 170n35
Heller, Herbert Jack, 47
Hengist, King of Kent, 51, 91, 151, 165n56
Henry IV, Part 2, 139
Henry VIII, 24
Henry, Prince of Wales, 132–3, 140
Henslowe, Philip, 25

Herbert, Sir Henry, 179–80n23
Herndl, George C., 48, 163n38
Heywood, Thomas: as collaborator, 4, 30, 98, 101, 115, 123, 150–1; and romance, 99. *See also titles of individual works*
Hillman, Richard, 166–7n78
Hirschfield, Heather Anne, 4, 13, 16–17, 18–19, 24, 156n69
Holmes, David M., 10, 155n35, 165–6n66, 166–7n78
Honest Whore, Part 1, The, 95–6, 149
Hope playhouse, 97, 103, 150, 177n91
Howard-Hill, T.H., 70
Hoy, Cyrus: and authorship attribution, 6, 22–4, 26, 28, 158–9n113, 159nn114, 117, 160nn134, 150; on critical approaches to collaborative drama, 3–4, 5–6, 32, 35; on date of *Match Me in London*, 179–80n23
humanism, 43
Hutchings, Mark, 4

If You Know Not Me You Know Nobody, Part 2, 99
Inner Temple Masque, or, Masque of Heroes, The, 4, 71, 74–5, 151

Jackson, MacDonald P., 6; on authorship attribution, 23, 24; on *The Changeling*, 22, 158–9n113; on *A Fair Quarrel*, 22, 29–30, 158–9n113, 160–1n151, 161n152; on methods of collaborative composition, 26; on *The Old Law*, 30, 123, 161nn156–7; on *The Spanish Gypsy*, 123; on *Wit at Several Weapons*, 28–9, 160n150, 171n62; on *The World Tossed at Tennis*, 22

James I, King: and absolutist monarchy, 137, 141–2; allusions in drama to, 68, 132–3, 136–8, 139–40; and the Bohemian crisis, 132–6; and Charles, Prince of Wales, 131–43; and Henry, Prince of Wales, 132; Middleton ghost-writes for, 108–9, 131; opposition to duelling of, 108–9, 118, 131, 135–6; performances presented to, 109, 118, 131–2, 150
Jameson, Fredric, 106, 173n9
Jocasta, 17
Johnson, Nora, 66, 70–1
Jonson, Ben, 16, 17, 18, 97, 167n5
Jowett, John: on authorship attribution, 23, 24, 32; on critical approaches to collaborative drama, 15, 32–3, 156n69, 161n164; on methods of collaborative composition, 24, 156n69; on Middleton and romance, 173n27; on Middleton and Shakespeare, 4, 33, 161n164

Kemp, Will, 67, 68, 74, 84, 170n38
Kernan, Alvin, 133
Kewes, Paulina, 18
King's Men, the: as performers of Fletcher and Rowley play, 82–3, 146, 151; as performers of Middleton plays, 5, 18–19, 67, 71, 150–1; Rowley's performances with, 5, 67, 71–2, 75, 82–3, 151; Rowley's status within, 19, 71, 75, 83, 146, 151
Kirsch, Arthur, 112
Kistner, A.L. and M.L., 117
Knapp, Jeffrey, 16, 17, 157n75
Knowles, Ronald, 73–4
Knutson, Roslyn L., 34

Lady Elizabeth's Men: distinctive boy actor in (*see under* actors); as performers of Middleton plays, 18, 97, 103, 118, 150; as performers of Middleton-Rowley plays, 5, 19, 83, 122, 126, 150–1; at the Phoenix, 128, 151; and Prince Charles's Men, 85–6, 103, 146, 150–1; and satire, 97, 103
Lady's Tragedy, The. See *Second Maiden's Tragedy, The*
Lake, David J., 6; on *The Changeling*, 22, 26; on *A Fair Quarrel*, 22, 25, 160–1n151, 161n152; on methods of collaborative composition, 25; on *The Old Law*, 30, 123, 161nn156–7; on *The Spanish Gypsy*, 178n6, 179n19; on *Wit at Several Weapons*, 28–9, 160n150, 171n62; on *The World Tossed at Tennis*, 22
Langbaine, Gerard, 18
Laroque, François, 73
Late Murder in Whitechapel, or, Keep the Widow Waking, The, 25, 123, 151
Lawrence, W.J., 134, 180–1n45
Leggatt, Alexander, 35, 173n27
Leinwand, Theodore B., 97, 172n6
Levin, Richard, 107, 112, 116, 170n35

Macbeth, 39, 45, 46, 150
MacLean, Sally-Beth, 34
Mad World My Masters, A, 97, 150
Magnificent Entertainment, The, 17
Maid in the Mill, The: auspices and date of, 146, 151; authorship attribution of, 23, 27–8; clown role in, 72, 73, 82–3; method of collaborative creation of, 27–8, 31
Maid's Tragedy, The, 23
Malcolmson, Cristina, 155n43, 166n69

Manley, Lawrence, 95, 96, 99, 103, 106, 114, 173n9
Marriage of the Old and New Testament, The. See *Two Gates of Salvation, The*
Marston, John, 16
Masque of Heroes. See *Inner Temple Masque, or, Masque of Heroes, The*
Masque of the Twelve Months, The, 135
Massinger, Philip: as collaborator, 18, 23, 30, 123, 159n117; as writer of clown role for Rowley, 71–2, 75, 78, 151, 169n28. *See also titles of individual works*
Masten, Jeffrey: on authorship attribution, 22, 24; on critical approaches to collaborative drama, 4, 6, 13–14, 156nn52, 69; on early modern attitudes to authorship in the theatre, 3, 6, 12, 15–17, 20; on *The Old Law*, 85
Match at Midnight, A, 149
Match Me in London, 130, 179–80n23
McElroy, John F., 112
McGann, Jerome, 156n50
McGee, C.E., 134–6
McLuskie, Kathleen, 10
McMillin, Scott, 34
McMullan, Gordon, 4: on authorship attribution, 26, 158n108; on critical approaches to collaborative drama, 11, 12, 14, 33
Measure for Measure, 151
Meres, Francis, 16
Metamorphoses. See Ovid
Mexia, Pedro, 175n42
Michaelmas Term, 96, 149
Middleton, Thomas: canon of, 149–51; on collaboration, 19–20; as ghost-writer for King James, 108–9, 131; and politics, 5, 11; and Prince Charles, 142–3; and religion, 5, 11, 46–52, 91; reputation of, 5, 14; and romance, 95–6, 117–18; and satire, 83–4, 91, 93–5, 96–8, 114, 117–18; and tragicomedy, 95, 97–8. *See also* Middleton and Rowley (playwriting team); *titles of individual works*

– collaboration with and/or revision of playwrights other than Rowley: Dekker, 17, 19–20, 95–6, 122–4, 125, 128, 149–51, 178n6; Fletcher, 85–7, 103, 160n150; Ford, 122–4, 125, 151, 178n6; Heywood, 30, 151; Massinger, 30; Shakespeare, 4, 33, 150–1, 161n164

– playing companies involved with: children's companies, 96–7, 118, 149–50; the King's Men, 18–19, 67, 71, 150–1; Lady Elizabeth's Men, 18–19, 97, 103, 118, 150–1, 157n88; Prince Charles's Men, 18–19, 93, 103, 150–1, 157n88

Middleton and Rowley (playwriting team): canon of, 4–5, 149–51; critical approaches to collaborations of, 3–4, 8–12, 13, 14–15, 33, 36–7, 118; and friendship, 13, 18–19. *See also* Middleton, Thomas; Rowley, William; *titles of individual works*

– differences between, 5, 6–7; in characterization, 61–5; in clown roles, 75, 90–1; of education, 4; of genre, 93–4, 114, 118, 148; of religion and representation of choice in tragedy, 5, 37, 41, 46–52, 57–65, 91, 148; of sensibility, 36–7, 64–5; of social status, 98; of sophistication, 9, 36; of style, 24, 26; of versification, 33

– methods of composition used by:

aim of creating unity, 11–12, 27, 59, 90, 115; division of labour, 8, 26–32, 36, 54, 115, 123–4; dominance and passivity in, 11, 21, 31–2; 'framing' technique, 26–32; separate composition, 36, 64, 154–5n30
Midsummer Night's Dream, A, 88, 129
mind, structure of the, 43–5, 46, 50, 52–3, 57, 63–4
Mooney, Michael E.: on *A Fair Quarrel*, 82, 118; on methods of collaborative composition, 11, 27, 29–30, 154n12, 154–5n30
morality. *See* choice
More Dissemblers Besides Women, 150
Morrison, Peter, 59
Moseley, Humphrey, 125
Mucedorus, 95
Munro, Lucy, 7, 34

Naremore, James, 168n10
natural law, 43–4, 141, 163n24
Neill, Michael, 55, 59, 63, 165n60
New Wonder, a Woman Never Vexed, A: auspices and date of, 98–9, 103, 106, 150, 174n34; clown role in, 72, 73, 82, 172n70, 182n78; as romance, 98–101; stylistic analysis of, 24
Nice Valour, The, 151
Nochimson, Richard L., 22–3, 24–5, 158–9n113, 160n134
Norton, Thomas, 17
No Wit, No Help Like a Woman's, 95, 97–8, 150, 173n27

offensive play performed at court, 132–3, 134, 136, 138, 151, 180n37
Old Law, The: attribution of authorship of, 30–1, 34, 122, 123, 161nn156–7; auspices and date of, 4, 138, 151, 181n57; clown role in, 72, 84–5, 87, 91, 171n56, 182n78; method of collaborative composition of, 30–1, 32; and the royal family, 35, 125, 130–1, 138–43, 148; and satire, 84–5, 87, 148
Oliphant, E.H.C., 178n6
Orgel, Stephen, 12, 14
Ovid, 38, 47–8, 162n6

Pacheco, Anita, 110, 112, 113, 115
Parker, Brian, 112
passion. *See* reason and passion
patrons as author-like figures. *See under* authorship in the theatre: and patrons
Peacemaker, The, 107, 108–9, 113, 118, 131, 150
Pelagianism, 42, 64, 162n14
Peltonen, Markku, 176n68
Pentzell, Raymond, 33
Perkins, William, 44, 45, 163n28
personae. *See under* actors: clown actors; actors: general
Philaster, 23
Phoenix, The, 149
Phoenix playhouse, 19, 126, 128, 130, 147, 151, 180–1n45
Pilgrimage to Parnassus, The, 68
playhouses as author-like figures. *See under* authorship in the theatre: and playhouses
playing companies as author-like figures. *See under* authorship in the theatre: and playing companies. *See also under* names of individual companies
Poets' War, 16–17
Porter's Hall playhouse, 103
post-structuralism, 8, 12–15, 32

predestination. *See under* Calvinism
presence. *See under* authorship in the theatre
Prince Charles. *See* Charles, Prince of Wales
Prince Charles's Men: audience of, 98–9, 118, 177n91; as author-like figure, 118–19, 124; at court, 109, 118, 131–4, 135–6, 139, 180n37, 181n46; at the Curtain, 92, 98, 118, 150; at the Hope, 150, 177n91; romance and satire in plays of, 93, 98–102, 103–19, 148; change of name, 174n31; and Lady Elizabeth's Men, 85–6, 103, 146, 150–1; as performers of Middleton-Rowley plays, 4–5, 19, 93, 103, 106, 118, 150–1; as performers of Rowley plays, 98–9, 101, 144, 150–1; at the Phoenix, 19, 146–7, 151, 180–1n45; and Prince Charles, 133; at the Red Bull, 150–1, 177n91; Rowley's performances with, 66, 71–2, 75, 83, 92, 150–1; Rowley's status within, 18–19, 20–1, 71, 75, 146, 150–1, 157n97
Prince Henry. *See* Henry, Prince of Wales
Prince Henry's Men, 95, 149–50
providence. *See* Calvinism: and predestination
Puritan, The, 97, 150
Puritanism, 11, 47

Queen Anne's Men, 98, 150

Rabkin, Norman, 11, 24
Randall, Dale, 62
reason and passion, 40–1, 43–4, 46–7, 50, 58–9, 163nn24, 38. *See also* mind, structure of the

Red Bull playhouse, 92, 98, 103, 150–1, 177n91
Reformation, The, 41, 42, 52–3, 64
repertory study. *See* authorship in the theatre: and playing companies
reprobates. *See* Calvinism: and predestination
Revenger's Tragedy, The, 47–9, 150
Reynolds, John, 55, 56
Ribner, Irving, 10, 165n61
Ricks, Christopher, 154–5n30
Roaring Girl, The, 19–20, 95–6, 150
Robb, Dewar M., 22, 158–9n113
Rollo, Duke of Normandy, 169n28
romance (genre of London comedy): and class relations, 95–6, 98–103, 114, 115–19; combined with satire, 106, 115–19; definition of, 95; parody of, 96, 97. *See also under names of individual companies, plays, and playwrights*
Rowe, George E., Jr, 173n27
Rowley, William: as leader of playing company, 4, 20–1, 71, 136; and popular culture, 98; and Prince Charles, 136, 142–3. *See also* Middleton and Rowley (playwriting team); *titles of individual works*
 – as actor: and acting as collaboration, 67–70, 90–1; allusions to, 143–8, 172n67; celebrity status of, 70–1; with the Children of Paul's, 169n29; as double act with another clown, 170n46; with the King's Men, 5, 19, 67, 71–2, 75, 82–3, 146, 151; with Lady Elizabeth's Men, 146; musical elements of performances of, 146, 182n78; as performer of roles written by himself, 35, 71–2, 75–91, 150–1, 171n52; as per-

former of roles written for him by others, 4–5, 35, 67–70, 71–2, 74–5, 151, 167n5, 169n28; persona of, 66–91, 148; physical characteristics of, 66, 71–2; with Prince Charles' Men, 4–5, 18–19, 20–1, 71–2, 75, 83, 92, 146, 150–1, 157n97
- collaboration with and/or revision of playwrights other than Middleton: Dekker, 25, 122–4, 125, 128, 143, 151, 178n6; Fletcher, 23, 28, 31, 146, 151; Ford, 25, 122–4, 125, 151, 178n6; Heywood, 4, 30, 98, 101, 150–1; Webster, 19, 25, 101, 151
- as playwright: on authorship and collaboration, 19–21, 167n2; canon of, 4–5, 149–51; critical neglect of, 5–7, 9, 10–12, 14–15, 21, 93, 154n24, 155n43, 161n166; for the King's Men, 19, 75, 82–3, 146, 151; for Lady Elizabeth's Men, 18–19, 146, 151; for Prince Charles's Men, 4–5, 18–19, 20–1, 71, 75, 101, 103, 118–19, 150–1; reputation of, 4–5, 9; and romance, 91, 93–5, 98–103, 114, 117–18; and satire, 83–5, 101, 117–18; as writer of clown roles for himself, 71–2, 75, 80–91, 124, 171n52; as writer of clown roles for other actors, 83, 124, 144
Rozett, Martha Tuck, 44, 45, 61, 163n28
Rule a Wife and Have a Wife, 72, 73, 151, 182n78

Sackville, Thomas, 17
Sargent, Roussel, 69
satire (genre of London comedy): and class relations, 96–7, 103–6, 114, 115–19; and clowns, 72, 83–4; combined with romance, 106, 115–19; definition of, 96–7; parody of romance in, 96, 97
Satiromastix, 179n19
Schoenbaum, Samuel, 21, 61, 155n35
Second Maiden's Tragedy, The, 51–2, 150
security. *See under* Calvinism
Sejanus, 17
self, the. *See* mind, structure of the
self-deceit. *See under* Calvinism
Shakespeare, William: and authorship, 16; and clowns, 67, 83, 88, 170n35; as collaborator and/or object of revision, 4, 24, 32, 33, 150–1, 161n164; as cultural construct, 14; and representation of choice in tragedy, 39, 45–6. *See also titles of individual works*
Shanke, John, 92
sharers, 19, 20–1
Shoemaker a Gentleman: auspices and date of, 151, 175n40, 183n10; clown role in, 72, 82, 182n78; critical neglect of, 5; as romance, 101–2; solo authorship of, 20; sources of, 175n42; stylistic analysis of, 24
Shoemaker's Holiday, The, 95, 99
Sidney, Philip, 168n11
Simmons, J.L., 11
sin. *See* choice
Sinfield, Alan, 39
Sir Thomas More, 13, 25
Sisson, C.J., 160n139
soul, the. *See* mind, structure of the
Spanish Gypsy, The: allusions to Rowley within, 143–7, 148; attribution of authorship of, 26, 31, 34, 122, 123–4, 128, 146, 178n6; auspices and date of, 125, 146, 151; and *The*

Changeling, 125–7; collaboration dramatized in, 120–2; and distinctive boy actor, 35, 124, 126–31, 143, 148, 179n19; performer of clown role in, 124, 145–7, 182n78
Stachniewski, John, 45, 47, 53, 60, 165n60
Stallybrass, Peter, 156nn50, 64
Staple of News, The, 167n5, 169n28
star studies, 168n10
Stevenson, Laura Caroline, 102, 174n28
Stork, C.W., 22
Stow, John, 99
stylistic analysis. *See* authorship attribution
Swan playhouse, 92, 97, 180–1n45
Swetnam, Joseph, 108
Swinburne, A.C., 9
Symons, Arthur, 36–7, 64, 162n1
synderesis, 43, 45, 50

Tarlton, Richard, 70, 84, 168–9n21
Taylor, Gary: admiration for Middleton and Rowley, 4; and authorship attribution, 26, 123–4, 128, 143, 146; on authorship and collaboration, 13; on date of *The Old Law*, 181n57; on *A Game at Chess*, 69; on sources of *The Spanish Gypsy*, 179n19
Taylor, John, 42
Taylor, Michael, 173n27
Thracian Wonder, The, 145, 149, 182n78
Timon of Athens, 33, 150, 161n164
'Tis Pity She's a Whore, 46
Tomlinson, T.B., 10
tragicomedy, 94–5, 97–8, 118, 142
Travels of the Three English Brothers, The, 150, 167n2

Trick to Catch the Old One, A, 96–7, 149
Turner, W., 92
Twelfth Night, 89, 172n73
Two Gates of Salvation, The, 47
Two Maids of Moreclacke, The, 168–9n21
Tyacke, Nicholas, 162n14–15

unconscious, the, 53, 55, 165n60
unity. *See under* collaborative drama
Unnatural Combat, The, 72, 75, 78, 151, 169n28, 182n78

Vickers, Brian, 3, 4, 7, 25, 32

Waswo, Richard, 45, 162n6
Webster, John: on authorship, 17; as collaborative playwright, 19, 25, 101, 115, 151. *See also titles of individual works*
Weimann, Robert, 170n35
Weldon, Anthony, 132
Welsford, Enid, 74
White, Peter, 162n14–15
White, R.S., 45, 46–7, 163n38
Whitefriars, 94
Widow, The, 150
Wife for a Month, A, 72, 75, 151, 182n78
Wiggin, Pauline G., 22, 64, 155nn35, 38
Wiles, David, 34–5, 67, 84
Wilkins, George, 150
Wilson, Robert, 169n23
Wit at Several Weapons: auspices and date of, 4, 85–6, 103, 106, 150, 171n62; authorship attribution of, 23, 28–9, 31, 85–6, 160n150; clown role in, 35, 72, 73, 86–91, 103, 106,

122–3, 148, 171n63, 182n78; disunity within, 90–1, 122–3, 148; as earliest Middleton-Rowley collaboration, 4, 18, 103; method of collaborative composition of, 28–9; 31; as revision of Fletcher play, 85–7, 103, 160n150; and satire, 87, 89–90, 103–6, 148
Witch, The, 150
Witch of Edmonton, The: allusions to, 144; auspices and date, 151; clown role in, 72, 80–1, 172n70, 182n78; as collaboration, 123
Woman Never Vexed, A. See *New Wonder, a Woman Never Vexed, A*
Women Beware Women, 48–51, 55, 61, 91, 151, 164n52, 164–5n53

World Tossed at Tennis, The: attribution of authorship of, 22, 31, 75; auspices and date of, 4–5, 66, 134–6, 142, 151, 180–1n45, 181n46; clown role in, 66, 71, 72–3, 75, 91; illustration on title page of, 71; Middleton's and Rowley's attitudes toward authorship of, 19–20; and the royal family, 35, 125, 134–8, 142, 148
Wright, Louis B., 96
Wright, Thomas, 43, 46, 57

Yachnin, Paul, 136
Yorkshire Tragedy, A, 150, 164–5n53
Your Five Gallants, 97, 150, 173n24

www.ingramcontent.com/pod-product-compliance
Lightning Source LLC
Chambersburg PA
CBHW020407080526
44584CB00014B/1212